THE BOY

Baden-Powell and the
Siege of Mafeking

Pat Hopkins

Heather Dugmore

ZEBRA

THE BOY

ZEBRA

First published by Zebra Press, an imprint of Southern Book Publishers
(a division of the New Holland Struik Publishing Group (Pty) Ltd.)
P O Box 5563, Rivonia, 2128, South Africa
Tel: (011) 807-2292
Fax: (011) 807-0506

First edition 1999

ISBN 1 86872 262 7

Photographs: kind permission of Mafeking Museum;
University of the Witwatersrand (History Papers) and Elleanor Cason

Cover design: Micha McKerr
Typesetting and design: PG&A, Gauteng

Set in 12 on 14pt Palatino

Reproduction by PG&A, Gauteng
Printed and bound by Creda Communications, Eliot Avenue, Epping II 7460

For Megan, Tiffany and Chelsea

DEDICATION

And the angels sing

There is nothing pretty about the place where the dead defenders of Mafeking are laid. It lies in a little square of brown stone wall, planted amid the dreary waste outside the town. There are no green lawns, no twisted yews, no weeping willows; the few fir trees hold themselves stiffly up ... and the great bushes of faded geranium only throw into relief the regular lines of limestone moulds, each with its prim wooden cross of advertisement.

FILSON YOUNG, CORRESPONDENT FOR
THE MANCHESTER GUARDIAN,
IN HIS BOOK THE RELIEF OF MAFEKING

Approximately 2 000 people died during the Siege of Mafeking. A thousand – Black, Boer and Briton – were killed in action, died of wounds, or expired from disease. The other thousand – all black except for one Dutch child – died of starvation. Everywhere there are monuments to these casualties of war.

In the veld, to the north of Mafeking, there are no memorials to the black starvelings – predominantly women and children – who perished in their scores after being forced from Mafeking by the British military authorities during the siege. These desperate people – if not hunted by Boers like wild beasts – sat down, sighed, sank back, closed their empty eyes and died. Their bones, picked clean by vultures, have long since turned to dust. It is to these people that this work is dedicated.

THE MAFEKING MAIL
SPECIAL SIEGE SLIP.

ISSUED DAILY, SHELLS PERMITTING. TERMS: ONE SHILLING PER WEEK, PAYABLE IN ADVANCE.

No. 72 **Friday, February 16th, 1900.** **127th Day of Siege**

The Mafeking Mail.

FRIDAY, 16TH FEBRUARY, 1900.

OUR BEEF PROVIDERS.

The appearance of some under-cut, juicy and succulent, on certain breakfast tables made us curious in this time of Siege as to its origin. We learned it was "Native beef," and the following account, which we prefer to give in its own picturesque language, is interesting in connection with the subject of our meat supply:—

"Mathakgong, the leader of "the expedition of 10th, whose loot was captured by the enemy a fortnight ago, said he would not have a quiet night until that fiasco had been blotted out; so on Friday he took four men with him to go and make another trial. Yesterday he and his companions were coming in with what appeared to be a span (12 head) of oxen they had captured close to Batho-Batho's, near Maritzani, at 5 p.m. They brought them down safely until they reached the Magogo Valley, where the Boers fired at them. The Boers first of all fired from their right and before they had time to reply another volley came from their left. They replied calmly, four men went to the right (where the heaviest fire was) and one to the left. The Boers soon shut up but not until they had wounded two oxen. One fell amongst the Boers and one just outside our advance trench, and 10 came in safely.

"Night before last (Saturday) 12 armed Barolongs left our advance trench, South of the Stadt, to go and annoy the Boers. They crossed their lines without being observed and were only fired at on their return. As soon as they returned the fire the Boers ran back to their trench and were silent for the night."

These people attacked the homestead of a Native farmer at Maritzani and exchanged shots, but the farmer made a vigorous defence and they retired.

WHERE'S GREITJE?

When the Boers were seen fiddling around the big gun on Wednesday and a letter under the cover of a white flag was sent in to keep us from firing while they rigged a derrick over "Greitje" preparatory to removal, some of the more hopeful took it as a sign that the damned old blunderbuss was wanted at Pretoria and that her unpleasant belch would no more twang its woeful discord on the harpstrings of our nerves. Alas, how disappointed must these optimists have been when the following afternoon the old scarifying sound was heard coming from about four miles due West instead of East, showing us that the openings to our dug-outs were all the wrong side about. However, we may comfort ourselves with the reflection that as we have borne bombarding for eighteen weeks there is no reason to funk anything these curs can do now. They have tried all the mean tricks their low cunning is capable of inventing, and now we are nearing the end, whether they take their guns to the East or West, can make no difference to us nor to the punishment they are soon sure to receive.

The Secretary to the Sports and Prizes Funds desires to acknowledge receipt of Ten Pounds Four Shillings, being proceeds from the Concert of Sunday afternoon last.

Mafeking Garrison.

GENERAL ORDERS
By Colonel R. S. S. Baden-Powell, Commanding Frontier Force.

MAFEKING, 16TH FEBRUARY, 1900.

Court of Summary Jurisdiction.—The Court of Summary Jurisdiction will meet on Saturday, the 17th February, at the Court House, at 10-15 a.m., for the examination of such prisoners as may be brought before it. President; Lieut.-Col. C. B. Vyvyan. Member: Major F. W. Panzera.

Officer Attached.—Major Baillie, Reserve of Officers, is attached for duty (without pay) to the B.S.A. Police from the 12th instant inclusive.

Assessment Committee.—The Assessment Committee will meet on Sunday, the 18th instant, at Dixon's Hotel at 10 a.m. Owners attending at the above place and hour will be informed about what time the Committee will arrive at their respective houses.

By order,
E. H. CECIL, Major,
Chief Staff Officer.

AUCTION SALE.

THE undersigned, duly instructed by Mrs. GIRDWOOD, will sell by Public Auction on

SUNDAY NEXT,
At 9-30 a.m.

1 Pony, 1 Gent.'s Saddle & Bridle, 1 Lady's Saddle and Bridle, 1 Cape Cart, 1 Set Double Cart Harness, 2 Shot Guns, 250 Shot Cartridges, 1 Gent.'s Bicycle, 1 Carpenter's Bench and quantity of Tools, a quantity of good secondhand Gent.'s Clothing, etc.

Also 1 Black Pony (Stallion)

in the Estate of the late Corpl. Armstrong, B.S.A.P.

ALDRED & ROSS,

Government Auctioneers and Sworn Appraisers.

Don't forget the time:
9-30 A.M.

NOTICE.

A.S.C. BUTCHERY & BAKERY.

THE following hours will hold good for issue or purchase of Bread and Meat:—

5-30 a.m.	9 a.m.
6-30 p.m.	8 p.m.

No one will be served outside these hours.

Bills for Bread and Meat.—Persons purchasing privately will be required to pay cash down. There is not sufficient Staff to justify running accounts being opened.

C. M. RYAN, Capt.,
D.A.A.G.B.

Mafeking, 16th Feb., 1900.

With the sanction of the Col. Commanding

CYCLE SPORTS

(Postponed on account of the condition of the Ground)

will be held at the

RECREATION GROUND,
— ON —

Sunday, February 18th,

Commencing at 3-30 p.m.

Lady Sarah Wilson has kindly consented to distribute the prizes, which comprise:

Watches; a Clock; a most handsome hand-painted "Watteau" Fan; Silver Glove Buttoner; Candlestick Mirror; Silver mounted Pipes; Amber Cigarette Holders; Cigarette Cases, &c.

Referee: H. H. Major Goold-Adams.
Judges: Major Godley; Capt. Cowan. Inspector Marsh.
Handicappers: Lieut.-Colonel Walford; Inspector Browne.
Starter: C. G. H. Bell, Esq., C.C. & R.M.
Clerk of Course } To be appointed on
Lap Scorer } the Ground.

The Totalisator
Will be upon the Grounds.
Under charge of Sergt. Major Merry.

PROGRAMME:

	Start
1. One Mile Siege Championship	3-40
2. Team Race of One Mile	4-0
Four members of: The Prot. Regiment, the B.S.A. Police, the Cape Police, the Bechuanaland Rifles, and the Town Guard.	
3. Half Mile Bicycle Race in Fancy Costume.	4-20
One Prize for Winner, and one prize for best Fancy Dress.	
4. Half Mile Ladies Race	4-40
5. Three Lap Race	5-0
Walk a lap. Run a lap. Ride a lap.	
6. One Mile Bicycle Handicap	5-30
POST ENTRIES.	

Bicycles will be provided for those who have not their own. Lots being drawn for them.

The distribution of Prizes will take place directly after the last race.

By the kind permission of Capt. Cowan the Band of the Bechuanaland Rifles will play during the intervals.

CONTENTS

Authors' Notes

Come then and spend a leisure hour in storytelling,
And our story shall be the education of our heroes.

PLATO, REPUBLIC, BOOK II

André Brink, arguably South Africa's leading author, cautioned in 1998 that most works being published to coincide with the centenary of the South African War would do little more than perpetuate myth and reinforce stereotypes. We predict that some will even attempt to create new fable for an event already teeming with lies.

The first great myth of the South African War was that it was a conflict solely between Boer and Briton — hence the discredited reference to the Anglo-Boer War. More specifically it was intended to be a 'white man's war', as if the calamity attendant on such an event could be contained as to have no effect on the black population. The second great myth is that the war was won by Britain and lost by the Boers. The reality is that Boers were the long-term winners and blacks the big losers — this achieved by a massive betrayal by Britain of her black allies during and after the war. The story of Mafeking is a contained clone of this nightmare.

The Siege of Mafeking left us many firsthand, day-to-day accounts of the drama to the extent that we know what the weather was on most days and who said and did what to whom. Because of these rich sources, which included diaries and memoirs, it was not necessary to use fictional tools in any part of the text whatever — truth, as they say, is often stranger than fiction and its telling does not have to be any less riveting.

Mafeking has officially been known by many variations of the name. It was originally Mahikeng, the British changed it to Mafeking and Bophuthatswana, the short-lived apartheid puppet state, decided on Mafikeng, which remains. We have used the official names as they were at the time and apologise for any confusion this may cause. While on the subject of names, the title *The Boy* may appear cryptic — it is meant to be. It refers to Baden-Powell's suspected lover, to Baden-Powell being the ultimate 'boy-man', to the Boy Scouts and, most importantly, as tribute to

Sol Plaatje and the long lineage of South African black men condescendingly called 'boys'.

We wish to caution those that are squeamish, favour stories that abound with 'nice' people, love happy endings and prefer myths to be perpetuated that *The Boy* may not be ideal reading. For the rest, including André Brink, we hope to pleasantly surprise you. While heroes — other than for Sol Plaatje and Mathakgong — are either deconstructed or are conspicuous by their absence, there are those whose magic is woven through the story and these we would like to thank. Without the kind and enthusiastic assistance of Geoffrey Phillips of the Mafikeng Museum, Michele Pickover, Elleanor Cason, granddaughter of David Taylor, the official Mafeking photographer, and Carol Archibald of the University of the Witwatersrand (Historical Papers) and Linda Boswell and Marius Basson of the Harold Strange Library of African Studies at the Johannesburg Library, this work would not have been possible. The same goes for Kate Rogan, Nicholas Combrinck, Jane Starfield, Gladys van Loggerenberg, Elsie Papenfus, Craig MacKenzie, Vicky Canning and Catherine Murray.

PROLOGUE

IT'S GOOD TO BE AN ENGLISHMAN

To the adoring world, the theatrical Colonel Robert Baden-Powell, besieged in Mafeking, wrote, 'All well. Four hours bombardment. One dog killed'. To his mother he wrote, 'It is horrible to sit here ... and yet not be able to see him and help soothe him.'

'Him', in Baden-Powell's missive, was 'The Boy', the impossibly comely Kenneth McLaren, his long-time friend who was a prisoner of the Boers. The angular, radiant, immaculately groomed Baden-Powell temporarily lost his carefully measured demeanour on hearing the news of his capture and his staff officers were forced to restrain him from declaring a truce so that he could rush to McLaren's side. Had they been unsuccessful Baden-Powell would have been debunked, with many of his peers in the South African War, as a buffoon. But, for the British, there was a happy ending to this imperial epic. On such whimsy do history and myth revolve.

On the evening of Friday, 18 May 1900, a Reuters telegraph reached London, which read simply: MAFEKING RELIEVED. Fleet Street churned out special editions that news-boys rushed out to give away. Announcements were made in theatres, dance-halls, hotels and pubs to patrons who stood as one to sing 'God Save The Queen'. Riotous pandemonium ensued.

Mother, may I go and 'maffick'
Tear around and hinder traffic?
                    SAKI

Whistling, singing crowds poured into the bunting-bedecked streets of London on Mafeking Night. Union Jacks unfurled from balconies, processions formed, top hats were flung in the air, streamers hurled and fireworks exploded. Improvised banners, outside Buckingham Palace, called for the appearance of 'The Queen of Mafeking'. Within an hour the masses, waving portraits of Baden-Powell, would bring the city to a week-long standstill that would necessitate troops being called out to restore order. A slightly piqued *Times* reported: 'There was certainly no trace of British phlegm in the demeanour of the crowds who filled the streets of London ... .White-haired old ladies were to be seen carrying a large Union Jack in each hand. And young women had colours pinned across from shoulder to shoulder. Sober-looking young men in spectacles stood at street corners blowing tin trumpets with all their might. In the city and the suburbs scenes were witnessed which have never been seen before in the history of this country. Well-dressed young women of usually proper demeanour traverse the roadways, arm-in-arm, six abreast, carrying flags and occasionally bursting into song.'

'They are behaving as though they have defeated Napoleon,' huffed critic William Blunt. *The Times*, trying to make sense of the 'intense excitement', commented: 'From a patriotic point of view, the spectacle presented by seven months of suffering and struggle has fired the spirit of the nation beyond all former precedent. The demonstration in London was unparalleled in recent times. There has been nothing like the defence of Mafeking in modern history.'

The Relief of Mafeking was the release of the British public from what Arthur Balfour, the deputy Prime Minister, called 'national humiliation'. In the build-up to the war the British, who prided themselves as defenders of the underdog, had been caricatured as brutal bullies. To make matters worse, during the opening months of hostilities, the British louts consistently had sand kicked in their faces. Mafeking was the bright spot. Here, a small town, against incalculable odds, stout-heartedly withstood a vengeful ruffian. The 'ewe lamb of the Empire' contained all the essential ingredients for a national fable that would restore Britain's faith in herself.

If England was what England seems,
An' not the England of our dreams,
But only putty, brass an' paint,
'Ow quick we'd chuck 'er! But she ain't!

RUDYARD KIPLING, 'THE RETURN'

The St George, the legendary hero who saves his country, in this tale was a man whose initials stood for British Pluck – Baden-Powell. He became the happy warrior of every English boy's dreams. Newspapers plastered pictures of him on their front pages for days on end. Queen Victoria promoted the Hero of Mafeking to Major-General for his deeds and sent him a telegram: 'The Queen to Major-General Baden-Powell. I and my whole Empire greatly rejoice at the relief of Mafeking after the splendid defence made by you through all these months. I heartily congratulate you and all under you, military and civil, British and native, for the heroism and devotion you have shown'. But the initials also stand for British Perfidy.

Baden-Powell. Knight, knave; saintly man, demonic boy; compassionate commander, genocidal tyrant; genius, idiot. British-Public.

Baden-Powell's disciples, in the bitter debate that is Mafeking, rate his defence of the town as one of the most gallant feats of arms in the history of the British Empire. His detractors write the investment off as a side-show conducted by a psychotic ringmaster. What bedevils the discourse is the core of the myth that the Siege of Mafeking was Baden-Powell and that Baden-Powell was the Siege of Mafeking. That this immensely contradictory man played his cards brilliantly, albeit with sleight-of-hand, is undoubted. But he was neither the dealer nor the hero. The luminaries emerged from the Tshidi-Barolong residents of the town – the dealer the British imperial government. Moreover, when the glossy cover is jerked from the fetid pit that is Mafeking, a crime unfolds that goes beyond denunciation.

> With heart at rest I climbed the citadel's
> Steep height, and saw the city as from a tower,
> hospital, brothel, prison and such hells,
> where evil comes up softly like a flower.
> BAUDELAIRE'S 'EPILOGUE'

Filson Young concluded his sojourn in the Mafeking cemetery thus:

> The graves are in prim uniform rows ... .arranged with military precision, row behind row, each row containing twenty graves or more. It is strange, amid the dreariness and stagnation of this place, to think of the jubilation at home. What cheering, what toasting,

what hilarity! But here the sparkle in the wine had died, leaving the cup that had brimmed flat and dull and only half full after all ... A strange place, you may say, in which to attempt the adjustment of mingled impressions ... In normal circumstances one may avoid such places, but after the din of arms and the shout of victory there was a sense of companionship to be found in the place that stood for the ending of disputes. Peaceful yes; but how was the peace gained? And peaceful though it be, the graveyard of Mafeking is a place to induce in Englishmen some searchings of heart.

Part I

A PLACE OF STONES

This is the ocean bright and blue
That the Armadale Castle plowtered through,
But if you turn it the other way
It's the lonely veldt on a cloudy day,
That is if you hold it upside down
It's the gathering storm on the desert brown;
And very seldom since Art begun
Could you get two pictures by drawing one.
                                    RUDYARD KIPLING

(A poem written by Kipling after he had been shown a painting by Baden-Powell. Mistakenly viewing it upside down, he thought it was a picture of the veld with a storm overhead rather than a painting of the sea.)

You thought of escaping the roaring (beast) and fled to the crouching one.
                                    TSWANA PROVERB

1

THE LILYWHITES

Here lies a man, who was an ape,
Nature, grown weary of his shape,
Conceived and carried out the plan
By which the ape is now a man

ANON
(FROM AN EPITAPH TO RAYMOND DART'S 'TAUNG BABY')

In London, on leave, on 3 July 1899, Colonel Robert Baden-Powell was having a raucous lunch with two friends at the Naval and Military Club, In and Out. A few tables away sat George Gough, aide-de-camp to Sir Garnet Wolseley, who, recognising the centre of attention as Baden-Powell, came rushing over.

'I thought you were in India,' said Gough. 'I have just cabled you to come home as the Commander-in-Chief wants to see you.'

Baden-Powell, after a quick briefing on the growing crisis in South Africa between the British and Paul Kruger's South African Republic (Transvaal), left for Wolseley's office where the following conversation, in Baden-Powell's words, is supposed to have transpired:

'"I want you to go to South Africa," said Wolseley.

With the air of a well trained butler I said: "Yes, sir."

"Well, can you go Saturday next?"

"No, sir!"

"Why not?"

Knowing well the sailing of South African steamers, I replied "There's no ship on Saturday. But I can go on Friday."'

It was one of Baden-Powell's favourite stories. It is, of course, embroidered, as there were ships leaving on the next Saturday that would dock in Cape Town.

Baden-Powell 'nearly danced home' to his mother after being accorded the title Commander-in-Chief, North West Frontier Force. As he sailed from London, with the cries of 'Bring back a piece of Kruger's whiskers!' still ringing in his ears, he was able to spend some time with The Boy, the only officer he had personally been allowed to select for his staff. Amongst those allocated to him were his second in command, Major Lord Edward Cecil, a gangly, melancholy, cadaverous and triumphantly dull younger son of the British Prime Minister, Lord Salisbury. Cecil was everything Baden-Powell despised in a man – the dislike was mutual. Accompanying Cecil was his beautiful and witty wife Violet, whose bewitching brown eyes flashed and entranced. Cecil was to regret, forever, bringing her along. Baden-Powell, his views on women well known, and his views on women accompanying their husbands on active service, even better known, would not have hidden his displeasure at her tagging along. Others among his allocated officers included Lieutenant the Hon. Algernon Hanbury-Tracy, his Intelligence Officer, and Captain Charles Fitzclarence, a descendant of William IV who would receive the Victoria Cross at Mafeking, and the Irish actress Dorothea Jordan. Little did Baden-Powell know, as the ship cut through a heavy green fog, that within a year he was to ascend into the swirling mists of Victorian mythology – to soar higher than even his fevered ambition could ever contemplate.

Robert Stephenson Smyth Powell came whooping into 'the Varsity of Life' in England on 22 February 1857. His aquiline, high-cheekboned mother, Henrietta Grace, a prodigious producer of children, was disappointed. She had wanted a daughter.

Robert Stephenson, known variously as Stephe, B-P, Baden-Towel, Barnum-Powell or Baden-Bowel, was christened in honour of his godfather, the inventor of the first successful steam locomotive – *Rocket*. His stern, tousle-haired father, Professor the Reverend Baden Powell, a theologian and Savilian Professor of Geometry at Oxford, and imperious mother, were parents from Hades. Their son inherited from the father, an anti-Semite and Darwinist thinker, his high-mindedness – on the surface anyway – and racism. His mother, a frenzied social climber, bequeathed to him his intellect, ambition and talent for embellishing the truth. So it is no surprise that the myth developed early. His claim to be the grand, grand nephew of Nelson was true; his assertion that he was a descendant of the seventeenth-century adventurer, explorer and soldier, Captain John Smith, of Pocahontas fame, was not. Add to this a gift for counterfeiting the past to conform to his wishes and the sum is a foggy life difficult to dissect.

When he was three, his father died. Many believed this to be divine intervention to bring him before a higher authority so that he could answer for his radical beliefs on creation. At this time, little Stephe would have been playing with his dolls and dancing in girl's skirts in front of the fire where his mother had once laid out the swaddled corpses of three of his siblings who died in infancy to keep them warm. On the Reverend Baden Powell's death, Henrietta Grace changed the family surname to Baden-Powell, a composition she so ardently stressed that she became known as 'Old Mrs Hyphen'. After this step, there followed, in London, a sycophantic journey to enhance the Baden-Powell name – no embroidery, no action, being beneath Henrietta's dignity. Baden-Powell was to acknowledge this by declaring, 'The whole secret of my getting on lay with my mother'.

To attract attention Baden-Powell created for himself a central role of entertainer; acting, fiddling, singing in a falsetto voice, telling stories, cavorting and painting – what a relief for Henrietta when John Ruskin, the English writer and social commentator, pointed out that his ambidextry was not a sign of grave mental illness. The freckle-faced boy, with a mop of curly red hair, was described by his younger sister Agnes as 'just a fun-loving English boy, full of kindness and delight in the joys of life's morning'. But, so precocious was he that William Makepeace Thackeray once gave him a shilling to get him out of his hair.

The London the Baden-Powell clan found themselves in after Baden Powell's death was the centre of the universe and capital of an empire ruled by a grumpy Teutonic empress who never got to see her vast domain. This was the heart of commerce and finance – its soul fired by a never-ending swirl of balls, receptions, garden parties, Epsom, Ascot, Henley and stirring tales of heroic adventures. Its streets were filled with the clip and clatter of horse-drawn delivery carts, hansoms, broughams and turnouts speeding past private gates guarded by gatekeepers. In the sweet-smelling air of Hyde Park, men doffed top hats to women in crinolines as horses high-stepped up the Row.

England! Oh to be in merry England! This was the nation of 'the best, most human, most honourable race the world possesses'. She gave the world Wilberforce, Dickens, Nightingale and Darwin and her offspring were streaming to all corners of the globe. Her power, industrially and militarily, was at its peak. Her navy ruled the waves of the Seven Seas, her explorers were opening up the savage wasteland of Africa and her missionaries were teaching the continent's inhabitants the concept of sin.

The real England, as Cecil John Rhodes saw it, was 'a stuffy little place, mentally, morally and physically.' It was covered with sprawling slums crammed with pallid people where children were forced to work 10 hours a day. The chimera of the healthy world of drawing-rooms, punting on the Thames and cycling on the South Downs was in reality the fine veil disguising a country filled with people so unhealthy that most men of fighting age were unfit for military service. Her great public schools — the kindergarten of Empire that prepared her upper-class boys for the rigours of imperial service — were overflowing with liars, cheats and sexual deviants. Charles Darwin did not need to travel far into this heart of darkness to witness a species ripe for decline.

The British upper classes were in trouble. They were a militarist, illiberal, undemocratic and anti-social anachronism, carried over from the chivalrous days of Lancelot, that was superfluous to a highly industrialised, commercial nation where the boundaries separating the classes were blurring. At the eleventh hour came the explorers, the lions of the hour, and the missionaries who paved the way for the upper classes to reinvent themselves as arch imperialists. In a flurry, the greatest imperial entity ever was opening up the world — facilitating the integration, for better or for worse, of the continents into a universal order. Wherever they landed these imperialists derided nationalism, yet imperialism was the most rabid and racist of all nationalisms and it would be a small step, in the next century, for Hitler, Mussolini and Verwoerd to walk down the same path. Britain's latter-day knights in shining armour, however, lulled the populace with a lie of wide skies, adventure, glory and mystique; of scarlet-coated officers, horse-drawn gun-carriages and pomp; of bugle calls and gunfire echoing off walls and across the veld; of God's Englishmen bearing the white man's burden.

Take up the White Man's burden —
  Send forth the best ye breed —
Go bind your sons to exile

> *To serve your captive's need;*
> *To wait in heavy harness,*
>   *On fluttered folk and wild —*
> *Your new-caught, sullen peoples,*
>   *Half-devil and half-child.*
> RUDYARD KIPLING, 'THE WHITE MAN'S BURDEN'

England's destiny to rule the world was magically captured by poets and authors such as Rudyard Kipling and Rider Haggard. They transformed Christianity, Civilisation, Commerce into romantic verse and prose. Into this broth was added a corruption of the work of Charles Darwin. The European races, or more specifically the upper classes, in this social-Darwinist scheme, naturally assumed a superior intellect. This belief in Caucasian intellectual distinction ensured they would always succeed, with the corollary that niggers would succumb. It was simply a matter of survival of the fittest. The imperial heroes, patently unfit, stepped forward as the Master Race. Occupying the bottom rung in this concoction were the primates, the people of Africa, supposedly without culture or history.

> *Ah what avails the sceptered race,*
>   *Oh what the form divine!*
> *What every virtue, every grace!*
> WALTER LANDOR, 'ROSE AYLMER'

Carlyle wrote 'nature herself is umpire and can do no wrong.' Harry Johnson blazed 'The Negro seems to require the intervention of some superior race before he can be roused to any definite advance from the low stage of human development in which he has contentedly remained for many thousands of years.' David Livingstone asserted ' ... and the people [of Africa] long in vain for a power able to make all dwell in peace.' John Speke declared of the African: 'He works his wife, sells his children, enslaves all he can lay his hands upon, and contents himself with drinking, singing, and dancing like a baboon to drive dull care away.' The time was ripe to intervene in Africa for Africa's sake — to save its people whose heads ' ... roll about them like a ball upon a wire' and whose 'eyes glaze over and look vacantly about as though vitality had fled their bodies altogether'. Africa could only be liberated through subjugation. Best of all, there was no need for sophistication when asserting authority, because, as

Frederick Selous, the great Rhodesian scout, noted, 'Savages do not understand such leniency, they take it for fear and at once take advantage!'

The morally pure upper classes of England were saved. John Ruskin thundered, 'Make your country again a throne of kings; a sceptred isle, for all the world a source of light, a centre of peace.' To make Britain the seat of emperors, a dispenser of civilisation, it was necessary to construct a martial ethos. Numerous 'little wars', which were little more than the scything down of native hordes, became the training ground for the jaunty officer class — a place where they could flaunt their 'fitness' and earn promotion. The myth was crude but effective. And the public loved these romantic reactionaries in their spectacular braided uniforms with headgear sprouting spikes and feathers.

Take up the White Man's burden —
The savage wars of peace —
Fill full the mouth of famine
And bid the sickness cease;
And when your goal is nearest
The end for others sought,
Watch Sloth and heathen Folly
Bring all your hope to nought.
RUDYARD KIPLING, 'THE WHITE MAN'S BURDEN'

After the explorers and the Bible came rape. The imperial myth was fired with tales of the Queen of Sheba and King Solomon's Mines. Suddenly there was an economic benefit. Pillage and piracy were elevated to an art form supported by supremacist Protestantism. Joseph Conrad echoed other anti-imperialist voices when he stated, 'The conquest of the earth, which mostly means taking it away from those that have a different complexion or slightly flatter noses than ourselves, is not a pretty thing when you look at it too much. What redeems it is the idea only.' But, the flag-waving nation, bedazzled by a sleight of gunsmoke and mirrors, refused to heed the warnings and called for encore after encore.

But, foreign affairs was becoming a hydra-headed monster — all the more so since Britain's competitors were catching up with her ageing industry and armaments. The sabre-rattling Germans, French and Russians seethed at this pompous little island's global boasts and exploits as they watched England's gunboats ferry troops from one colonial insurrection to another – cheering whenever her nose got bloodied.

This was the age in which Baden-Powell grew up – an era in which a boy's character was shaped by the school he attended. Thackeray wrote that Charterhouse School was an institution of 'infernal misery, tyranny and annoyance'. It was a Gothic-Christian concentration camp focusing on 'character education' – this meant that it concentrated on competitive sports, rigorous discipline, ritual and extreme physical hardship at the expense of intellectual pursuits. Its contribution to Victorian England was a steady stream of emotionally floundering intellectual dwarves. Baden-Powell loved Charterhouse from the moment he arrived in 1870 as a boy of 13.

Greek was Greek to him and so were mathematics and French. Far better to be shinning up the goalpost (he was goalkeeper for the first XL) and terrifying the approaching opposition with wild Indian war-cries than applying oneself to academic pursuits. During idyllic periods of free time, he would disappear into the adjoining wooded copse – a Never-Never Land where he read Robert Louis Stevenson and stories of pirates; danced and played hide-and-seek by himself, teaching himself to move silently and lie quietly for long periods; studied the tracks of small animals and birds, then, creeping up on them, killed and cooked them over a smokeless fire; and, when danger approached in the guise of Redskins (the schoolmasters), he would fly up trees and hide in the highest branches. In his first year he fagged for, and was infatuated with, Edward Parry, Captain Perrywinkle, who would go on to play soccer for England. In turn, Charterhouse loved Baden-Powell from the moment he arrived.

His intellectual advancement at Charterhouse was so minute that his godfather, Dr Jowett, was forced to reject his application for admittance to Balliol, Oxford. His results in the entrance examination were so appalling that not even the intervention of his mother could get the decision rescinded. In a huff – at about the same time Sol Plaatje, the pre-eminent black South African political leader of the early twentieth century, was born – he sat the Army Examination, a test designed for his intellectual peers, in which he came second in Cavalry and fifth in Infantry. These results would propel him into dark continent adventures which he called 'howling good sport'. Later these escapades would lead to the founding of the Boy Scout movement; contribute, unwittingly through his bigotry, to the founding of the forerunner to the ANC (his actions at Mafeking were a major incitement to Sol Plaatje, one of the founders of the South African Native National Congress in 1912); and launch him into the mythological league of Wellington and Nelson.

Being placed in the top six meant he was exempted from a two-year spell at Sandhurst and was gazetted into the 13th Hussars — the 'Lilywhites'. A few weeks later, in 1876, he received orders to ship-out to join his regiment at Lucknow in India. On board the overcrowded *Serapis* Baden-Powell, on a voyage to live his dreams, briskly paced the deck as he witnessed children perish from the intense heat and the cook go insane and throw himself overboard. The eternal 'boy-man', watching this side-show, had grown into a real ripper. His short, well-groomed body was energetic and hard. His thinning, neatly trimmed hair had the teeth marks of a wet comb frozen in. His sharp-featured, handsome face, made more adult by a clipped moustache, appeared open and friendly. The only aspect in doubt were his cold, steely blue eyes — but that ruthlessness was camouflaged behind a chirpy, gregarious mask of exploding cigars, comic song and practical jokes. In reality he was an aggressive fascist and PG Woodhouse's bumbling Brabazon Plank — but the world chose to see him as an ingenious hero, with a flair for bending rules. He was Stalky, saintly soldier and *Boy's Own* magazine hero. Little did he know, as he paced the deck, that his initials would come to stand for British Pluck, the soldier whose wounds only hurt when he bathed his brain with laughter, and that Boy Scouts would write He with a capital when referring to Him.

Baden-Powell was a night person — the darkness imparting its power to him. Under the protective cloak of the night sky — sometimes red, sometimes blue, purple or black — he did mental battle against the dark schizoid forces that waged a capricious civil war within. One moment he was duelling with a death drive that would lead him on many hazardous adventures — escapades that he nevertheless felt necessary to gild and enrich — and the next he would be dousing the flames of his crippled sexuality.

He was consumed with a terrible fear of masturbation. He was petrified that this vice, of 'misusing ones private parts', would cause him to become an idiot, rot away the inside of his mouth and render him blind. The solution, when he found the strength, was to dunk his genitals in cold water. At times he would ponder less serious matters that were curiouser and curiouser. Wet dreams, a gratuitous waste of semen, led he believed to decay as the body recycled unused sperm to build strength. On happier occasions he would reflect on his good health achieved by breathing through his nose when he slept, drinking a glass of hot water before bedtime and having a jolly good 'rear' everyday. He would pass these quaint idiosyncrasies on to over half a billion children, mainly boys, in the next century.

His first tour of India was a fever-filled disaster made worse by murderous Afghanis he encountered in the sun-seared 'howling, rocky desert' of Afghanistan who believed their passport to Paradise was dying in battle against the English infidel; injuries he sustained when he accidentally shot himself in the foot; and impecunity. In between supplementing his income with sketches, stories and articles which the public at home devoured, he sent numerous pleas to his mother to get him transferred.

If his first tour of India was a journey to the underworld of the damned, his second was to Shangri-La. It was love at first sight when he laid eyes on Lieutenant McLaren at the start of this Indian tour. Had it just been the infatuation of a suppressed homosexual, the matter would be of no interest. The reason he was instantly besotted was that he mistook McLaren for a 14-year-old boy – hence his pet name, The Boy. McLaren, in fact, was 20 at the time and also an officer in the Lilywhites. This relationship would do much to fuel speculation that Baden-Powell was a homosexual with paedophiliac tendencies.

'The Little Prince', as McLaren was also known, was a great horseman and champion polo player. The happy pair were soon setting up home together and appearing opposite each other in plays. In their first performance together, in *The Area Belle* – in which Baden-Powell played Tosser and McLaren played Penelope – McLaren's opening song began 'I'd choose to be a daisy if I might be a flower.' In Muttra (south of Delhi where they were stationed), as the sunsets glowed rich and red and the band played the day away, the devoted couple would sit outside their beautifully decorated bungalow and watch as their dogs played with the fox terriers of the regiment and 'a nigger got a dozen with a cat o' ninetails'. During these blissful days, their neighbours would hear The Boy, normally a depressive, laughing a lot. They would wish him less cheer because his laugh was an intensely irritating hoot, much like the high-pitched wheeze of a train whistle.

In these early years of his career, Baden-Powell faced a dilemma. He had risen rapidly through the officer ranks through a mixture of natural leadership, luck and arrant self advertisement. The stories of India he wrote were dedicated to officers who could make a difference to his career. The recipients of this toadying, in case they were unaware of the honours bestowed on them, were sent copies of the stories by his mother. The public was beginning to see his paintings and read the exaggerated tales in which he was portrayed as a character straight from an adventure book. The fact that he was coming to be regarded as a 'delightfully breezy beggar' – who was a master of such puerile games as 'I am the Bouncing Brother of the Bosphorous' – was immaterial as he was rapidly approaching the ceiling of his career.

A senior officer had two options for advancement – he had to have made a name for himself in a 'little war' or have passed the Staff College examination. Considering his humiliation at Oxford, the idea of sitting another examination was horrific. A 'little war' became his holy grail. For two decades he chased niggers from Cape Town to Cairo and from Calcutta to Kandahar. It was all a great game and the world, in particular India and Africa, his playground. Sadly, other than for a few skirmishes and village burnings, his only action was confined to the stage. Wherever he went the niggers refused to oblige with a fight.

In frustration he unsuccessfully tried spying. When spying in Russia he took with him a full-dress and undress uniform as well as his own passport. He was arrested and sent home. But espionage had another purpose, clues to which were littered in his travel stories. Homosexuality was widely practised in Victorian England, but regarded as an act of beastliness and thus a dreadful risk for those who did not remain firmly barred and bolted in the closet. Places away from the prudish spotlight were ideal for the occasional romp. In one of his stories, set in North Africa, he had as his companion Hadj Ano, which literally translated means 'up anus'.

Then, suddenly, the light of 'happy circumstance' began to swing his way. His ray of destiny shone on Africa. In 1895 Major Baden-Powell received the longed for 'pink flimsy' telegram that had him treading air. 'It is the great thing for me,' he gushed as he read the order to 'proceed on active service as commander of a Native Levy in Ashanti' in what is today central Ghana. The terror of Staff College could now be shelved. It did not work out like that, but importantly he had entered the aloof and patrician Sir Garnet Wolseley's inner circle – the famed 'Garnet Ring'.

The Ashanti were synonymous with unspeakable terror in Victorian England. The exaggerated stories of their fetishes and sacrificial practices sent shivers down the spines of England's citizens, confirming the worst of the truths about the savage inhabitants of Africa. Wild reports had begun to reach Wolseley in 1894 that the Ashanti king, Prempeh, was refusing to pay the indemnity of 50 000 ounces of gold levied after Wolseley's own expedition 20 years before. Moreover he was getting restless once more for independence.

The expedition was sent off by the tumults of over a million cheering Londoners.

Oh Prempeh, Prempeh
You'd better mind your eye;
You'd better be civil,
Or else you'll have to die,
And your kingdom of Ashanti,
You'll never see it more,
If you fight to old West Yorks
And the Special Service Corps
       W S ADAMS, EDWARDIAN PORTRAITS, 1957

The troops would have been better for reading Stanley: 'Fatal Africa! One after another, travellers drop away. It is such a huge continent, and each of its secrets is environed by so many difficulties – the torrid heat, the miasma exhaled from the soil, the noisome vapours enveloping every path, the giant cane-grass suffocating the wayfarer ... the unspeakable misery of life within the wild continent ... in the land of blackness'.

The fronds of palm trees hung tiredly in the decaying air crawling with mosquitoes and thick with the odours of rotting fish as the ship docked at Cape Coast Castle on the Gold Coast. But what a 'wag' it was for Baden-Powell to learn that local chiefs were referred to as kings. The amusement was all the greater for his being able to urge monarchs from their hovels at the end of a stick. 'Without undue swank,' he wrote, 'there is great joy in cursing a real live king, especially when one is merely in one's pyjamas.' The fun, unhappily, was quickly dampened by reports that Prempeh's belligerence was overstated. The indemnity was an impossible burden which he wanted to negotiate. Baden-Powell prayed: 'That the Ashanti will fight is the great hope of those who toil through the long hot hours in this steaming, fetid atmosphere.'

As he reconnoitred ahead, cutting a swathe through the dark, damp, oppressive carpet of jungle, he was able to note, from the hammock in which he was carried when the heat became too intense, just how lazy the people of Africa were. On these occasions he was inclined to administer a lick of a whip, which, to these primitive brutes, whom he described as 'not far removed from the monkeys they hunted', was, but a small thing! He was also able to observe, as he barked orders, that 'a dog would grasp your meaning in one half the time.'

The worst happened. Baden-Powell found Prempeh – wrapped in a collision of colourful cotton and smothered in gold jewellery – at Kumasi, sucking on a mango, and unsportingly friendly. Baden-Powell was greeted with a welcome of beating drums, yells and blasts of ivory horn. He was devastated. When the main body of the expedition arrived with the governor, Colonel Sir Francis Scott, Prempeh was made to kneel before Scott and hug the governor's knees. Even this profound insult would not light the spark. When the gold was demanded, less than 700 ounces were produced. Baden-Powell was given the task, one he undertook with relish, of finding 'hidden' treasure. The spree of destruction that followed enraged the Ashanti but hardly assuaged Baden-Powell's frustration. Prempeh, his mother and their family were arrested and the grass houses of Kumasi torched. As the British set off back for Cape Coast Castle – with black palls of smoke billowing sluggishly into the air behind them – Staff College once again beckoned.

While avoiding Prempeh's spitting mother, a foul-tempered harridan with folds of skin hanging off her back, Baden-Powell had time to reflect on the quality of the malarial, acridly-sweating British troops being carried piggy-back through the jungle. 'Tommy Atkins', evaporating in the tropics, vomiting blood and covered in a heat rash, was the unhealthiest species of all.

If the British upper classes were the knights, then their intellectual equals, the lower classes, were their fodder. While the officers flaunted their stuff at home, it would not do to have troops too literate or perceptive to see through their thin veneer in the field. Drawn from the teeming, unwholesome slums covered by crushing soot and layers of greasy smoke, the average British soldier was shot through with diseases, the most common being syphilis and alcoholism. Poorly paid and trained, they were the unthinking species despised by all — their only duty 'to look smart in times of peace and get killed in times of war.'

When the 'arf-made recuity goes out to the East
'E acts like a babe an' 'e drinks like a beast,
An' 'e wonders because 'e is frequently deceased . . . .
RUDYARD KIPLING, 'THE YOUNG BRITISH SOLDIER'

The awaiting calamity that Baden-Powell foresaw of putting British troops to the test against stern opposition was not long in coming. General F Fuller would write, at the beginning of the South African War, 'We had not been trained for war, we knew nothing about war ... about anything at all which mattered and upon which our lives might depend ... We could march tolerably well, could form advances and rearguards exactly as our ancestors had done one hundred before; we could fire volleys, fix bayonets, cheer and blow whistles; not for a moment did it enter anyone's head that we should be found wanting in this way'. They must have improved, because when the Ashanti expedition docked in London the army could not even get the whistling and cheering right. Their ship docked at the same time as the vessel bearing the disgraced Dr Leander Starr Jameson, the leader of the failed Jameson Raid, from South Africa. Dr Jim was packed off to prison with the triumphant sounds of the celebrating British brass band meant to welcome the expeditionary forces.

O it's Tommy this, an' Tommy that, an' 'Tommy, go away';
But it's 'Thank you, Mister Atkins,' when the band begins to play,
The band begins to play, my boys, the band begins to play,
O it's 'Thank you, Mister Atkins,' when the band begins to play.
RUDYARD KIPLING, 'TOMMY'

Baden-Powell wrote a mainly fictional book, *The Downfall of Prempeh*, within four days of his return. He was promoted, at the age of 36, to brevet lieutenant-colonel. Prempeh, for his part, was exiled to the Seychelles, returning many years later to Ashanti as president of their Boy Scouts movement.

Shortly after Ashanti, came the precursor, for Baden-Powell, to the real thing. The interlude in Matabeleland — later, with Mashonaland, to form Rhodesia in southern Africa — was to provide him with 'the best adventure of my life' and introduce him to the game that was 'better than any other game' – man hunting, or, in his own words, 'the sport of nigger hunts'. He had found the supreme animal prey. But Matabeleland was more than just an amusement park. From childhood he had demonstrated a deep love of scouting and here he was able to elevate his skill to a new level.

Before Matabeleland, Baden-Powell had foreseen the benefits of scouting in warfare. He believed that military success rested on an accurate knowledge of an enemy's actions, movements, strengths and preparations and on the quality of scouts – the eyes and ears of the military – who would gather this information. Moreover, he believed that basic training in the principles of scouting would make the normal soldier more alert. These ideas were published in 1884 in his first book, *Reconnaissance and Scouting*, dedicated to Wolseley. In Matabeleland he would articulate the next step, by expropriating the ideas of Frederick Brunham, toward establishing the largest youth movement in history – an organisation whose primary aim would be to cure the deficiencies he witnessed in the average British soldier.

Burnham was an American prospector and Civil War hero who, seeing the taming of the American frontier, looked to the frontiers of Africa as the source of the untold wealth hinted at in *King Solomon's Mines*. Like many frontiersmen he built castles in the air. He had, with his family, driven up from Durban to Matabeleland on a Studebaker buckboard. Though he would later become a successful businessman in America, his Rhodesian adventure is remembered for his scouting services to Rhodes during the wars against the Matabele. Burnham, whom Baden-Powell referred to as 'a better class Buffalo Bill', became his scouting mentor.

Matabele anger had simmered, boiling over from time to time, ever since Rhodes bamboozled them out of their land and Jameson defeated them in the bloody Matabele War of 1893. Their best land was taken from them and given to Frederick Selous's Pioneer Column; their men forced to provide labour; and a hut tax imposed on them. The Rhodesian authorities, when the rinderpest struck, did not bother to consult with the tribe as they set about destroying the cattle that were their economic lifeblood. The Jameson Raid, in late 1895, and the rounding up of the raiders made up largely of British South African Police, left few colonial police in the country and the Matabele seized a golden opportunity. The early stages of the 1896 Matabele Uprising took the form of attacking isolated settlers and prospectors. By April, Bulawayo was surrounded and, in June, the Mashona of Mashonaland had joined the rebellion. The

16

situation, for the settlers, was desperate. For Baden-Powell it was heaven, he had his 'little war'. He very nearly spoilt it.

Baden-Powell was sent to Matabeleland in May 1896 as chief-of-staff to Sir Frederick Carrington. He arrived in Bulawayo from Mafeking on a regular 'Buffalo-Bill-Wild-West' Deadwood Coach and immediately loved what he saw. 'The streets were filled with crowds of the most theatrical looking swashbucklers and cowboys ... All men dressed in Boer hats and puggree, flannel shirt, breeches and puttees; so sunburnt it is hard to tell at first sight, whether a man is English, half-caste or light kaffir.' These were the courageous, resourceful men whose spirit was the frontier spirit − a restless, impatient yearning to cross the next river or line of hills. These larger than life characters were, like himself, convinced of the inherent superiority of their kind. On the enemy side were the thrillingly wild Matabele − bedecked with feathers and wearing tails, brandishing ox-hide shields, their assegais flashing − capable of great feats of endurance, strength and bravery. What a pleasant change they made from the cowards of Ashanti.

The Matabele operated in small guerrilla bands, avoiding frontal assaults. This was an ideal scenario for Baden-Powell's talents and thirst for adventure: 'lion or leopard, boar or buck, nigger or nothing, you never knew what was going to turn up', he wrote. The country brought out the cowboy in him. He began to wear the pinched Stetson and neckerchief that would later become part of every scout's uniform. He wore a bright red shirt and from his hips hung twin revolvers. While hunting 'the laughing black fiends' over 'the weird jumbled mass of bush and boulders' of the Matopo Mountains, he wrote, 'Didn't my heart go pit-a-pat the first time the Matabele saw me on foot among hill-side boulders. But when I found I could ... skip away faster than they could follow, it became a cheerier adventure'. In fact, they spotted him often until he realised his red shirt was a beacon − it went and the next item, the khaki flannel shirt, was added to the uniform that would become that of the Boy Scouts. Such was his romanticised view of the Wild West that the collapsible bath and scented lavender soap that went everywhere with him were not the slightest bit paradoxical.

His Matabeleland adventure was seminal in the lead-up to the formation of the Boy Scout movement. Burnham introduced him to the science of woodcraft − the knowledge of the wild that permitted a man to survive, even thrive, in the wilderness without help from the civilised world. Burnham also told him stories of the laagers at Salisbury and Victoria in 1893 where the old men and boys as young as seven carried bandoleers so that they could pass out shells to the men in the defences. Those too small to carry arms were told to carry water and act as messengers. Most importantly, it was here that the concept of taking boys from industrialised, urban environments and inculcating in them tribal values, clean living and moral virtue began to formulate.

The veld bestowed a vitality essential to his very being. Here was his Eden and he felt as remote and difficult to subjugate as his surroundings. The wide, sun-warmed open spaces, teeming with life and given its leopard-spots by the flat-topped acacias and thorn scrub, conjured up magic for him. This was his Africa. Not the green, stagnant, rotting world of Equatorial Africa, but the open primal savannah, which stretched as far as the eye could see, was his paradise. The birds called and chirped to each other and, when they were still, he could hear the wind swish through the grass. The searing midday sun, the nights wild with stars and alive with screeching owl and flitting bats, the scent of grass and shrub, everything was sharp, clean. The enchantment was heightened by the freedom and adventure of being in an area where the only law was your own.

The Matabele came to know him as 'Impeesa' — 'the hyena that skulks by night'. Baden-Powell reworked this to mean 'the wolf that never sleeps' — a sobriquet he wore with pride. The Matabele had come closest, with this name, to labelling him for what he was, a scavenging creature of the night. But it was his blood lust tinged with voyeurism that was nearly his undoing.

Matabeleland's Somabula Forest was teeming with rebels. The Cape authorities, as well as Sir Frederick Carrington, had issued written instructions that captured rebels were not to be shot. Baden-Powell, while burning villages and blowing up caves to flush out tribal people who had taken refuge, captured the big-fish, Chief Unwini, who had refused to lay down his arms and exhorted the Matabele to keep on fighting. Baden-Powell decided to court-martial the injured warrior. The trial was a farce and Unwini was sentenced to be shot by firing squad at sunset before a parade of tribespeople and Matabele prisoners. It was a day Baden-Powell had dreamt of.

'Ooh! It will be a long time before I get over that catastrophe,' mourned Baden-Powell after missing a public execution in Algeria. He would dream of what it must have been like. 'PRRR-AH! The volley flies; and through the light-brown whisk of smoke one sees him hanging limply from his arms, head down and knees all loose and swaying'. All his life he kept a photograph, in his Matabele Scrapbook, of three 'spies' that had been hanged from a tree in Bulawayo − he titled it 'The Christmas Tree'.

It is not recorded if Chief Unwini, 'the fine old savage', obliged with the necessary twitches and sways to satisfy Baden-Powell's curiosity as his life gurgled away in the purple afterglow of evening. It did lead to an order from Cape Town that Baden-Powell be arrested. Carrington refused because Baden-Powell's luck was in full cry. The rebellion had begun to peter out and Baden-Powell was able to claim that his action had contributed to ending the crisis and restoring the prestige of Britain. A court of inquiry dismissed all charges against him, and, on his return to England, he was promoted to full colonel and returned to India as commander of the 5th Dragoon Guards. Unwini, rather than blot his record, was to have a profoundly positive effect on his career. Baden-Powell, in Rhodesia, was regarded as a British hero who got things done.

It was because of this, and a belief that his unconventional methods closely approximated how the Boers would fight in the event of war between the British and the South African Republic, that he was chosen to play them at their own game. His orders, given him by Wolseley at their meeting, remain an item of intense debate. There is no doubt that he broke them by investing himself in Mafeking. On the surface his orders were a nebulous nonsense given to him by people Lord Kitchener described as thinking Mafeking 'was the nearest seaport to Pretoria'. But, Baden-Powell's orders only make sense when peering beyond the smokescreen cloaking a nudge-nudge-wink-wink collusion of powerful cronies. Though no direct evidence exists to Rhodes's involvement, the circumstantial evidence is sufficient to detect 'the spoor of the Cape sorcerer in this'.

Baden-Powell's orders were to raise two regiments − which would include the police of Rhodesia and Bechuanaland − of mounted cavalry and to mount, equip, train and supply them with the least possible delay. In the event of war, he was to organise the defence of the Rhodesian and Bechuanaland frontiers and as far as possible keep the forces of the enemy occupied in that direction away from the main forces and the port cities of the Cape Colony and Natal. The essence of these orders was to keep mobile. The fact that Baden-Powell did the very opposite has led detractors to accuse him of cowardice and worse and supporters to praise him as a deeply insightful commander. Neither assessment is true. Amongst all his faults there is no evidence of faint-heartedness. Nor did he ever display a talent for perspicacity other than in matters of defence. His gifts were to take the ingenuity and ideas of others and promote them as his own and to ride good luck whenever it presented itself. The reality, in the field, was always going to be, as was the case with Jameson a few years earlier, that Baden-Powell would neither be able to raise a substantial force of more than a thousand men nor would such an irregular force be any match for the hard-riding, sharp-shooting Boers. It appears that what the cabal required this time was only a show of 'make-believe' to bring the stubborn Kruger to his senses and force him to back down.

Cecil Rhodes, notwithstanding the personal disaster the Jameson Raid had proved, still carried a vast amount of influence in London and in South Africa, particularly Cape Town, and still cherished the hope of a federation of Southern African states. Shrewd, ruthless and — ironically for a social-Darwinist — sickly, Rhodes, the 'Uncrowned Emperor of South Africa', still desired the downfall of Kruger. But, for him to promote the brand of imperialism in which he played the leading role, the problem posed by Kruger required resolution through the extension of British influence by means other than conquest. The 'Robber Baron' was acutely aware that, in the event of war, the British would inevitably be victorious and his interests would be subject to a more sophisticated plunderer.

Rhodes was not just concerned about a British victory in the 'crisis' Sir Alfred Milner, the High Commissioner to the Cape Colony, was working nicely toward. He was also worried that the war would be altogether a different proposition from that being sketched in smoky rooms. There was a danger behind the lie, growing out of all proportion with the help of bellicose speeches and jingoistic headlines, that the threat posed by Kruger's 'trumpery little state' was risible. Kruger, Milner's 'snuffy, mendacious savage' was pilloried. Surely, Britons thought, this primeval man with greasy hair and beard fanning out across his chest, with shrewish eyes that had saddle bags beneath them, who spat in public, left his pipe sticking out of his pocket and believed the earth was flat, could be no match for their mighty regiments. The Boers were derided as ignorant, dirty backvelders. They were portrayed as obstinate, single-minded bigots with their heads buried in Bibles. The short, sharp lesson they were to be given, was for their own good. Yet Kruger's regime was more stable than most in Britain realised. By the end of the war Churchill would praise these fiercely independent people, with their stolid features, blue cloth jackets, wide-brimmed hats green with age, each with a fine horse, excellent Mauser and double bandoleer, as 'the most capable mounted warriors since the Mongols'. They were not lacking in military hardware either, being provided with the latest by Britain's many adversaries.

Joseph Chamberlain, the Colonial Secretary, known variously as Emperor Joe, Pushful Joe, Radical Joe or Judas, owed Rhodes an enormous debt of gratitude for not disclosing his role in plotting the Jameson Raid. Rhodes was in London at the time Gough sent the telegram for Baden-Powell to present himself to Wolseley. He was also to arrange the two crucial 'chance' meetings Baden-Powell was to have in Cape Town with the Wilsons and Benjamin Weil, the largest wholesaler in Bechuanaland. On his return to Cape Town he was confident that the crisis Milner was working up to would not take place and that Kruger would back off. 'It is too ridiculous,' Rhodes declared. 'There is not the slightest chance of war.' Baden-Powell was the perfect choice to make this happen as he was a proficient actor, supposed 'action man' and had the trust of 'Rhodes's settlers'. He could be relied on to create a crisis by his mere presence on the north-west frontier that would frighten the Boers into negotiating a satisfactory peace. This was classic Rhodes, the adventurer conspirator, using *agents provocateur* to create the chaos within which he could further his aims. But, the mistake he made with Jameson was to intimately involve a *Boy's Own* hero in his vision and planning – the mistake he made with Baden-Powell was not to involve him. Or maybe his problem was simply a reliance on *Boy's Own* heroes to do his bidding. Whatever the case, Baden-Powell, like Jameson, threw away the script and wrote a new drama in which he was the lead player.

Baden-Powell's troubles began when he arrived in Cape Town, 'a fourth rate provincial town full of cads'. He had expected red carpet treatment on his arrival but no one was there to meet him. WP Schreiner, the Prime Minister of the Cape Colony, and Sir William Butler, the General Officer Commanding the Cape, treated him with undisguised animosity as both anticipated that the matter with Kruger would be solved without dramatics. Believing Baden-Powell a dangerous interloper, they openly obstructed and frustrated his orders. No, he could not recruit men in the Cape Colony; no, they would not advance him money for supplies; no, he could not enter Mafeking; and, no, he could not wear a uniform in the Cape Province.

Little concerned, he turned to the ambitious Sir Alfred Milner – the hawk who even looked like a raptor. Milner, his delicate face long and thin, his expression mobile with grey hooded eyes under arched eyebrows, immediately saw through Baden-Powell's orders. He cursed Wolseley because if anyone could dash his perfectly laid plans it was Baden-Powell – a schoolboy hero from the Rhodes-Jameson mould. Milner's plan was to work up to war whilst showing Kruger to be the aggressor. His programme was running smoothly until Baden-Powell and Cecil presented themselves. The disastrous consequence could well be peace before a shot was fired. Milner rebuffed Baden-Powell and Cecil before his predatory eyes fell on the delectable Violet. Whilst Edward Cecil was having a beastly time in Mafeking, Alfred and Violet would be practising archery on the lawns of Government House, riding bicycles through the mist under Table Mountain, galloping down to Green Point and generally getting to know each other more intimately. This cooing couple would marry in 1921 after the death of Edward.

Baden-Powell had two other meetings in Cape Town, both of which he thought were chance, but would make his stay worthwhile. He met Benjamin Weil from Mafeking, who agreed to accept a 500 000 pound letter of credit from Cecil, a note he knew neither Baden-Powell nor Cecil had the funds to cover or authority to issue. Weil, for his part, forgot to mention that he had foreseen war coming and was in Cape Town to buy in as much stock as he could as prices would soar at the outbreak of hostilities and that Mafeking, in any case, was flooded with supplies that had been built up in anticipation of a levy being imposed on goods exported to Rhodesia. The levy, because of political uncertainty, was shelved and business people were left holding tonnes of speculative goods. The other meeting, at Rhodes's residence, Groote Schuur, was with Captain Gordon Wilson, Lady Sarah Wilson's husband, and an officer of the Royal Horse Guards, who Baden-Powell appointed his second aide-de-camp.

Baden-Powell saw no point in remaining in a town stifled by bureaucrats. He left Cecil to organise the supplies and caught a train, with the Wilsons, for Bulawayo. The train wound its way from Cape Town and on through the Boland. A verdant canvas of rolling hills bordered by purple mountains, brushed with a veil of haze, flashed by. It steamed through Kraaifontein,

Klein Drakenstein, Worcester and De Doorns before huffing and puffing its way over the Hexrivierberge, whose granite switchback pinnacles were polished silver by millennia of heat, winds, storms and withering erosion. In the desolate Karoo the train passed ostriches and flocks of sheep that sweltered by day and shivered by night as the heat quickly dissipated in the azure skies. It stopped at sidings — whistling and bleating impatiently — in countryside that appeared impossible to support human habitation, where well-wishers called goodbye to family and friends: Laingsberg, Beaufort West, Kimberley, Vryburg and on to the dreary, thorny, raw sienna plains of Mafeking, burnt by overexposure to the sun, that has the text of all contemporary South African history imprinted in its dust. On, through the ancient mopani and acacia plains, teeming with game and studded with rocky outcrops and the haunting, tapering trunks of Africa's most potent symbol — the baobab — to Bulawayo, where the only talk was of war. There a force was quickly recruited and placed under Colonel Herbert Plumer. Baden-Powell set up a second recruiting station at Ramatlhabama, near where Jameson had launched his raid, and placed this force under Lieutenant-Colonel Charles Hore — a man out of his depth in even the shallowest puddle.

Secret messages were whispered through the grapevine that Baden-Powell was looking for men. Those who responded were a sorry collection unlikely to terrify the Boers: tailors, jockeys, musicians, farm workers, carpenters, decorators, male nurses, florists, stewards and waiters flounced in. Most were loafers who had never ridden a horse or handled a rifle — they were little more than an 'organised crowd'. At the same time, news was filtering through of larger than expected concentrations of Boer commandos gathering on the western frontier of the South African Republic. Baden-Powell set about training this force at Ramatlhabama, a few kilometres from Mafeking, just inside the Bechuanaland border.

Ramatlhabama is a wretched place — treeless, dusty, sweltering, fly infested. The first few weeks amongst a shambles of collapsed tents were high farce. The horses provided Baden-Powell were unbroken. A lot of time was spent picking up recruits — who had arrived trim in their uniforms, cocked slouch hats and high boots — who were shortly sprawled in the bleached dust. Shooting practice was little better as bullets flew in every direction except at their targets. Pressing daily pleas came from Mafeking requesting Baden-Powell to protect the town. At first he was unwilling to commit any of his wholly inadequate forces to defend a town the Cape authorities had seemingly abandoned. But Hanbury-Tracy concluded toward the end of August that the situation was hopeless, approached Baden-Powell and laid out the only option he had of success.

The intention of Baden-Powell's published orders, as he interpreted them, was to draw away a large force of Boers from the harbours of the Cape and Natal while Wolseley rushed troops to South Africa. Mafeking, its location and tenuous links with the outside world making it the most vulnerable town in the Cape Colony, fitted the bill perfectly. The Boers, in the event of war, were determined to take Mafeking. As a town it was relatively insignificant, but it was an important railhead and contained a mountain of supplies. Most importantly, as the town was at the cross-roads of all competing interests in South Africa, it was a hothouse from which powerful men had fomented mischief and, as a consequence, an emotional sore in Boer consciousness. It was on the 'missionary road' as well as Rhodes's visionary road from Cape Town to Cairo; it was the jumping off point for Frederick Selous's Pioneer Column into the interior; and it blocked the Boer road to the west that would allow them to join with German South West Africa.

Mafeking, the capital of the white man's badlands, was a town reeking with character, history, adventure and intrigue. Mzilikazi, king of the Matabele, tore through, as did the outlaw Scotty Smith and the Griqua chief Nicholas Waterboer. Baden-Powell was well aware of its historical, albeit logistic, significance. He would have been aware that the Boers hated it because the Tshidi-Barolong tribe, based here, had bested them more than once in the battle for land and it was hereabouts that Jameson launched his fateful raid. Baden-Powell immediately saw the possibilities sketched out for him by his intelligence officer. His irregular force, laughable in the field, would be more than adequate if taken from their horses and placed behind defences and in trenches. It was from this point he began to prepare for and engineer the siege that would catapult Mafeking into international consciousness. Mafeking would be the bait in an elaborate trap – he was suddenly the master of his own destiny.

While awaiting permission to enter the town, Baden-Powell held secret meetings with the mayor, F Whitley, the resident magistrate, Charles Bell, and the resident high commissioner, Major Hamilton Goold-Adams. When permission came in mid-September, he wasted no time in moving his Ramatlhabama force into Mafeking – leaving the Bulawayo contingent under Plumer, whose force included The Boy as one of his officers, to harass the Boers along the north-west frontier – and immediately set about preparing for a long siege. Unbeknown to the residents of the town, their relief palpable as the sounds of bugles filled the air and cavalry rode in by the hundred, their whinnying horses kicking up a fine dust that hung swirling in the morning air, their town was to become the stage for Baden-Powell's most enduring drama.

Mafeking. Its name and history evokes red-cheeked little girls in frilly dresses, zealous priests promising eternal life and a honky-tonk hellbroth of politicians, prostitutes, soldiers, adventurers, brigades, desperados and renegades. It recalls an eccentric village of geometric Victorian trimness nestling on the willow-boughed banks of the warm, languid, muddy Molopo River whose waters become incandescent each evening as it flows into the setting sun. It awakens the sounds of hagglers, clanking blacksmiths, a boy twanging a Jewish harp and the ghostly droning of fly shrouded carcasses hanging in the butcher's shop. It conjures up the layered aromas of noisome sweat, stale ale, urine and freshly baked bread perfumed by a wisp of camel thorn wood-smoke. And, it would come to invoke outrage at its unwarranted, shabby treatment of its black neighbour, Mahikeng – A Place of Stones – the picturesque *stadt* of round houses with roofs pointing into the morning sky where eagles soar on rising thermals.

Baden-Powell took over Dixon's Hotel as his headquarters and acquired the adjacent attorney's office as his own. After placing two framed photos of McLaren on his desk he lifted his head and peered out of the window. As his eyes flashed round the bustling Market Square, Baden-Powell would have seen the photographer, with a pencil stub behind his ear, battling to get a girl to sit still for a portrait; the chemist dispensing pills; the bicycle shop filled with cycles with pedals attached to the front axle; queues at the Standard Bank; and fleetingly caught the headlines of the day's *Mafeking Mail and Protectorate Guardian* as a copy was lifted into the air by a sudden gust of wind. He would have smelt the odours of the farm stalls – selling milk, cheese and a rainbow of fresh fruit and vegetables – intermingling with the sounds and music from the rowdy saloon of the hotel before wafting over the wide veranda and up the red bricks. He would have heard irritable horses, secured to hitching posts, stamping their feet and rattling their halter chains as they tried in vain to rid themselves of the flies that hummed round their heads.

To the north of Market Square, beyond the recreation ground, was the recently completed Victoria Hospital and newly built convent of the Irish Sisters of Mercy. To the west was the railway compound with its well equipped workshops, an engine house, numerous sidings and a bungalow camp for its employees. Across Railway Street, in the Commercial Hotel bar, presided over by a greasy barman, unwashed men sipped brandy in a fog of tobacco smoke. A mile out, to the north-east, was the racecourse with a tin-roofed grandstand. To the south of the racecourse, toward the river, the old Brickfields. To the south-west, on either bank of the river, was the native *stadt* of Mahikeng and halfway between the black and white towns, close to Warren's Fort, were the barracks and stables of the British South African Police, above which hung a Union Jack, dejected for want of a breeze.

The residential heart of the town consisted of a shabby grid of dusty, single-storey, red mud brick, tin-roofed, porched houses — filled with a litter of furniture — that lined the unpaved streets that carried Zeederburg Coaches and Cape Carts to the interior. From the houses came a clash of cooking utensils, the scent of a dinner of fried meat and coffee and the wail of a tired child. Mangy dogs squirmed and panted in grassless gardens, fowl cackled and fluffed their feathers while pigs grunted over slops in the back of others, here a flower, there a cabbage patch. Dotted between these residences were several churches from which the crucified figure of Christ gazed down on supplicants, two schools, another two hotels where men sauntered in and staggered out, a Masonic lodge, the Mafeking Club, a cemetery, courthouse and jail. Beyond the outer limits of this featureless town lay the Kalahari to the west, Bechuanaland a few kilometres to the north and the Transvaal even closer to the east.

From mid-September, as news of Baden-Powell's investiture spread, the town began to fill with refugees from the surrounding farms seeking shelter. At the same time the neighbouring native *stadt* of Mahikeng was swollen by some 2 000 desperate refugees, mostly from the mines in Johannesburg, who sought protection. These people, to the inhabitants of the white town, were different. They were unwelcome intruders bringing filth and disease. Baden-Powell, however, temporarily needed their digging skills to dredge the trenches and bunkers he planned as an integral part of the town's defences.

From the outset he set about preparing to withstand a long siege. At first he was not going to include Mahikeng in his defences, only changing his mind when he realised that the enemy would be able to enter Mafeking, unseen, from that quarter. Even so, he refused a request from the Barolong to arm themselves, reiterating what Magistrate Bell had told them: this was to be a white man's war. All able-bodied men were enlisted in the town guard under Colonel Vyvyan, stock taken of all supplies in the town and arrangements made for women, their eyes raw and red rimmed from tears, and children to leave for Cape Town. For those refusing to leave, who had inadequate bunker protection, Baden-Powell hastily erected an enclosure, to the north of the *stadt*, on Mr Rowland's farm. This Women's Laager, intended as a refuge, was shelled often, and, because of overcrowding and disease, became a squalid, miserable place. It was not easy persuading the remaining women, mainly of Dutch origin, to go to the camp. Magistrate Bell noted in his diary that one woman, on being dragged there, declared that she hoped the lintels of the houses in Mafeking would be smeared with the blood of English women and children.

The coloured population, drawn mainly from the labourers of the surrounding market gardens, were placed in a corps of Cape Boys and railway employees organised themselves into the 'Railway Volunteers'. Irrespective of what was stated publicly, non-Barolong black residents of the Fingo Location were organised into the Black Watch. Sixty women of the white town volunteered as nurses and the Sisters of Mercy hastily organised a casualty ward and equipped an operating theatre. The west and south-west were to be protected by 500 armed Tshidi-Barolong and 21 officers and 448 men of the Protectorate Regiment under Colonel Hore. The southern approaches at Cannon Kopje were the responsibility of the Tshidi and 10 officers and 81 men of the British South Africa Police (BSAP) under Colonel Walford. The north-east was to be held by the five officers and 11 men of the Bechuanaland Rifles under Captain Cowan. Brickfields was the responsibility of the four officers and 168 men of the Cape Police and Cape Boys under Inspectors Marsh and Browne and the north and north-west were the responsibility of the 116 men of the Railway Volunteers. Rail track was laid along the northern defences so that a mobile patrol could be mounted.

The shrub to the north-east of the town was cleared and thorn bush dragged down. On the open veld on the south-west fringe of the *stadt* earthworks were raised, rifle pits dug and trenches sited. The outer perimeter of the defences, Baden-Powell's aggressive line from where attacks could be launched, consisted of 60 strong points. These were connected by a zigzag of trenches dug by the black refugees. The strong points, the first time such technology was used in war, were connected by telephone to Baden-Powell's headquarters. An inner defence system was created, manned by the 300 members of the town guard and also connected to headquarters. Once these works were complete, the black refugees were put to work digging bunkers for the white residents of the town.

The town's defenders were reasonably well equipped with Lee Metford and older Martini Henry single loaders. The artillery was spectacularly inadequate. Of the four muzzle loading 7-pounders, two had been abandoned by Warren at Warren's Fort 15 years ago. Gerans, the local wagon builder, and his foreman, Green, managed to repair them but they could only fire two kilometres. For the rest there was a 1-pounder Hotchkiss, a two-inch Nordenfeldt, seven .303 Maxim machine guns and two small quick-firers. The three steam engines, *Mosquito*, *Firefly* and *Wasp* were armoured and 'boogie-trucks' reinforced with rail track welded to their sides to act as mobile fortresses. Mule teams were laid on for transport and ambulances constructed.

Above Baden-Powell's office a tower was erected from where he could view all his fortifications. A hole was cut through the floor of the building so that he could bark commands into the mouthpiece connected to the telephone exchange below. The captain was on the brig and in command. He could scan the surrounding landscape for enemy activity, or the horizon for a sudden attack. Still, these defences were a paper tiger against the might of the Boer force, under General Cronje, massed on the frontier. Baden-Powell resorted to bluff.

Beyond the outer perimeter he began to lay an extensive 'minefield'. He buried thousands of little black boxes, manufactured in a 'secret laboratory', and marked them with cautionary signs. These boxes were filled with sand, but the Boers were not to know that. Amid great publicity he ordered trials of the mines in which a few well-placed explosions were enough to give the impression that there really was a minefield. He manned some forts with dummies and laid out imaginary barbed wire over which people would step with great care. It never occurred to the Boers, before and during the siege, that cattle could meander safely over the mines and through the barbed wire.

In the days before the start of the war tension reached fever pitch.

Mafeking was the centre of world news. The build up of Boer forces could best be observed from the town. Hard drinking, hard living correspondents began arriving by train. *The Times* sent John Angus Hamilton, Reuters Vere Stent and Parslow for the *Daily Chronicle*. J Emerson Neilly of the *Pall Mall Gazette* reported that 'Mafeking [was] in a state of excitement … Crowds were at the railway station, women and children were preparing to quit what they believed was a doomed town, and everyone talked of the coming war. There were frightened faces, faces that had anxiety printed on them … '

On the streets people gathered in knots, all discussing the burning issues. Merchant dignitaries waited in high-collared white shirts, hunters, a preacher or two and barkeepers forgot their differences in the maelstrom of fear and excitement. Then, suddenly, Jameson, released shortly after his imprisonment, arrived to ostensibly help with defences. Rhodes was in Kimberley organising the defences of that town and it would not be beneath him to send his able lieutenant to rescue the situation from a maverick. His appearance nearly gave Baden-Powell a heart attack. On the pretext that the Boers would have stopped at nothing short of tearing the town apart brick by brick if they suspected him of being there, Baden-Powell sent him packing.

He also made hasty plans to rid himself of Rhodes and Jameson's friend, Lady Sarah Wilson. But she could wait while he dealt with more dangerous 'spies'. Baden-Powell was, justifiably considering his covert intentions, paranoid about spies. Had the real position regarding dummy fortifications and deliberate misinformation been leaked to the Boers, his bait to lure them to Mafeking would not have been taken. The town was, because of its proximity to the Transvaal, a suspected hotbed of spies. On 7 October he published an order.

Spies
There are in town today nine known spies.
They are hereby warned to leave before 12 noon
tomorrow or they will be apprehended

Fear swept through Mafeking. The effect of the notice was that neighbour began to inform on neighbour and friends on each other. Mr Heald, the jailer, began to make room for an influx of Boer 'agents'. Men in bars toasted Queen Victoria more vigorously.

On 8 October Baden-Powell received a preview of the ultimatum to be issued by Kruger, to the British, on the following day. Baden-Powell, realising the terms were impossible to meet, knew exactly when war would start. He despatched *Mosquito*, under Lieutenant Nesbit and 15 men, to go and pick up artillery he was expecting from Vryburg. The Boers under General Koos de la Rey, with prior knowledge of the train's itinerary, ambushed and derailed it at Kraaipan. The first shots of the war were fired as the locomotive thrashed impotently in a great swirl of noise and smoke on the morning of 12 October.

On the same day, *The Times* reported: 'The position is critical. Colonel Baden-Powell has warned the inhabitants to expect an attack ... Our defences are completely organised. Every available man has been mustered, and the women are in laager. A native tribe, the Barolong, under Chief Wessels, are co-operating in outpost duties'. That night Baden-Powell sent a staff officer to order Lady Sarah Wilson out of town before it was besieged. Disappointed, but with no alternative as she was an officer's wife, she was forced to obey.

That 'joyous little dodge' was about to start. Amongst the last mail from Mafeking, before it was besieged, were the corrected proofs of Baden-Powell's latest book, *Aids to Scouting For NCO's and Men*. As his fame grew in the event that supposedly wrote a new chapter in the annals of Victorian courage, boys who could get their hands on a copy found in it a new game and social workers discovered in it a scheme for reaching children in Britain's mean urban dwellings.

2

THE FISHING FLEET

I'm a regular Randy Pandy, oh!
A swell and a toff and a dandy, oh!
With a big moustache that's all the mash
In the great Mashonalandy, oh!
AN INSERT IN A MUSICAL BURLESQUE, 'JOAN OF ARC',
PRODUCED AT THE GAIETY THEATRE

M any publicly mourned the passing of 'Little Randy' from syphilis on 24 January 1895. Lord Randolph Churchill died prematurely, from a disease presumed to have been contracted during a drunken orgy while a student at Oxford. Despite his agony, few of those close to him grieved.

Lord Randolph, the father of Winston Churchill and the idolised older brother of Lady Sarah Wilson, had been a lisping, dandified figure before he lost his mind. He loved nothing more than to dress in the latest glories – flashing jewellery, coloured shirts, silk hombergs, beautifully cut suits and, when not wearing starched collars, a riotous cravat. Grandiloquent, eccentric, pugnacious and opinionated, he exhibited an abundance of all the insufferable traits of the grand House of Marlborough from which he was descended.

Lord Randolph, the *enfant terrible* of British politics, left a trail of resentment and enemies wherever he went and it is not surprising that his rapid rise to the lofty positions of Leader of the House of Commons and Chancellor of the Exchequer is remembered for his spectacular plummet from grace. He was a leading light of the ultra right-wing of the Tory Party and a champion of 'Tory Democracy' – a feudal philosophy that pitted the mythical alliance of the landed aristocracy and peasantry against the bourgeoisie who were responsible for tearing down Camelot. His fabled, fiery rhetoric made him the icon of the working class but, more importantly, the target for those who held the strings of power. They tugged, he fell.

The wreck of Lord Randolph's career and the loss of his substantial ministerial income was a disaster. The maintenance of his flamboyant lifestyle and the public school education of two sons were an enormous drain on his resources. As his financial situation became more desperate, he began to grasp at any illusory straws cast his way by Midas.

Lord Randolph was the perfect prey for Cecil Rhodes. Unfortunately for Rhodes, he did not get to see Lord Randolph's medical records. Had he done so the Churchills may never have become so closely linked to southern Africa. Rhodes did little to temper Lord Randolph's grandiose dreaming. Rather he fired it. With detailed maps spread before them, Rhodes demonstrated to Lord Randolph that Mashonaland was the crock of gold at the end of a rainbow. He painted a perfectly logical picture, illustrated by the substantial diamond finds at Kimberley and the rich discoveries of gold on the Witwatersrand, of a sub-continent that was a veritable treasure trove. All that was left to do when Rhodes finished was for Alfred Beit, Rhodes's goblin fixer, to finalise the details of the drooling Lord Randolph's trip to Mashonaland.

Lord Randolph, on the pretext of visiting Mashonaland to investigate state-subsidised emigration to the promised land, set up a syndicate of family members, financiers, newspaper proprietors and friends while signing a lucrative deal with the *Daily Graphic* to provide them with 20 stories. Rhodes, meanwhile, thought he had covertly recruited a figure of great influence to promote his ideas and vision. It was a public relations coup which filled him with enormous hope. Unbeknown to Rhodes, he had enlisted an albatross who would severely embarrass him and cause the shares of his British South Africa Company and De Beers to nose-dive.

Lord Randolph's voyage, to Cape Town in 1891, on the *Grantully Castle*, was a nightmare of sea-sickness, boredom and unappetising food. To make matters worse, the trip was crowned by a raging fire on board. He was so irritable by the time the ship docked in Cape Town on a grey and windless day that the royal greeting he received, from a cheering crowd, was not enough to stop him from longing for a quarter hour at the Amphytrion – a yearning he was happy to proclaim at every opportunity during his harrowing trek through the subcontinent. But, it is not Lord Randolph's unhappiness and discomfort, but his penetrating insults for which this gambol is remembered.

Some of 'Yahoo' Randolph's bespatterings would cause an outcry in Britain among vexed women and have ireful Boers reaching for their Mausers. On visiting a diamond mine in Kimberley he declared, on being shown a beautifully crafted piece of jewellery, ' ... whatever may be the origin of man, woman is descended from an ape'. But, his most mordant vitriol was reserved for the Boers on his visit to the South African Republic. He opined that ' ... they will pass away unhonoured, unlamented, scarcely remembered either by the native or the European settler' and that they would leave, on the pages of African history, 'a shadow, but only a shadow, of a dark reputation and an evil name'. He would so upset the Boers that they would parade his effigy through the hissing streets of Pretoria and burn it. These, however, were only asides. His real venom was reserved for the hand that fed him.

Lord Randolph left the seething South African Republic at Rhodes's Drift and crossed the Limpopo River into Mashonaland. He entered the region saying, promisingly, 'After all I have seen of the Transvaal, that the country of the Matabele and Mashona have been rescued in the nick of time, owing to the genius of Mr Rhodes and the tardy vigour of the British Government, from the withering and mortal grasp of the Boer' and that the country offered Britain the best opportunity for clearing her foul slums since the opening of Australia.

In charge of Lord Randolph's cumbersome wagon train, that became a standing joke wherever it bogged down, was the easygoing Percy Fitzpatrick. The young Percy, a future politician and literary luminary, would need all his considerable breeziness to deal with this expedition that was concerned only with his Lordship's every comfort. He light-heartedly brushed off the moans and groans as they inched slowly through the African bush in search of a suitable camp site so that the accompanying team of chefs and their unfortunate assistants could prepare the champagne-swilling Lord Randolph's dinner of baked partridge, loin of kudu, mounds of vegetables and cleansing, hot stewed prunes while the nobleman dashed off his next destructive missive.

From Mashonaland, Lord Randolph spewed a stream of the usual slanders that ranged from questions regarding the sobriety of the British South Africa Police to the discourteous observation that the Zimbabwe

Ruins were a pile of rubble. These damning and embarrassing utterances were interspersed with Churchillian idiosyncrasies that included the feeding of gin to horses to ward off horse-sickness. *Punch* derisively labelled him 'Grandolph the Explorer'. While those in power held their breath for the next instalment, young Winston and the readers of the *Daily Graphic*, whose circulation grew by the day, relished his successive pronouncements from the 'land where the Rudyards cease from Kipling and the Haggards ride no more'.

The calamity came with Lord Randolph's proclamation on the viability of Mashonaland. He declared that Mashonaland was not fit for human habitation. The hellish heat, the scissoring storms, the savage natives, debilitating malaria and the treacherous roads that shook up one's inside 'like an omelette in a frying pan', were suited only for the barbaric inhabitants of the land. While he railed against the living conditions, his mining expert, Henry Perkins, wrote reports on the non-existent prospects for substantial gold finds. South African land shares crashed on the London Stock Exchange.

Lord Randolph, notwithstanding his injurious statements, covered his bets by purchasing the Matchless Mine with Alfred Beit. On his return to Cape Town, via the Missionary Road through Mafeking, he, surprisingly, considering the dent he had made in Rhodes's plans for Central Africa, stayed there as the guest of Rhodes. While Rhodes undertook a damage control exercise, Lord Randolph was persuaded to purchase shares in another gold mine – this time on the Witwatersrand. During his stay with Rhodes they discovered a subject on which they were in agreement. Both were convinced that the entangled problems of Southern Africa had been created by a combination of Kruger's stubbornness and British jingoism. Kruger had to go. War was not the solution, the Uitlanders in Johannesburg were. The two gentlemen concluded that this issue could simply be unravelled by increasing the numbers of expatriates in the South African Republic to the point where the Boer government would be swamped and washed away by a tide of progressive forces. Lord Randolph undertook to work toward encouraging large-scale emigration to the Witwatersrand instead of the now discredited Mashonaland.

Lived a woman wonderful,
(May the Lord amend her!)
Neither simple, kind, nor true,

But her Pagan beauty drew
Christian gentlemen a few
    Hotly to attend her.
                RUDYARD KIPLING, 'SOUTH AFRICA'

As Lord Randolph, at home a few years later, lay dying violently —
tortured and contorted by paralysis, his words seized by a loss of
articulation and his hearing all but gone — Lady Sarah Wilson, a minor
shareholder in the mining syndicate, took control of its affairs. With the
face of a pug and the nature of a bulldog, she was a frightening likeness of
her brother before his illness. Winston, her hated nephew, called her 'a
cat', many others referred to her simply as 'that bloody woman'. The feud
between her and Winston — soured by her distrust and low regard for
him, and his jealousy of her relationship with his father and perception of
her as a meddlesome mischief maker — was, however, little more than a
clash of powerful and forceful personalities.

A bedrock of self importance and self interest, with a snub nose and
large bulbous eyes set wide, Lady Sarah Isabella Augusta Spencer-
Churchill, the youngest daughter of the seventh Duke of Marlborough,
was every bit a Churchill. Consuela Vanderbilt, married to a nephew of
Lady Sarah, remarked bitterly that the squat Lady Sarah was as 'hard as
her polished appearance . . . and [that] her harsh and sarcastic laugh .. made
me shudder'. Yet, beneath Lady Sarah's seemingly frigid exterior — further
constricted by high-boned collars, pinching shoes and corsets — burnt a
spirit of adventure that could not be doused even in the claustrophobic
gloom of Blenheim Palace. Her mind, however, strangled by the aridity
and rigidity of life within the stately home, dulled her to the implications
of the growth of women's liberation round her. Thus, despite her own
desire to break loose, she fervently opposed the growing suffragette
movement.

In 1883 Lady Sarah's father died, leaving her, the only child still at
home, as her fearsome mother's constant companion. Her eldest brother
became the Eighth Duke of Marlborough and Lady Sarah and her mother
were forced to move to Grosvenor Square. Matrimony became
imperative. To get married, for most Victorian women, was to get
buried in the same breath. For Lady Sarah it was the only means of escape.
But her forlorn looks and truculent temperament, in a land where society
women outnumbered eligible men, were enormous barriers. Then, just as

her prospects seemed terminal, she found the prosaic Gordon Wilson, a lieutenant in The Royal Horse Guards.

The gentle, round-shouldered, insipid Gordon was a career soldier. His father, Sir Samuel Wilson, had made his substantial fortune in Australia as a cattle rancher and was a neighbour of the Churchill's. Gordon's only achievement, other than his success as a racehorse owner, was to save the life of Queen Victoria on the platform of Windsor station when he knocked the gun from a potential assassin's hand. He and Lady Sarah did, in their own self-seeking ways, complement each other. She regarded Gordon and his money as her passport to freedom; he considered her the ideal wife for an army officer facing the prospect of many foreign postings. Their wedding, whilst Lord Randolph was in Mashonaland, was the society event of the season.

Lady Sarah, as her two sons found, had no maternal instincts — moolah was her passion. Her fascination with wealth and the well-heeled was to last a lifetime. This and her hankering for adventure drew her to the affairs of the mining syndicate and ultimately lured her to South Africa, where she was to fulfil her wildest fantasies. The walrus-moustached Gordon was to slip forever into the background.

It was preposterous of Lady Sarah to expect anyone to believe that the timing of her first trip to South Africa, in December 1895, was happenstance. She professed that the journey was broadly to familiarise herself with the mining industry in southern Africa and specifically to inspect the syndicate's investments — malarkey! She boarded the *Tantallon Castle* in Southampton with Alfred Beit and many of the Johannesburg plotters of the Jameson Raid to take place later that month. The boredom normally associated with a sea voyage was, for her, blissfully absent on this exciting trip.

Lady Sarah, as the passengers above played deck quoits and the band below performed a waltz, indulged in a far more exhilarating game. Clandestine meetings in smoky rooms, devious schemes, surreptitious plots, powerful men, mystery, drama, delicious heart-stirring stuff. Her role in this epic that would lead directly to the South African War, is not altogether clear. She had never met Rhodes so it can only be assumed that her part would have been to lend legitimacy to what was ultimately a predatory criminal act. She would have known, before embarking, of the plot, but, in all likelihood, would have been ignorant of the details of such matters as Jameson's force waiting near Mafeking at Pitsani — a horrid little station in a strip of Bechuanaland that had been awarded to Rhodes by Chamberlain so that Jameson could position his invading force at the most accessible point to Johannesburg in order to rush, in the shortest possible time, to the Witwatersrand when he received the signal from the plotters. These intriguing titbits would only have been added to the hush-hush atmosphere during the voyage.

Lady Sarah soon sensed, however, that her plotter companions were paper tigers, a realisation which may explain her reticence, later, in admitting any involvement in the affair other than as a fortuitous observer. What she detected, her powers of perception honed by growing up in a house heavily larded with political talk, was that the Johannesburg plotters were engaging in bravado. 'I must admit,' she recalled, 'that it was the fiery-headed followers who talked the loudest − those who had nothing to lose and much to gain. The financiers while directing and encouraging their zeal, seemed almost with the same hand to put on the brake and damp their martial ardour.'

It was clear that the rebels had no intention of converting insurrectionary ideas into action or of using the weapons covertly smuggled into Johannesburg in oil drums by De Beers and stashed at Standard Bank. For all their grumbling, these gilded mining magnates' fortunes were booming. Beneath their bluff she observed them for what they were − rich, spoilt little squabbling boys so deeply divided that they could not even decide on the design of a future flag, let alone anything else. The disaster, when it came, would not surprise her. However, in the thrall of their wealth, she would never denounce them.

The *Tantallon* was blown into Cape Town by an icy south easter. Like her brother, Lady Sarah's initial opinion of the city, a metropolis in the grip of 'King Slump', was uncomplimentary. The rickety hansom that transported Gordon and her from the docks was ancient and, when not held up by bullock carts, shook and rattled over untidy, poorly paved streets. She wished she was in Melbourne or Sydney. Unlike her brother, her initial perception of Cape Town was to change dramatically and she would soon come to regard it as the most beautiful, albeit pathetically dull, city in the world.

She and Gordon moved into the Grand Hotel in Newlands, then, after a few days, into the rustic Vineyard Hotel in the same suburb. They spent summer days driving round Cape Town doing some late Christmas shopping before Beit brought the news that he had secured an appointment for them to meet Rhodes on 22 December 1895. It was a meeting she awaited with relish.

The drive along the cathedral-nave of the Scotch fir avenue to Groote Schuur, Rhodes's home, while enveloped by perfumed air from the surrounding gardens, was intoxicating. Ahead, hazy Table Mountain melted into a lush rolling plateau carpeted with an azure sea of hydrangeas amongst which cannas and arum lilies floated. A herd of playful wildebeest and skittish zebra grazed on a terrace while, a little further back, under an oak tree, a tan eland calf suckled, its snout punching its mother's udder. Lady Sarah was mesmerised as the road took a serpentine sweep and the house, its right wing covered with scaffolding, came into view. In front of the thatched, gabled, recreation of a traditional Cape Dutch manor house stood Cecil Rhodes, the Prime Minister of the Cape Colony, deep in conversation with his architect, Herbert Baker.

Rhodes, tall and burly, with a rugged countenance defined by entrancing blue eyes, was dressed in white flannel trousers, tweed coat and a floppy slouch hat. As his visitors approached, he removed his hat and slid a hand through his ruffled hair. The diffidence in his high-pitched voice when he greeted them was unmistakable. This would surely have been aggravated by his previous experience in dealing with the 'Churchill lot'. He left Baker to get on with his work and ushered the party into the house. Rhodes, however, soon felt at ease in Lady Sarah's company and from that first meeting they became lifelong friends.

His nerves, jangled by the ceaseless attentions of what was euphemistically called 'the fishing fleet' – those unbridled, rampaging society women looking to land the biggest catch of all – were calmed by Lady Sarah's sharp turn of mind and absence of coquettishness. She took a place in his life he normally reserved for men. Whether this friendship was ever sexually consummated is a matter for conjecture. Princess Radziwill, a renowned temptress and admiral of the 'fishing fleet', certainly saw Lady Sarah as her arch rival. But it does appear that their fondness for each other was no more than the cerebral meeting of two like minds.

Little of substance was discussed during that first meeting. It was a social call and Rhodes showed the Wilsons through his home. The teak-panelled interior of the airy, high-ceilinged house, through which a cooling breeze fluttered, was filled with the scents of a thousand flowers and the sense of powerful men discussing issues that would affect history. Rhodes wanted to have everything as authentic and theatrical as possible.

There was no electricity, and the mansion was lit only by tallow candles and the final rays of red-stained sun that glowed through the open sash windows to envelop the antique Dutch porcelain, inlaid high-backed chairs and priceless oriental rugs that decorated the cavernous rooms. Everything, down to the collection of Zimbabwean phallic symbols, was blended in perfect harmony and each item had found its precise place and space.

'Passing through the rooms,' enthused Lady Sarah in *South African Memories*, 'we came to the wide verandah, or stoep, on the other or eastern side. This ran the whole length of the edifice, and was used as a delightful lounge, being provided with luxurious settees and armchairs. From here Mr. Rhodes pointed out the view he loved so well, and which comes vividly to my mind to-day. In front three terraces rise immediately beyond the gravel courtyard, which is enclosed on three sides by the stoep. These, bright with flowers, lead to a great grassy plateau, on which some splendid specimens of Scotch firs rear their lofty heads; while behind, covered with trees and vegetation, its brilliant green veiled by misty heat, Table Mountain forms a glorious background, in striking contrast to the cobalt of the heavens.' As they prepared to depart, Rhodes invited his new friends to join him for lunch on Christmas Eve.

The day of the Wilsons' second visit was sultry. Rhodes dispensed his ideas freely. He was not eloquent, but, the man who believed himself to be the reincarnation of the Emperor Titus had no need to be, because his ambitions did all the talking required. Africa would be painted red from Cape to Cairo and that was only the beginning of his ideas to extend British rule throughout the world. His vision took in the occupation by 'British settlers of the entire continent of Africa, the Holy land, the Valley of the Euphrates, the Islands of Cyprus and Candia, the whole of South America, the Islands of the Pacific .... the seaboard of China and Japan, the ultimate recovery of the United States of America ...!' The only hindrance to this crusade was Kruger – or, more precisely, Kruger's gold as Rhodes had not found enough of his own in Mashonaland to finance his mirage. As the poet Dryden remarked: 'War seldom enters, but where wealth allures'.

Rhodes and Kruger hated each other and conflict was inevitable. Rhodes's views on Kruger, according to Lady Sarah in *South African Memories*, were the same as Cape Judge Coetzee's; 'Kruger is only a white kaffir chief, and as such respects force, and force only. Send sufficient soldiers and there will be no fighting'. Rhodes and Kruger, despite their mutual antipathy, were remarkably similar. Their defining difference was Rhodes's rashness conceived from too many improbable victories as opposed to Kruger's patient pragmatism learnt from innumerable setbacks. Kruger, even though Rhodes had outwitted him many times, waited for the perfect opportunity to exact his revenge. 'Take a tortoise,' he counselled his burghers. 'If you want to kill it, you must wait until it puts out its head, and then you cut it off.' Rhodes's head popped out in late 1895.

The South African Republic had been desperately poor before the discovery of gold on the Witwatersrand in 1886. The news of rich seams of gold on the Witwatersrand reverberated round the world and prospectors flocked in their thousands to the new Eldorado. A short distance away in Pretoria President Paul Kruger, holding a poisoned chalice, watched as the dark forces of Mammon rumbled into his promised land.

Johannesburg, the new Sodom, housed nearly 100 official brothels, over 600 licensed bars, a race track, a permanent circus and a frenetic stock exchange where champagne was served to those who had struck it rich. Rooster and gander hung enticingly from the butcher's ceiling and the smell of raw sewage and the finest perfumes permeated the air. Hagglers haggled, hustlers hustled and whisky-soaked drunks tottered through the traffic of fast-moving carriages. By day, crowds thronged the unpaved streets and greeted each other with 'Here's luck!' before relinquishing the streets to housebreakers and thieves by night. Flora Shaw, the journalist, commented that Johannesburg was ' ... hideous and detestable, luxury without order; sensual enjoyment without art; richness without refinement; display without dignity.' Olive Schreiner, the writer, only needed one word to describe it. 'Hell!'

Kruger, desperate to retain power and preserve Boer culture and society, resorted to oppression and injustice. He granted mining rights but withheld valuable concessions for transport and mining equipment – monopolies he gave to his trusted pals. Taxes, without corresponding political rights or the provision of basic services, were extortionate. He wrung levies on imports from the Cape; refused to co-operate with his British neighbours; and stubbornly frustrated any efforts to establish a railway between Johannesburg and Cape Town. The Uitlanders began to get restless and bar-rooms were filled with calls for revolution. The situation went from crisis to crisis. It was the perfect scenario for Rhodes.

Lady Sarah was hypnotised by Rhodes's turbulent make-believe world – a world normally the preserve of playground children. The one observation she made during that lunch was that Rhodes appeared overly worried. He was. At the beginning of December he had had second thoughts about the scheme he had orchestrated of a Johannesburg uprising coupled with a raid into the South African Republic to topple Kruger. Jameson, who was to lead the incursion on a trumped up appeal from the 'women and children' of Johannesburg, had talked him round, but Rhodes was concerned that the Johannesburg conspirators were not ready. Had he compared notes that day with Lady Sarah, the Jameson Raid might never have happened.

Even though she had entered Rhodes's confidence, she had no role to play in the conspiracy, other than the decorative. After Christmas she caught a train for the 'deadly respectable' town of Kimberley so that she could be well placed to join the 'triumphant plotters' in Johannesburg after New Year. She visited De Beers – 'the moving spirit, the generous employer, and the universal benefactor' – and played games of croquet on the lawn of the Kimberley Club to while away the seemingly endless days.

While Lady Sarah waited anxiously, Jameson and his force prepared to 'ride, ride together, forever ride into history'. Once Jameson decided on something, he, like Rhodes, was incapable of stopping. He seethed at the continued delays; then messages began to come through ordering him to abort. The Uitlanders sent Captain Harry Holden and a flame-haired American, Major Maurice Heaney, to Pitsani to implore Jameson to sit tight. But the pair liked what they saw and joined the rebels. Then Rhodes cracked and sent Jameson a telegraph commanding him not to move. Jameson, or so he claimed, never received the instruction.

The Jameson Raid has been referred to as a fiasco – it was more like high farce. The two drunken members of the 478-man force assigned to cut the telegraph line to Pretoria snipped a farmer's fence instead. Kruger, with the help of a humming overhead telegraph line, was able to track Jameson's ride, which began on 30 December 1895, from the outset. This was not the only assistance the Boers would get from the accommodating raiders. At the time the farm fence was being vandalised, the petite Johnny Willoughby, 'a wonderful transport officer', was in Mafeking, loading the personal effects of Jameson's officers, including those of the Honourable Bobby White. Amongst White's paraphernalia were his despatch case containing the names of all the Uitlander conspirators as well as copies of every secret document relating to the planning of the attack. This evidence was in code – fortunately, Bobby, who never anticipated that the raiders might be apprehended, had packed the key.

The poem, 'Jameson's Ride', by Poet Laureate Alfred Austin, an 'absurd little cock-sparrow of a man', appeared soon after General Cronje called an end to this drunken frolic at Langlaagte. This ode, described as 'spirited doggerel', is a fitting memorial to Jameson's tragic joke:

> *Wrong! Is it wrong? Well, may be:*
> *But I'm going all the same.*
> *Do they think me a Burgher's baby,*
> *To be scared by a scolding name?*
> *They may argue and prate and order;*
> *Go, tell them to save their breath:*
> *Then, over the Transvaal border,*
> *And gallop for life or death!*
>
> *Let lawyers and statesmen addle*
> *Their pates over points of law:*
> *If sound be our sword, and saddle,*
> *And gun-gear, who cared one straw?*
> *When men of our own blood pray us*
> *To ride to their kinsfolk's aid,*
> *Not Heaven itself shall stay us*
> *From the rescue they call a raid.*
>
> *There are girls in the gold-reef city,*
> *There are mothers and children too!*
> *And they cry, 'Hurry up! for pity!'*
> *So what can a brave man do?*
> *If even we win, they'll blame us:*
> *If we fail, they will howl and hiss.*
> *But there's many a man lives famous*
> *For daring a wrong like this!*
>
> *So we forded and galloped forward,*
> *As hard as our beasts could pelt,*

First eastward, then trending northward,
  Right over the rolling veldt;
Till we came on the Burghers lying
  In a hollow with hills behind,
And their bullets came hissing, flying,
  Like hail on an Arctic wind.

Right sweet is the marksman's rattle,
  And sweeter the cannon's roar,
But 'tis betterly bad to battle,
  Beleaguered, and one to four,
I can tell you it wasn't a trifle
  To swarm over Krugersdorp glen,
As they plied us with round and rifle,
  And ploughed us, again — and again.

Then we made for the gold-reef city,
  Retreating, but not in rout.
They had called to us 'Quick! For pity!'
  And He said, 'They will sally out.
They will hear us and come. Who doubts it?'
  But how if they don't, what then?
'Well, worry no more about it,
  But fight to the death, like men.'

Not a soul had supped or slumbered
  Since the Borderland stream was cleft;
But we fought, ever more outnumbered,
  Till we had not a cartridge left.
We're not very soft or tender,
  Or given to weep for woe,
But it breaks one to have to render
  One's sword to the strongest foe.

I suppose we were wrong, were madmen,
  Still I think at the Judgement Day,
When God sifts the good from the bad men,
  There'll be something more to say.
We were wrong, but we aren't half sorry,
  And, as one of the baffled band,

> *I would rather have had that foray*
>   *Than the crushing of all the Rand.*

The news of the failed raid exploded like a bombshell. Cape Town was in uproar, Rhodes resigned as prime minister of the Cape Colony and Lady Sarah rushed to his side. This simple act, when everyone else was disowning him, brought her into Rhodes's inner circle. When he left for London 'to face the music' she accompanied him on to the ship, *Moor*, that was to take him to England. Their conversation on board is not recorded, but Lady Sarah appears to have been given the task by Rhodes of trying to gather as much information on the disaster as quickly as possible. As she left the ship, Rhodes promised her that his career was not over.

'I am quite sure it is not, Mr Rhodes,' replied Lady Sarah to reassure him, 'and what is more, I have a small bet with Mr Lawson [a family friend and special correspondent to the *Daily Telegraph*] that in a year's time you will be in office again, or, if not absolutely in office, as great a factor in South African politics as you have been up to now.'

'It will take ten years; better cancel your bet,' replied Rhodes after a minute's thought.

Soon after, Sir Hercules Robinson, the High Commissioner whose appointment had been engineered by Rhodes, managed to find Lady Sarah a berth to Durban on the troopship *Victoria*, which was being sent to take Jameson and his raiders back to England for trial. The mission of the *Victoria* was top secret and the placing of a civilian, who had been fully briefed, on board, as an 'indulgence passenger', was highly irregular.

It was a greasy, steely day when the *Victoria* arrived in Durban. The green sea was a rolling mess, the stormy sky a hostile purple-grey and the air glazed with the smell of fish. Waiting to board, as Lady Sarah disembarked, were the bedraggled raiders — in flannel shirts, khaki breeches, high boots, and the large felt hats of the Bechuanaland Border Police — who had not seen a change of clothing since their capture. She greeted her friends White and Willoughby before approaching the hawkish, slim, round-shouldered, balding Dr Leander Starr Jameson. Dr Jim, tense as a strung bow, was hardly the picture of the hero of Rudyard Kipling's poem 'If'.

While in Kimberley, Lady Sarah would have heard friends speak adoringly of the cavalier Dr Jim. They would reverently have told her that this charismatic charmer held Her Majesty's commission as Administrator of Rhodesia and was holder of the distinguished Order of Commander of the Bath, and was passionately loyal to Rhodes. They would not have added that his gentle humour and easy manner were a magnet that attracted all sorts of men while camouflaging a ruthlessness that rendered the Hippocratic Oath and medical ethics meaningless. His deliberate misdiagnosis of an outbreak of smallpox – calling it a minor virus – to protect anxious mine owners concerned about losing production by being forced to quarantine their labourers, led to the death of many blacks. Both Matabele and Mashona died as a direct result of his dealings north of the Limpopo while Administrator and Rhodes's emissary, and Piet Grobelaar, Kruger's envoy to Lobengula, was stabbed to death on Dr Jim's orders. Lady Sarah's friends were unlikely to mention, though she might have seen the twinkle in their eyes, that he was purported to be a notorious womaniser and that his bedside manner, with pretty patients, went way beyond the restorative.

If, in the month of dark December,
  Leander, who was nightly wont
(What maid will not the tale remember?)
      BYRON

The only question that Lady Sarah had for Dr Jim, at that brief meeting in Durban, and she asked him straight out, was why he had ignored all the orders not to move. Jameson replied indifferently that he had 'thought it best to make up [Rhodes's and the Uitlanders'] minds for them'. Lady Sarah, who appeared instantly smitten by Jameson, described the man – who dreamt of himself as the British hero Clive and whose rallying cry was 'Clive would have done it' – as a hero of 'absolutely fearless disposition'. Better authority has it that he 'shook like a leaf' on his capture.

From Durban, Lady Sarah caught a train to Johannesburg and mining magnate Sir Abe Bailey's mansion, Clewer Lodge. Even though the city was quieted in the wake of the Raid, she liked Johannesburg's youthful recklessness and exuberance from the moment she arrived. She first inspected the barred and barricaded offices of Goldfields, the padlocked Standard Bank where the arms had been stored and the depressed Johannesburg Stock Exchange, where the 'call of shares' had been reduced to only 20 minutes. On route, to survey the site where General Piet Cronje had waited for Jameson at Langlaagte, she passed a black township – an experience that repulsed her. The rancid air, the houses patched out of flattened, rusted paraffin tins and mouldy canvas, the smoke of wood fires and the filth disgusted her. But, it was not only the unsightly shelters or noisome odours that were abhorrent but the dirty, lice-plagued kaffirs – the cheap, virtual slave labour of the mining magnates – that offended her. She heaved a sigh of relief as their cart negotiated the last rank puddle – round which naked children played – that stood between them and happy escape from these pernicious surrounds. She wrote, after this encounter, ' ... for downright brutality the nigger is hard to beat, and it is also quite certain that whom the latter does not fear he will not love. I have personally experienced great devotion and most attentive service on the part of natives ... but it has often made me indignant to hear people, who have had little or no experience of living in the midst of a native population, prate of the rights of our "black brothers", and argue as if the latter thought, judged, amused themselves, or, in short, behaved, as the white men do, who have the advantage of hundreds of years of culture'.

In Pretoria, shortly before she left to return to Cape Town for England and while visiting Sir Abe and the Johannesburg plotters in prison, she caught sight of 'Oom Paul' Kruger. 'There,' she remembered in *South African Memories*: 'we saw the little primitive "dopper" church where the President always worshipped, overshadowed and dwarfed by the magnificent Houses of Parliament, built since the Transvaal acquired riches, and by the no less grand Government Offices. As we were standing before the latter, after the fashion of tourists, our guide suddenly became very excited, and told us we were really in good luck, for the President was just about to leave his office on his return home for his midday meal. In a few minutes the old gentleman emerged, guarded by four armed burghers, and passed rapidly into his carriage. We took a good look at this remarkable personage. Stout in figure, with a venerable white beard, in a somewhat worn frock-coat and a rusty old black silk hat, President Kruger did not look the stern dictator of his little kingdom which in truth he was.'

Back in London, Lady Sarah was suddenly the belle of the social whirl. The Randlords, as they had been called for a decade, were the stars, able to bring a shiver of pleasure to any social event. Lady Sarah was now an insider, able to summon a visiting mining celebrity at a moment's notice.

Colonel (later Lieutenant-General) Robert Baden-Powell – the Commander-in-Chief,
North West Frontier Force, who would later found the Boy Scout movement.

Veldcornet Sarel Eloff,
President Paul Kruger's grandson,
who unsuccessfully attempted to take
Mafeking on 12 May 1900.
(Mafikeng Museum)

Magistrate Charles Bell,
who looked remarkably like Cecil Rhodes.
(Mafikeng Museum)

The blindfolded Petrus Viljoen just about to start for the Boer lines
in exchange for Lady Sarah Wilson.
(Eleanor Cason)

Lord Edward Cecil, without hat and seated alongside Baden-Powell, telling funny stories outside the staff dugout. Also in the picture are Captain Ryan and Major Hanbury-Tracy (seated), and Captain Gordon Wilson and Lieutenant McKenzie (standing).
The two boys on either side are unidentified.
(MAFIKENG MUSEUM)

Baden-Powell sketching on his verandah in Mafeking.
MAFIKENG MUSEUM)

The Colonial Fingoes under Mr D Webster. (ELEANOR CASON)

Baden-Powell seated between Magistrate Bell and Mayor Whitley. On the ground is the drunk,
The rest are Baden-Powell's principal officers. Seated l to r: Major Godley, Lieutenant-Colonel V
Lieutenant-Colonel Hore and Dr William Hayes. Standing l to r: Major Panzera, Captain Ryan,
Captain Wilson, Captain Hanbury-Tracy and Captain Cowan.
(MAFIKENG MUSEUM)

The Mafeking Cadet Corps drilling.
(Mafikeng Museum)

A party of Boer prisoners, captured on 12 May 1900,
being marched into Mafeking.
(Eleanor Cason)

: Moncreiffe.
ll, B-P, Whitley,
eener, Lord Cecil,

The Mafeking Siege Orchestra Society.
(MAFIKENG MUSEUM)

Major Lord Edward Cecil
– son of the British Prime Minister and
Baden-Powell's second-in-command.
(MAFIKENG MUSEUM)

Impeesa, 'the hyena that skulks by night',
as Baden-Powell was known by the Matabele.
(MAFIKENG MUSEUM)

The court of summary jurisdiction. Plaatje, with beret and leaning on windowsill, interprets in a case where the accused black 'spy' was sentenced to death.
(Mafikeng Museum)

Jimmy Quinlan, the stationmaster and an Irish nationalist, prior to the siege.
(Mafikeng Museum)

Lady Sarah Wilson posing at the entrance to her bunker excavated in front of
Benjamin Weil's house.
(MAFIKENG MUSEUM)

The most sought after prize, after Rhodes, was Jameson who had been sentenced to 15 months' imprisonment but was released after four on the grounds of ill health. Unshackled, his recovery was miraculously swift and he developed a close friendship with the Wilsons. The farce that was the Raid, rather than make Dr Jim a laughing stock, had launched him as a hero who would have succeeded in his laudable mission but for the betrayal of his friends. For Lady Sarah, Dr Jim appears to have become more than an idol.

Lady Sarah, in May 1899, with Gordon, Dr Jim and her German maid Metalka, boarded the *Norman* for a second voyage to Cape Town. Again she claims the timing of this trip, one that would transport her on a journey of high adventure and thrust her into the international limelight as the 'heroine of Mafeking', was coincidental. Hooey again! Rhodes was in London at the time Baden-Powell's mission was being formulated and Lady Sarah and Dr Jim were two of his closest cronies. There is no doubt this pair would have been intimately involved in any devilment Rhodes conjured concerning southern Africa — the place to be in these electrifying times.

Docking in Cape Town, the party caught a train for Rhodesia where Dr Jim handed them over to his friend Maurice Heany, who would be their host until they got word from Rhodes. Sarah was overjoyed to be back in Africa. 'A curious thing about this continent,' she wrote in her *South African Memories*, 'is; you may dislike it or fall under its charm, but in any case it nearly always calls you back. It certainly did in my case.' In Bulawayo, the Wilsons and Dr Jim kept updated with the escalating drama and rising tensions in the region while indulging their great passion, hunting. It was here that Lady Sarah was to fall in love with the African bush, especially camp life.

She retained joyous memories of sitting round an orange fire dreamily admiring the star-pierced sky that was velvet except in the west where it was still pink from the remnants of the day. 'I can recommend this life as a splendid cure for any who are run down or overworked,' sighed Lady Sarah. On these hunting trips her party would be accompanied by Wilhelm, Dr Jim's Zulu servant, who Lady Sarah called Vellum. The lean, friendly, sparkling eyed Vellum was to accompany her on her Mafeking adventure and become her devoted confidant. She would write that beneath his skin 'beat a heart of gold' and that 'to him I could safely have confided uncounted treasures'.

The eagerly awaited message from Rhodes, sent from London, for the Wilsons to join him at Groote Schuur, came five weeks later. Arriving in Cape Town before Rhodes, in early July, they were fortunate that their accommodation was assured because the city had become a circus packed with the greatest armada the 'fishing fleet' had ever mustered. Singing 'Soldiers of the Queen', Cape Town was their new playground and the just completed Mount Nelson Hotel their headquarters. The gentle-women of London society invaded every hotel in their march to net a man in uniform. Babbling balls, frivolous soirees, champagne picnics and breezy canters through the wooded lower slopes of Table Mountain were the bait for a dashing husband. Many, on this matrimonial mission, made themselves busy hosting charity bazaars or working in hospital wards. Others – 'they are so daring' sighed Milner – squabbled for rail passes to get close to potential hotspots. But, the vast majority of these parasoled ladies only wanted to have tittering fun.

The day Rhodes returned was declared a public holiday and the route from Cape Town to Groote Schuur, now with a tiled roof after the fire that had engulfed it and burnt it to the ground shortly after her last visit, was decorated with a rainbow of banners, bunting, flags and arches. That night, at a huge public meeting at the Drill Hall, Rhodes mounted the dais to 'cheering [that] went on for ten minutes, and was again and again renewed, till the enthusiasm brought a lump to many throats'. The triumphant Rhodes was once again summiting the peaks of political power that threatened to be a serious match for the pushy ambitions of Milner.

Lady Sarah, while awaiting the 'chance' meeting with Baden-Powell later in the month, was Rhodes's constant companion. She accompanied him on his morning rides, had breakfast with him, sat with him while his portrait was painted by P Tennyson Cole, attended the Cape parliament when he was speaking and, in the evening, helped him perfect his bridge game. Lady Sarah, after the meeting with the future hero of Mafeking, accompanied Baden-Powell and Gordon to Bulawayo in late July.

Gordon spent most of his time at Ramatlhabama, which left Lady Sarah some much needed privacy with Dr Jim. Long days were spent socialising with officers, sight seeing or practising applying bandages to the lanky arms of black children while tiresome early evenings were spent rehearsing for the play 'Geisha Tea'. By contrast, idyllic nights were spent with Jameson. Then came the news, in mid September, that Baden-

Powell had broken his orders and entered Mafeking. She rushed to the town, with Vellum, intending to find out what was going on before heading for Cape Town. The adventure and suspense-charged atmosphere of Mafeking, however, seduced her and she did not complete her journey, choosing, like Baden-Powell, to make history.

Lady Sarah's two weeks in the sand-bagged, locust-plagued Mafeking were a blur. She was unsure whether Baden-Powell would let her stay and play a part in the drama, or decide the stage was too small for both of them. To display her potential usefulness she took an ambulance course and tried to get involved in the hospital. She rented a cottage to indicate the permanence of her presence; underlined her status by fraternising with her cousin Fitzclarence and friend Edward Cecil; and, on 7 October 1899 wrote her first report for the mass circulation *Daily Mail* which had tried in vain to coax her nephew to be their South African war correspondent. This report, written by the 'only female war correspondent' in South Africa, 'recording the events on the frontier from a woman's perspective', was a blockbuster for her reputation and a boost for the circulation of the newspaper. She wrote of the chaotic, taut conditions of a nervous, nearly hysterical community where the town militia rang the alarm bells so frequently that the residents were forced to sleep in their clothes. But, despite the disruptions and discomfort, she enjoyed the build-up to war immensely. 'We eat and drink and have our joke, even play a game of bridge after dinner,' she gaily reported from Dixon's Hotel.

It is unclear what decided her fate in Baden-Powell's mind. The fact that she bought a white polo pony, Dop, and took to riding out to inspect the fortifications twice daily must have been an irritation. But, it is most likely that the arrival of Dr Jim made up his mind. Baden-Powell must have known of Lady Sarah's and Dr Jim's close relationship which, during a protracted siege, could prove unsettling. He must also have suspected that the presence of Rhodes's closest allies was more than chance. Jameson he disposed of straight away. Lady Sarah would have to wait her turn. On 8 October Baden-Powell received a preview of Kruger's 48-hour ultimatum to be served on Britain the following day. Baden-Powell now had his timetable and included in his final preparations was the need to rid himself of all unwelcome guests. Lady Sarah was top of that list.

On the evening of 10 October he sent a staff officer to Lady Sarah to notify her of his decision to evict her. The timing of the delivery was brilliant, the messenger was not. Baden-Powell wanted her to leave, at first light, for Kanye, an isolated oasis in the Kalahari some 100 kilometres to the north, in Bechuanaland, where she would be well away from all her tools of mischief. Giving her the notice as the ultimatum ticked away would allow her no time to rally the support of powerful friends. With no option but to obey she convinced the messenger that Kanye was not suitable as it was too remote and its supplies might run dry. They agreed that she go to Setlagole, a trading post 70 kilometres south of Mafeking, en route to Kimberley.

It turned unseasonably cold that night as the rising wind whipped black clouds across the face of the moon. She made her way to Major Gould Adams's house and arranged a Cape Cart, six mules and a driver. She roused Vellum, told him of the order, and returned to pack. She and Metalka packed two handbags that were strapped to the cart. She hardly slept as the wind increased to a gale which howled angrily through the town. The dust-storm shook loose sections of corrugated iron that flapped noisily, furiously twirled a rusty weathervane and caused a neighbouring door to bang through the tempestuous night.

The evictees clattered over the railway line at daybreak in what Lady Sarah called the most vile of all forms of transport. The cursing driver cracked his curling whip above the ears of the mules to urge them on while Vellum brought up the rear on Dop. As the searing sun rose and the gale increased, the day became suffocatingly hot. The sun threw flaring beams through the sky boiling with dust as they drove through a countryside that could only maintain a few starved bushes and stunted clumps of hardy grass. The occasional bleached skeleton attested that there may have been other life in this wasteland, but it was not then evident.

Late that afternoon, as they jolted across the ragged course of a dried-up river and lunged up the far bank, they were able to see Setlagole. Streaks of sun were climbing up the trellised grey house, and the adjoining ramshackle store, and casting long shadows. A donkey grazed close to the front door while another drank at a murky trough. Fowls pecked and turkeys gobbled in a rough pen and a horse whinnied in the stables a stone's throw away. A group of loafers, black and white, lounging against the store, studied the new arrivals who were trying to shake off the dust that permeated every pore. As the gold-tinged sun dropped away the Frasers, a 'nice old Scotch couple', showed Lady Sarah and Metalka to two neat rooms. Shortly after they had settled in,

50

Sergeant Matthews, in charge of the Setlagole Mounted Police depot arrived to report that several hundred Boers were waiting in ambush along the railway line at nearby Kraaipan and that he was riding to intercept the train and warn the driver.

That night Lady Sarah again could not sleep. The incessant howling of a dog at the full moon nearly drove her out of her wits. Then, as dawn broke, the sounds of gunfire, from Kraaipan, came rumbling through the air. Sergeant Matthews had got to the train and warned the driver, who stopped and refused to continue. Nesbit, transporting Baden-Powell's artillery to Mafeking, commandeered the train and drove it into the first Boer bullet of the South African War — fired by gunner Jaap van Deventer, who, ironically, was knighted, later in life, for services to the British Empire.

3

THE BLACK ENGLISH BOY

Son: *Daddy, How do fish live in the sea?*
Father: *Why — as men do on land —*
            The big ones eat the small ones.

S olomon Tshekisho Plaatje's mortal wounds were not sustained on a blood-soaked battlefield; rather, his untimely death, at the age of 55, can be attributed to the emotional injuries he suffered from exertion and despondency while fighting for the freedom of all South Africans. The sum of traumas — borne from endlessly summiting, peak-after-pinnacle, over the political obstacle course and dead-ends laid for black South Africans — is incalculable. 'One of the greatest of the sons of South Africa,' acclaimed Vere Stent, editor of *The Pretoria News*, on hearing of Plaatje's death. GA Simpson, editor of the *Diamond Fields Advertiser*, eulogised, 'No mere words ... can adequately pay tribute to ... the memory of one who was an outstanding figure in the life of the people of South Africa.'

Plaatje's short, fragile stature and scholarly, youthful appearance are hardly the images of myth. Yet his is the tale of passion, foresight, penetrating intelligence and endeavour that is the essence of legend. His original mind, range of talents and depth of courage made him the perfect foil to the betrayal, savagery, insults and humiliation that so characterise the melodrama that is South African history. He was a man of peace, yet his achievements mark him as a revolutionary. That his contributions to the diverse cultures of South Africa and its ultimate liberation have faded into the mists of history should be blamed on incompetent historians rather than on the man.

52

Plaatje, the sixth son of the influential Johannes and Martha Plaatje, was born on 9 October 1876 on an isolated windswept outstation of the Berlin Mission Society's main mission at Pniel near Barkly West. The powerful clout the Plaatjes commanded within the local Berlin Mission Society – an authority garnered as a consequence of being one of the first Barolong to convert to Christianity – brought relative affluence through the privileged use of various Society farm lands.

The slight, impish Martha Plaatje treated the disappointment of not giving birth to a coveted girl as a chiding from an irate God. Plaatje's devoutly Christian parents christened him Solomon after the sage biblical character and Tshekisho, 'Judgement', in repentance for God's admonition. The Plaatje's atypical surname was originally Mogodi, the new form developing from a nickname, 'Ou Plaatje' – squat one – given to Plaatje's great-grandfather by the Dutch-speaking Griqua tribe. This change in identity was not superficial, because the same forefather also embraced Christianity. Though there is no direct evidence to suggest it, it would appear that the acquisition of a new Western-flavoured surname was the symbolic manifestation of a break between the Plaatje family and traditional Tswana culture.

The Plaatjes, of the peaceful Barolong tribe of the Tswana, could trace their ancestry to King Modiboa, the eighth chief in a line of monarchs stretching to Morolong, the founder of the Barolong. The Barolong, a society in turmoil and transformation forced on them by external factors, were caught in the unremitting vice of nineteenth-century regional history. From the east – in the wake of the upheaval and scattering caused by Shaka's consolidation of power among the Zulu in an event known as the *difaqane* – came the terrifying 'People of the Cat', the Tlokwa, of the axe-throwing cannibal, Chieftainess Mmanthatisi. She, in turn, was consumed by the assailing hordes of the Matabele under the leadership of Mzilikazi. From the west, looking for space uncontaminated by English, came the Boers, soon followed by their intrusive foe. From the heavens, across which flashed Haley's comet in warning of the coming pestilence, came drought, plagues of locusts and the rinderpest. From the depths of the earth came gold and diamonds, followed by kleptomaniacs and the pious 'reverend imperialists' who, in the long run, would do more damage to Barolong culture and contribute more to the conditions that would open blacks to exploitation and enslavement than all the rest together. The devil could not have played a better hand.

The Berlin missionaries, like most of their divine peers, were profoundly ignorant of the intricate fabric of African culture and arrogant in their contention that indigenous ways of life were meaningless. They tore down centuries of communal life, shattered traditions and violated codes and customs without replacing them with anything substantial other than a basic education. Fortunately for the young Solomon, his family, in particular his mother, never forgot their rich tribal roots. Martha told Plaatje the stories of the Barolong past in ethereal language that would ensure that the young boy's heart, no matter how far his horizons expanded, remained anchored in traditional values.

One of the stories Martha told Plaatje was the intriguing tale of the founding of Mahikeng — A Place of Stones. This story would have Plaatje trembling at night in terror of the Matabele and shaking with anger at the ingratitude of the Boers.

Mzilikazi and his invading Matabele arrived like a 'swarm of locusts' to settle at Inzinyani, south of the Limpopo River and to the north east of present-day Mafikeng, on land that belonged to Chief Tawana of the Tshidi-Barolong. The Matabele, after forcing the Tshidi, the most powerful and autonomous Barolong tribe, into submission, imposed a hut tax on the tribe, to be paid each spring. The presence of the Matabele together with their offensive habit of walking about stark naked amongst the conservative Barolong, was a persistent source of malice and young Tshidi men itched for the opportunity to prove themselves against the provocative intruders. The moment was not long in coming for Chief Tawana had one of Mzililazi's tax collectors, Bhoya, and his assistant assassinated.

Sol Plaatje narrates the story in *Mhudi*, an epic of South African native life a hundred years ago and the first novel in English by a black South African, published in 1930 by Lovedale Press.

> '[Chief Tawana]' the messenger went on, 'received the [tax collectors] with indifference and, without informing his councillors in any way, he commanded some young men to take the two to the ravine and "lose them", which is equivalent to a death sentence. The tax collectors were dragged away without notice and almost before they realised their doom they were stabbed to death.

> 'I am told,' said the narrator, 'that, before his death, Bhoya, with his hands manacled, gesticulated and cried: "you dogs of a Western

breed, you are going to suffer for this. You will pay with your own blood and the blood of your children for laying your base hands on the courier of King Mzilikazi. A Matabele's blood never mingled with the earth without portending death and destruction. Kill me with your accursed hands, you menial descendants of mercenary Hammersmith's, and you have sown the seeds of your own doom. Do you hear me?"

'He was still speaking when Rauwe stabbed him in the breast. He fell forward, gave a gasp and a groan, rolled up the whites of his large dull eyes, and, after uttering a dread imprecation, sank back lifeless.'

Revenge was swift and Tawana sent messengers to prepare his people for attack:

Hello: Hello Everybody: The enemy has been sighted:
Matabele of Mzilikazi; At the source of the Molopo:
All regiments — Old Guards and fresh conscripts, to
The Kgotla [tribal meeting place] immediately: By order of the King.

A regiment of Matabele swept all before them. Hideous cries rent the air as men and women were speared and babies' heads smashed upon rocks before being skewered and held aloft. Towns were torched and the flames from hundreds of homes licked 'the air in a reddish glow that almost turned the night into day'. These scenes transformed the surrounding bush into 'howling pandemonium' as petrified Barolong fled in every direction.

The victors celebrated with a feast. Warriors, a cluster of furry tails about the waist, rhythmically marked time to the rattle of assegais on shields while praise singers, bedecked in fantastic head-dresses, leaped and sang to the beat of drums. The vanquished began a flight south to Thaba Nchu, a Wesleyan Mission station, to join up with other refugee Barolong tribes under the supreme leadership of Chief Moroka. It was here that Molema, a younger son of Chief Tawana, converted to Christianity.

Into this murky soup, in 1834, arrived the Boers, under Sarel Cilliers, 'dragging moving white houses'. This trail-blazing group of Voortrekkers with their ox wagons was to be joined by Andries Hendrick Potgieter, whose dour party included a young boy named Paul Kruger. The Boers fared little better than the Tshidi against Mzilikazi. Shortly after they came on the scene, at Vegkop, near present-day Heilbron, they were relieved of all their livestock. 'This fight marked the beginning of the tragic friendship of Moroka and the Boers,' commented Plaatje. 'Word reached Moroka that the Boers, having lost all their cattle, were now exposed to starvation and further attacks. The chief rose nobly to the occasion. He sent teams of oxen to bring the Boers back to Thaba Nchu. On their arrival he levied from among his people gifts of milch cows and goats and also hides to make sandals and shoes for the tattered and footsore trekkers and their families, whom he settled at a place called Morokashoek. If South Africans were as romantic and appreciative as white people in Europe and America, Morokashoek would be a hallowed spot among the Voortrekker descendants, and efforts would surely be made to keep the memory of the benefactors of their ancestors.'

Potgieter and Moroka entered upon an alliance which in 1837 was to drive the Matabele north of the Limpopo. Chief Tawana agreed to lend Tshidi assistance on condition that if the coalition succeeded his tribe would be allowed to reoccupy their plundered lands around the Molopo basin. With the defeat of Mzilikazi, the joyful Tshidi returned 'home'. Peace did not last as the Boers reneged on the pact. The bitter effect of this was that the Tshidi under Tawana and his successor Montshioa were to contest with the Boers, until 1885, the right of the tribe to occupy their ancestral lands. In the ebb and flow of conflict the Tshidi continually retreated and regrouped, but after each confrontation found themselves squeezed a little harder.

Montshioa, to uphold his claims to his lands, sent his five brothers and an uncle to establish protective outposts to defend and demarcate his territory. One of these brothers, the Christian Molema, along with 12 Christian families, was ordered to build a settlement on 'the Missionary Road' as close as possible to the South African Republic's western border. Montshioa's intention was twofold. Molema and his turbulent literate followers were, Montshioa believed, emasculating his followers and secretly building the foundation of an alternate power base so, by expelling them, he was ridding himself of a powerful internal threat. Further, Montshioa wanted the educated Molema to establish this outpost at the crossroads of regional politics so that he had a worldly-wise emissary who could negotiate on his behalf.

Molema selected a treed spot on the Molopo characterised by a rocky outcrop. He called it Mahikeng. He chose so well that this spot became the focus of growing Boer territorial frustration exacerbated by continued Tshidi calls for British intervention. Montshioa eventually moved his Tshidi headquarters to Mahikeng as the tempestuous epicentre of regional politics zoomed in on the settlement. Martha, as she recounted this story to Plaatje, would have cursed the Boer betrayal of the Tshidi by growling: 'Across the colour bar, the Boer perspective becomes so blurred that they can see no distinction between friend and foe'. She would have revered Montshioa for his savvy in sending Molema to found this strategic settlement and for finally persuading the British to give the Tshidi protection. She could not then have seen the hand of Rhodes behind the scenes. He would have to wait for a caustic descendant of Molema's who remarked that Montshioa's 'victory', in soliciting Britain to help him defeat the Boers, was the difference 'between drowning in clean water and dirty water. The end result is the same, namely death'.

It is very easy, but mistaken, to ridicule Montshioa for calling in Lucifer to save himself from Satan. Montshioa, like most black leaders, failed to recognise that the British and the Boers were more closely allied than they appeared. This quarrelsome pair were not merely competing white tribes — rather, they were kinsfolk of a fundamentally different order of things involved in an extended blood-feud. These whites, moreover, were in absolute agreement that the black societies they found themselves among were entirely alien cultures of a lower order.

Matters, for affected blacks, were complicated by the overwhelming changes wrought on southern Africa in the last three decades of the nineteenth century by the discovery of diamonds and gold. Prior to 1870 most South African blacks still lived in independent chiefdoms — by 1899 none did. And as quickly as blacks lost their freedom, so they lost their land and their ability to support themselves. The only options, for most blacks, as they were deprived of their domains, was to starve or offer themselves as cheap migrant labour. Add to this the teachings of the missionaries that it was ordained in the scriptures that one group were natural labourers while another were masters and it is not difficult to discern the yolk of impending slavery.

O execrable son, so to aspire
Above his brethren, to himself assuming
Authority usurped, from God not given:
He gave us only over beast, fish, fowl

57

Dominion absolute; that right we hold
By his donation; — but man over men
He made not lord, such title to himself
Reserving, human left from human free.

> MILTON, PARADISE LOST, BOOK XII, 64–71
> (QUOTED IN S M MOLEMA'S
> THE BANTU, PAST AND PRESENT)

But, this was the exacting world in which Sol Plaatje was raised.

Plaatje's pre-school education, on the various outstations of the Berlin Mission Society, was little different from what other boys of the Barolong would have received. It was invaluable when he later formulated his complex, holistic ideas. The countryside, as he herded his father's long-horn cattle, was the perfect environment in which to come to grips with the patterns of the natural universe. He studied the rivers, the plants, the climate and the cosmos and, in due course, amalgamated what he observed with teachings about the ancestral world, Tswana concepts of community and Christian values in a rhythmic, evolving, all embracing cycle of life that never appeared contradictory.

In the early 1880s Plaatje's family moved to Pniel, the headquarters of the Berlin Mission Society. This move was to complete the circle of his childhood and be remembered as 'the best and happiest days' of his adolescence. Pniel was a severe Teutonic monument that sullenly glared at Barkly West across the Vaal River. Its lush, tonsured grounds, irrigated by dams and chugging steam pumps, were a contrast to their arid boundaries fringed with clumps of brown grass and shrubs that fought for survival in a land beaten by drought and sun. The cutaway river bank of the mission estate was lined with weeping willows and shady karee in which a multi-hued gathering of birds trilled. Inland, white butterflies fluttered among neat rows of blooming flowerbeds and laden bees struggled from the orchards. Close to the muddy river were the adjoining church and school. From the stern, tin-roofed church — its virginal, reproachful interior smelling of melting tallow — built in the shape of a cross, the discordant sounds of off-key hymns floated through Gothic windows.

All was not well, however, in Eden when the Plaatjes arrived at Pniel. Plaatje's doctrinaire father, 'a man who thought he knew a lot', as a church elder, had been summoned to restore spiritual confidence amongst the flock while the Society repaired the parlous state in which the mission and the school found itself. The discovery of diamonds in the region, and in particular on the estate, began a contagion of corruption that galloped through the mission like a cancer. Priests, who had never before entertained evil thoughts, suddenly entered a lascivious world where they gleefully explored 'gross carnal sins' and demonstrated signs of 'severe disobedience'. The man specially sent by the hierarchical and strict Society to restore order was Ernst Westphal, the son of a wealthy businessman, who arrived at Pniel, with his wife Elizabeth, at about the same time as the Plaatjes.

The Plaatjes built a huge stone and thatch house on the edge of the mission lands at the foot of a rocky ridge. Around the home were planted vegetable gardens, while the family's considerable accumulation of livestock grazed on the verdant surrounds. Plaatje's stern, opinionated father, because of his pre-eminent position, tended to uplift the spirits of the Pniel congregation. His sons, while not attending the mission school, shared the duties of looking after the family assets.

All black children living on mission lands were required to attend the church school. There was nothing philanthropic about these Dickensian institutions. Their intention was to provide children with a basic, primary education so that they could be confirmed into the church and be able to read their Bible. Yet, most black children floundered badly in these elementary schools which only reinforced Social Darwinist and other pseudoscientific ideas that black people were of lesser intellect.

At Pniel, the language of instruction, to mainly Tswana children, was Cape Dutch, from English handbooks, taught by people whose only proficient language was German. More precisely, the children — with the rare exception of a handful of linguistic geniuses such as Plaatje — only heard gobbledegook. Plaatje, for whom this impossible situation was merely a challenge, would go on to speak eight languages fluently and be able to write in four of them. The big-boned, bearded Westphal soon took an interest in this talented pupil and gave him extra tuition, which brought Plaatje into contact with Westphal's wife. The ivory-skinned Elizabeth, her almond eyes exaggerated by hair pulled severely back into an elaborate bun, appears to have seen deeper into the boy than anyone else. She introduced him to the works of Shakespeare, Goethe, Milton and Sir Walter Scott, while teaching him to play the piano and violin and nurturing his strong singing voice.

Plaatje thrived on the rigid discipline of the mission. Over and above deciphering what he was taught at school, his domestic chores, music lessons and singing training, he took responsibility for the church choir, did odd jobs to earn money for books and, when he reached Standard III, the highest grade offered at the school, became a pupil-teacher assisting Westphal in the classroom. His limited free time, when not reading, would be spent deep in thought on the river bank. It must have been during one of these idyllic private moments in 1884 that Plaatje came to the decision – a bombshell for the Westphals who were afraid of the unrestrained temptations of the flesh for a country boy – to leave Pniel for Kimberley. This was not the last time he would show independence.

By the time Plaatje arrived in Kimberley, a town synonymous with human hope and greed, to take up a job with the Post Office as a messenger, the town had most of its rough edges cut and polished. Kimberley, the foremost South African industrial city, was dominated by Rhodes's De Beers Consolidated Mines Limited. The adventure camp of hype and fortune seekers had largely been replaced by an ordered town directed by a monopoly whose enormous profits could largely be attributed to the driving ambition of Rhodes and the authoritarian organisation of the black labour force into regimented labour camps or compounds. One Kimberley suburb that avoided this systemised sterilisation was the polyglot Malay Camp of some 20 000 inhabitants, amongst whom Plaatje lived.

Sol Plaatje's rich baritone voice gave him the imposing presence his delicate frame lacked. His neatly trimmed hair, parted on the left, crowned a wise, oval, high cheeked face that suggested youth but was by no means young. Though he was to join the Eccentric Cricket Club he was not in the least sporty and it appears unlikely that he ever graced a cricket pitch. By day he endured one of the few jobs open to blacks – outside of manual labour – and showed all the necessary deference, politeness and respect for his white superiors that the position required. Then, at the end of the day – avoiding the dangers of being arrested by municipal police intent on bolstering the number of 'convicts' required for night soil duties – he would enter an optimistic *avant-garde* world that represented, in the late nineteenth century, the cutting edge of black thought and aspirations in South Africa.

The dusty evening air would be burning golden when Plaatje reached the Malay Camp. As he walked through the ramshackle collection of shanties, tin homes and mud houses, whose walls were decorated with a web of spidery cracks, he would smell the air musty with wood smoke and sharp with cooking meat. The road, where he carefully negotiated mule droppings and mounting litter, quaked with the pulse of beating drums and an accordion. When he reached the lodgings he shared with Isaiah Bud-M'belle he would change out of his knickerbockers and dress smartly for a night amongst the dynamic group of black intelligentsia that had welcomed him into their midst.

I am black but comely O ye daughters of Jerusalem
As the tents of Kedar and the curtains of Solomon,
Look not upon me because I am black
For the sun has looked upon me.
            SONG OF SONGS,
            QUOTED IN SOL PLAATJE'S *NATIVE LIFE IN SOUTH AFRICA*

The constant flow of ideas and deep-rooted humanity of the group Plaatje made his friends had a remarkable influence on him. Drawn from all over South Africa they were the élite that had passed through the mission schools — mainly Lovedale College and the Healdtown Institute — and occupied the prime positions open to blacks. Their credo was black improvement through progress; and advancement was achieved by an all-embracing education, diligent work, individual achievements and, most importantly, by introducing the 'enlightened' English to their cause. They presumed the chasm that divided black from white would rapidly be breached. 'We are just emerging from barbarism,' said John Knox Bokwe, a leading black spokesman, in *Imvo Zabantsundu*, 'and have to find our way, and by degrees gain [Britain's] confidence. By and by we shall attain, if one here and there shows capacity for positions of trust and responsibility, and creditably discharges the responsibility.'

These aspirant black Englishmen embraced Queen Victoria as their monarch and 'God Save the Queen' as their anthem. They established cricket, soccer and rugby clubs and a Philharmonic Society. And, when they went to the theatre, they dressed in black coats and starched white shirts that screamed for attention. They studied and dissected English literature — particularly Shakespeare — and fawned on the political institutions of the Cape Colony and British Empire. They specially valued the limited non-racial Cape franchise and chimerical concept of equality before the law. Euphoria permeated their ranks as they envisaged the significant role awaiting them in Cape politics and their imminent welcome into 'civilised' English society. It was a fatally flawed fantasy.

What they did not realise was that the 'Native problem' did not refer to rural blacks or the labourers necessary for menial and manual tasks below the dignity of whites. The educated, who did not know their place in the great scheme of things and threatened to take white jobs, were the pests. 'If the whites maintain their position as the supreme race, the day will come when we shall be thankful we have the natives in their proper place,' promised Rhodes during the debate on the Glen Grey Act, the precursor to the infamous 1913 Natives' Land Act, which sought to drive sharecroppers from Cape land and turn peasants into wage labourers. It was obvious where the natives' proper place was and it certainly was not at a performance of *Hamlet* in the Queen's Theatre in Kimberley to which Plaatje went.

The circle in which Sol Plaatje moved in Kimberley consisted mainly of pioneers whose naiveté can be excused for its good intent. What this group conceived was the far-fetched idea of a united non-racial South African society where the quality of individuals rather than the colour of their skins were the determinants. But, if resentful whites thought these aspirant blacks reached beyond themselves, the overwhelming majority of their black, tradition-bound countrymen believed they were being too hasty. While the chill-wind of racism blew from the front, the hot-breath of tribalism and custom breathed down their backs.

Plaatje experienced the latter when he fell in love with and married Isaiah Bud-M'belle's beautiful, dimpled and bewitching sister Elizabeth, who charmed and enlivened him.

> I long for the solitude of the woods,
> Far away from the quarrels of men,
> Their intrigues and vicissitudes;
> Away, where the air was clean
> nd the morning dew
> Made all things new;
> Where nobody was by
> Save Mhudi and I.
>
> Speak not to me of the comforts of home
> Tell me of the village where the antelope roam;

Give me my hunting sticks and snares
In the gloaming of the wilderness;
Give back the palmy days of our early felicity
And we'll be young again — Aye:
Sweet Mhudi and I.

SOL PLAATJE, MHUDI

Elizabeth was of the Hlubi tribe and both families vocally and resolutely opposed the union. So heated was the debate that Plaatje recalled the fate of Romeo and Juliet when he wrote; 'My people resented the idea of my marrying a girl who spoke a language which, like the Hottentot language, had clicks in it; while her people likewise abominated the idea of giving their daughter in marriage to a fellow who spoke a language so imperfect as to be without any clicks. But the civilised laws of the Cape Colony [he married by Special License] saved us from a double tragedy in a cemetery.'

Then, in 1898, the sought-after position of court interpreter to the Mafeking Magistrate, Charles Bell, became available. This career, for a black person in the Cape Colony at the turn of the century, was considered highly responsible as it was the tangible link in giving fair legal treatment to blacks in what, for most, was an alien institution. Plaatje was fascinated by law — the supreme arbiter. He had long before begun formulating his legal ideas and ideals based on customary, natural and cosmic laws which were ultimately answerable to divine law long before these became the principles entrenched by the South African Native National Congress, the forerunner to the African National Congress, which he helped found in 1912. Bell, who received his application — together with a strong recommendation from the influential Silas Molema, a family friend of the Plaatje's and a younger brother of Joshua Molema, the successor to the founder of Mahikeng — had no hesitation in giving Plaatje the post. Plaatje, before taking up the position at the end of October, took the heavily pregnant Elizabeth to stay with his family at Pniel.

He could never have foreseen that accepting the position of Mafeking court interpreter would catapult him to the forefront of the battle to free South Africa from all forms of racism and discrimination. Nor could he have imagined that this burning, tireless passion, ignited by his first-hand experience of British betrayal, would consume his energies, leaving little for the growing family he left at Pniel.

Plaatje, on his arrival in Mahikeng, moved into Moratiwa, the book-crammed house of his benefactor, Silas Molema. Mahikeng was no Malay Camp. The 350 kilometres that separated the two settlements represented the yawning gulf between trend-setting vibrancy and bumpkin conservatism. Yet Mahikeng was an important centre with a handful of progressive black thinkers. They were mainly to be found amongst the Mfengu, of the Fingo Location situated slightly east of Mahikeng and south of Mafeking. They had been part of Rhodes's Pioneer Column into Rhodesia in the early 1890s but refused to go further than Mafeking and settled and prospered here. This influential educated group — who gave their allegiance to the Molemas — aspired to western ways, built western-style housing and sent their children to the school Silas Molema founded. With deep porches, gables, creaking wooden floors and high pressed ceilings, Moratiwa was the most impressive of these homes and the focal point for the followers of the Molemas. But, the vast majority of the 5 000 Tshidi residents — for whom Mahikeng was the centre of the universe — owed their loyalty to the hard-drinking, illiterate Chief Besele, whose name had been corrupted to Wessels by the whites of the town, but who embodied the ancient traditions and archaic customs of the tribe.

Mahikeng was prettily situated on the banks of the Molopo River which meanders through the sallow plains that were once the hunting grounds of the Tshidi. Molema, when he founded it, had forbidden anyone to cut down any of the many trees among which the round, thatched huts, plastered with red mud and decorated with floral and animal designs, were built. The *stadt*, as it was known, was filled with a carnival of sounds and odours. On hot summer afternoons the breeze would be scented by the promise of a storm and the smell of wood smoke.

Goats and the occasional cow browsed. Gaunt old men, sucking curved pipes, would still speak savagely of the rinderpest that had recently decimated their wealth. Plaatje described the scourge as sweeping 'through Bechuanaland like a blizzard [which] denuded [Montshioa's] territories of nearly every beast — Buffaloes and wildebeest in the forests perished like domestic kine and many flourishing cattle posts were reduced to ruins. So that where formerly large herds or sleek fat oxen swarmed over the grasslands as a moving testimony to Barolong wealth, only heaps of whitened skeletons remained, the only vestige of the animal life that once throve there. It was a heartbreaking situation. The misery of his people being a thing terrible to contemplate. Hyenas and wild hounds gorged themselves to excess, while flocks of carrion birds and other scavengers of the woods were attracted by the stench of rotting carcasses'. Among these scavengers were the emissaries of the labour recruiting agencies who, before the plague of 1896, had never considered it worth their while to 'collect boys' among the Tshidi for the mines in Kimberley and Johannesburg.

Angus Hamilton, war correspondent for *The Times*, on visiting the *stadt*, gave his impressions of the dress of the male inhabitants of the town: 'Their attire was a weird mixture of effete savagery and of the civilisation of the sort which is picked up from living in touch with white Africa and missionary societies. Many black legs were clothed in trousers, many black shoulders wore coats. Here and there, as relics of the past, there was the ostrich feather in the hat, the fly whisk, composed of the hairs from an animal, the iron or bone skin-scraper with which to remove the perspiration of the body. A few wore shoes upon naked feet, a few others sported watch chains and spoke English ... a few ... were garmented with skins of animals upon the naked body.'

Plaatje enjoyed his work — which included clerical duties, translating letters and documents and writing up the civil and criminal record books — in the kennel-like courthouse in a building described as not having 'much architectural pretensions and quite inadequate for the purpose required. In one gable end justice is dispensed, in the other — postage stamps'. His job satisfaction was heightened by the arrival, after Christmas, of Elizabeth and his infant son, Frederick York St Leger, and by the fact that he got on well with Bell — who looked remarkably like Cecil Rhodes — the Cape Colony's most experienced magistrate and a talented linguist who was thorough, efficient, witty and courteous. Plaatje insatiably studied legal procedures and terminology and began preparing himself to sit the Cape Civil Service examination so he could be considered for promotion to the Supreme Court and, of more immediate importance, considering the birth of his son, now nicknamed 'Sainty', an increase in salary. The one thing that incensed him about his new job was that the white employees in the understaffed magistrate's office, even those of junior rank, treated him as if he were a lowly messenger.

Plaatje was acutely aware of the growing tension, in 1899, between Boer and Britain and, in August, sent his wife and son to the safety of her parents in Burghersdorp. Most reliable information on Boer movements and military build-up on the western borders of the South African Republic was supplied by the Barolong. Plaatje and the élite Barolong believed that should they support Britain in the event of war the institutions of the Cape Colony they so admired would automatically be extended by a victorious and grateful England to all the people of South Africa. Plaatje proudly declared his allegiance to England by pronouncing, 'we are citizens of a town of subjects of the richest and strongest empire on earth'. It was absolutely and utterly inconceivable that, at the end of the war, their champions would prefer their white enemies to their black allies. Once again educated blacks were trapped by the myopia of euphoria even though the warning signs, such as Milner's declaration that you only had 'to sacrifice the Nigger completely and the game is easy', abounded.

The British let the blacks of South Africa know loudly and clearly that this was to be a 'white man's war', as if the calamity attendant on such an event could be contained so as to have no effect on the black population. But, the British, as well as their Boer opponents, had every reason for declaring the spectator status of blacks. Blacks, armed with an education, already constituted an irritating and growing nuisance. Equipped with the tools of modern war, they could become a truly frightening third force which could destabilise the labour market and even challenge for power. Logistically neither white combatant could conduct a war without black labour or support – both knew this, they just could not say it, because it would seriously have undermined their contention that they were members of a superior race.

Jan Smuts, the young State Attorney in the South African Republic, summed up the conundrum. 'The peculiar position of the small white community in the midst of the very large and rapidly increasing coloured races and the danger which in consequence threatens this small white community and with it civilisation itself in South Africa, have led to the creation of a special code of morality as between the white and coloured races which forbids inter-breeding, and of a special tacit understanding which forbids the white races to appeal for assistance to the coloured races in their mutual disputes. This understanding is essential to the continued existence of the white community as the ruling class in South Africa, for otherwise the coloured races must become the arbiters in disputes between the whites and in the long run the predominating political factor or casting vote in South Africa. That this would soon cause South Africa to relapse into barbarism must be evident to everybody.'

The Cape authorities issued instructions to all magistrates that blacks were not to be armed and that they were to be confined to their locations during hostilities. The Barolong, with news reaching them daily of the growing crisis, were keenly aware of the Boer position regarding Mafeking generally and Mahikeng in particular. Revenge — should Mafeking be overrun — on the scale of that exacted by Mzilikazi on the Chief Tawana was a distinct possibility. To no avail did Wessels and his headmen bombard Bell with entreaties to arm the Tshidi so that they could defend themselves. At the beginning of October the Tshidi demanded a meeting, with the authorities, at which Plaatje was to be the interpreter.

Bell tendered mild and reassuring platitudes to the hard, angry men that sounded, to Plaatje, as if Bell was referring to 'an impending Parliamentary election rather than to a bloody war'. The defiant Tshidi, whose efforts would prove decisive during the siege, were having none of it. Plaatje takes up the story:

> The magistrate replied each time with confident assurance that the Boers would never cross the boundary into British territory. The Transvaal territory is only ten or twelve miles from the magistracy. The assurances of the Magistrate made the Natives rather restive ... The Chiefs told the magistrate that they feared he knew very little about war if he thought that belligerents would respect one another's boundaries. He replied in true South African style, that it was a white man's war, and if the enemy came, Her Majesty's white troops would do all the fighting and protect the territories of the chiefs. We remember how chief [Wessels] and his councillor Joshua Molema went round the Magistrate's chair and crouching behind him said: 'Let us say, for the sake of argument, that your assurances are genuine, and that when trouble begins we hide behind your back like this, and, rifle in hand, you do all the fighting because you are white; let us say, further, that some Dutch men appear on the scene and they outnumber and shoot you: what would be our course of action then? Are we to run home, put on skirts and hoist the white flag?'

> Chief Motshegare pulled off his coat, undid his shirt front and baring his shoulders and showing an old bullet scar, received in the Boer-Barolong war prior to the British occupation of Bechuanaland, said: 'Until you can satisfy me that Her Majesty's white troops are

impervious to bullets, I am going to defend my own wife and children. I have got my rifle at home and all I want is ammunition'.

This frustrating meeting was followed by a letter from the chiefs addressed to the Cape Government, through Bell, which never went further than his desk. At the same time as the British were brushing off the headmen, 2 000 refugees swelled the ranks of Mahikeng. Plaatje, whose duties had now been expanded to include acting as interpreter in Lord Cecil's Court of Summary Jurisdiction, could not have helped noticing the muscles built from physical labour of the fleeing Shangaan mineworkers, who sought protection in Mahikeng and were placed in a camp north of the *stadt*. He could also not but help being struck by the poor state of those pouring in from the surrounding countryside who, unbeknown to themselves, were marching to the doom that would revolt Plaatje and partly inspire his crusade to fill his people with a dignified vision of themselves.

Part II

EVERYTHING IN THE GARDEN IS LOVELY

'Everything in the garden is lovely.'

BADEN-POWELL IN A LETTER TO HIS MOTHER
DURING THE SIEGE OF MAFEKING.

'. . . one asked oneself what it was that had held these ordinary-looking people
to so heroic an intention.'

FILSON YOUNG, WAR CORRESPONDENT FOR THE
MANCHESTER GUARDIAN

Yet ye were saved by a remnant (and your land's long-
    suffering star)
When your strong men cheered in their millions while
    your striplings went to war.
Sons of the sheltered city – unmade, unhandled, unmeet –
You pushed them raw to the battle as ye picked them raw
    from the street.
And what did ye look they should compass? Warcraft learned
    in a breath.
Knowledge unto occasion at the first far view of Death?
So? And ye train your horses and the dogs ye feed and prize?
How are the beasts more worthy than the souls, your sacrifice?

KIPLING, 'THE ISLANDERS'

Not to the swift but to the most enduring.

TSWANA PROVERB

'When the history of this war comes to be written, people who should know
are of the opinion that Mafeking will be found to have no small part in the
huge task of holding South Africa.'

LADY SARAH WILSON

4

THE LUCK OF THE OIRISH

I of my own free will, and without any mental reservation whatsoever
will obey all orders transmitted to me by the Irish Invincibles
nor to seek nor to ask more than is necessary
in carrying out such orders, violation of which will be death.

THE OATH TAKEN ON BEING INDUCTED INTO
THE IRISH NATIONAL INVINCIBLES

'With 6 000 to 7 000 Boers camped within 10 miles of us, I have just a little bit of responsibility,' boasted Baden-Powell in a letter to his mother at the commencement of the Siege of Mafeking. How great this accountability was, was amply illustrated with this notice pinned outside Dixon's Hotel when Baden-Powell received news, brought in by Barolong scouts, that Boers were cutting the fence and crossing the frontier:

> In consequence of the armed forces of the South African Republic having committed an act of war, by invading British Territory, I give notice that a state of war exists, and that the civil law is for the time being suspended; and I proclaim martial law from this date in the Bechuanaland Protectorate.

He concluded the letter to his mother with: 'It is a most interesting experience especially as my first act was to proclaim Martial law ... I have already got the jail full of suspected spies ... and I keep them there with no proof of guilt ... I am a regular Jack-in-Office!'

During the first days of the war, work on Mafeking's defences continued apace. More trenches were dug, a few more strategic 'forts' constructed and the 'minefields' extended. From the first reports of Boers entering the Cape Colony, Baden-Powell expected an attack. On 11 and 12 October 1899 he had sent the armoured train out, and squadrons north, south and east to intercept the Boers but none were sighted. 'It was an extremely enthusiastic scene', reported J Emerson Neilly of the *Pall Mall Gazette*, 'and had a pathos of its own. Who knew how many of these brave fellows would come through the fire unscathed.'

The tension in the town, on Friday 13 October 1899, was palpable. The telegraph lines had gone dead shortly after the disquieting news reached Mafeking of the ambush of *Mosquito* at Kraaipan under Lieutenant Nesbit while transporting artillery to Mafeking. Boers had not yet been sighted, but scouts reported that Mafeking was encircled and the railway line was torn up to the north and south of the town. In the morning, the hot sun cooled by a gentle breeze, the armoured trains, *Firefly* and *Wasp*, under the command of Captain Williams of the British South Africa Police (BSAP), rumbled over the metal bridge that spans the Molopo River and headed south. Shortly after the trains had disappeared behind Jackal Tree Hill, the rat-a-tat sounds of the Maxim gun was heard for the first time and this was followed by the deeper thud of the Hotchkiss. 'To give a short account of what I found war to be,' enthused Sol Plaatje in the first entry in his famous Siege Diary, 'I can say: no music is as thrilling and as immensely captivating as to listen to the firing of the guns on your own side. It is like enjoying supernatural melodies in a paradise to hear one or two shots fired off the armoured train; but no words can suitably depict the fascination of the music produced by the action of the Maxim, which to Boers ears, I am sure, is an exasperation which not only disturbs the ear but also disorganises the free circulation of the listener's blood.' When the trains steamed back Williams reported that they had dispersed Boers tearing up the lines and that Hooper, of the BSAP, had fired the first shot to kill a Boer horseman. This report was incorrect because the casualty was one of Baden-Powell's Barolong scouts who had mistakenly been fired on by the exceedingly jumpy British troops.

Baden-Powell, shortly after the train returned, received information that two truckloads of dynamite he had ordered be sent to Bulawayo were still in Mafeking. The stockpiles in the town were a Godsend, the oversupply of dynamite was not. Baden-Powell had ordered James Quinlan, the Irish stationmaster, to get rid of the incendiary surplus to preclude the risk of the Boers raising the flaky red tin roofs of the houses of Mafeking. Quinlan, much to Baden-Powell's fury, delayed fulfilling the instruction. That this deferment was to be a stroke of fortune for Baden-Powell is by the bye – Quinlan's luck had temporarily run out.

Baden-Powell hurriedly ordered the two truckloads of dynamite shunted up the line in the direction of Bulawayo. The assigned engine driver nervously shoved the trucks some 10 kilometres from Mafeking until he sighted a group of Boers a kilometre ahead. He quickly uncoupled the trucks and dashed back to Mafeking. The Boers, believing the trucks a Trojan horse, fired on them. The resultant explosion rattled every sash window in Mafeking and the credulous Boers believed, throughout the siege, that the wrecked cars were detonated by remote control. This simple belief heightened their fears of Baden-Powell's 'mines' laid round the defences.

When the relieved engine driver returned, dragging ballooning clouds of black smoke, he witnessed soldiers questioning railway employees as to why the dynamite had not been sent to Bulawayo as commanded. Macullum, the manager at the Railway Refreshment Bar, was just then passing on a snippet of information to the interrogators. He claimed that he had heard Quinlan, whom he had known since Quinlan came to Mafeking over a year ago, proclaim in an alcohol-soaked outburst that he was a Fenian, proud of it, and that 'a man is not a man unless he is a Fenian'. Quinlan was, on this paltry evidence, circumstantially linked to another Irishman, Wellan, who was found in possession of a sophisticated military cipher, and, *voilà*, found himself in jail facing charges of high treason for an act of laxness. That a huge injustice was afoot is undoubted. But, in a town which should have become renowned for invidious behaviour rather than heroism, the case of Quinlan would have been a trifle but for two massive twists in the tail.

Quinlan normally swaggered, but, today – heart pounding frantically, mouth dry and spirit shattered and woebegone – his smile was wiped from his leathery face. When he was dragged into the small, bleak courtroom to face Lord Edward Cecil, the charges against him had swollen with improbable accusations of conspiring with the Boers, planning to blow up Mafeking and divulging the schedule and purpose of the *Mosquito* to General De la Rey. Quinlan would have been shot that afternoon but for the spindly nature of the evidence.

Quinlan would undoubtedly have been aware of Nesbit and *Mosquito*'s undertaking and he would certainly, as an Irish nationalist, have sympathised with the Boer cause against the British. It is also unquestioned that someone had tipped off De la Rey. It is, however, probable that Quinlan was being framed.

Then Cecil took a closer look at the accused squirming before him. Cecil's frustrated, quizzical expression was of a man trying to match a name to a face. The penny dropped. Quinlan was a known Irish nationalist. That part was right, but Cecil lied to embellish the story. He accused Quinlan of being an Irish National Invincible and implicated him in Dublin's Phoenix Park murders of 6 May 1882, claiming that he, Cecil, sat on the Royal Commission to investigate the twin assassinations. Cecil was lying: when that Commission sat he was a schoolboy. He, had, however been involved in countering Irish nationalism and would have known all the players involved – particularly those with links to as notorious a society as the Invincibles.

Little did Sol Plaatje know, as he sat at the scuffed table for officers-of-the-court, that this moment marked the end of his own quiet life. And, standing at the crossroads, as Quinlan's short hearing continued, he could have acquired a flash of insight, a premonition, of the future path southern African blacks might have to walk. Plaatje must have felt a pang of fraternity as Quinlan was dragged off to prison to await trial after the siege and then be deported to London to be tried as an accessory in the Phoenix Park murders, which would almost certainly have resulted in his execution – because, soon, the lapsed revolutionary's life would be saved by another act of laxness, this time on the part of the Magistrate's Court in Mafeking. The supporting evidence for the charges against him were mysteriously removed from the case file after the siege, and it is strongly suspected that Plaatje was the culprit.

This is the skeleton of the story of Jimmy Quinlan.

Gladstone's Land Act of August 1881, which moderately reformed Irish landlord-tenant farmer relations, was regarded as a great legislative achievement. Prior to the Act, the aristocratic Anglo-Irish landlords were an oppressive and avaricious law unto themselves who subjected their Irish tenants to a tyrannical system of feudalism that closely approximated slavery. The land-owning nobility – who had been able to extort exorbitant rents, evict tenants and suppress dissension as they saw fit – had had the full backing of the colonial system with the sheriff and the Royal Irish Constabulary riding in tandem with them where necessary. The counter-attack by Irish nationalists on the system of landlordism, that led to the introduction of reforming legislation, was not intended to improve the system of bondage Irish farmers found themselves in, but as a kick in the groin in the greater battle to make the bloody cost of occupying Ireland too great for England.

However, while the Land Act solved many of Ireland's land problems, it had a disquieting effect on the radical wing of Irish nationalism which required a broad base of oppressed citizens to sustain viable insurrectionary activity. They needed cold-blooded landlords, chaperoned by the unquestioning, baton-wielding forces of the establishment, to continually harass and evict tenant farmers. The sounds of landlords clubbing screaming barefoot children and shrieking defenceless black-shawled women, to the triumphal accompaniment of rebel songs and the crackling and spitting of tenants' torched huts, were the driving music of revolution. The risks, therefore, of a substantial segment of the persecuted breathing a collective sigh of relief at the reform of iniquity imperilled the urge to nationalism. Gladstone was, thus, a more dangerous enemy than any that had gone before.

What Gladstone either failed to recognise or did not have the strength to rectify was that Irish patriots wanted the abhorrent English robbers of their land to immediately give it back and go home so that Ireland could be free. It appears that feebleness drove the British premier because the warning had already been vividly delivered by Robert Emmett, the Darlin' of Erin. The firebrand nationalist hero, in his speech from the dock after being sentenced to death, had bellowed, 'When my country takes its place amongst the nations of the earth, then, and only then, let my epitaph be written'.

The Land Act, thus, rather than bringing peace, escalated the conflict. A stupefied Gladstone cried that Irish anarchists were 'marching through rapine to the dismemberment of Empire'. He was painfully getting the point, at the end of a pike, as a wave of violence shot through the country. Ireland 'reeked of blood' as two bailiffs were pumped full of bullets and flung into Loch Mask; a collaborating tenant farmer, his wife, son and daughter were executed for moral cowardice; and a juror, who had served on a jury that convicted a man of murdering a policeman, was dismembered. Eager judges, prosecutors and policemen could not have slept easily as fiery meetings damned them. Britain resorted to coercion, much to the joy of the patriots, because, as they trumpeted, 'When we are pleasing the English, we are not winning'.

But matters were not all going the way of the patriots. The Land Act was proving a success amongst individual farmers who promptly lost sight of the big picture of nationhood as the fug of their desperate lives lifted. Even Charles Stewart Parnell, of the Irish Party, who straddled the great divide between nationalism and the administration, became concerned at the anarchical levels of turmoil that were pushing Ireland to the brink of dissolution. The radical Ford section of Clan-na-Gael, in America, the largest financiers of the Irish nationalist movements, fearing Parnell was becoming a reactionary even though he was being held without trial, cut off his subsidy in October 1881. The Clan diverted these funds to further ignite the tense situation by establishing, the following month, an assassination society that would target British officials, starting with the Chief Secretary and Under Secretary to Ireland. This arcane brotherhood, the Irish National Invincibles, armed with foot-long, razor-sharp surgical knives, were given the coveted assignment of mortally piercing the ribs of the British devil.

The Invincibles, limited to 450 élite warriors, were more extreme than anything that preceded them. Under the ultimate leadership of the mysterious 'Number One', only the bravest and most determined members of the Fenian Brotherhood were inducted into self-contained Invincible cells. The 50-strong Dublin section, under the chairmanship of James Mullett, a member of the Supreme Council of the Fenian Brotherhood, used Mullett's pub as their headquarters. Mullett, however, was in prison and played only a limited role in the plots hatched in the smoky bar decorated with an aslant portrait of Daniel O'Connell, a sepia photograph of the Manchester Martyrs and other loyalist knick-knacks.

On 2 May 1882 Parnell was released from detention in a deal, that came to be known as the Kilmainham Treaty, brokered with Gladstone. This promised a diminution of the land agitation; the possibility of closer ties between Gladstone's Liberal Party and Parnell's Irish Party; and the immediate ending of the harsh Coercion Act.

Outraged patriots on one hand and the hard-line Chief Secretary to Ireland, WE Forster, on the other, saw this double-dealing pact as a disaster. Forster was livid that Gladstone had not forced Parnell to renounce violence and boycott politics. He believed that the liberal British government was making a treasonous deal with scoundrels, terrorists and anarchists. He resigned in a rage, as did Lord Cowper, the Viceroy to Ireland. Gladstone accepted their resignations, seeing them as an opportunity to further calm the Irish question by sending a liberal Viceroy and Chief Secretary to that vexatious island. It was widely expected that Gladstone would select Joseph Chamberlain, the forceful mayor of Birmingham, as Chief Secretary to Ireland. Chamberlain, and the watchful press, were enraged when Gladstone unexpectedly chose Lord Frederick Cavendish to accompany Lord Spencer, the new Viceroy, as Chief Secretary to Ireland.

The florid Cavendish, his face netted with a regular pattern of burst blood vessels, was the second son of the Duke of Devonshire and married to Gladstone's niece. This forty-something man – described as an amiable lunatic by his friends and as immoderately stupid by his detractors – was as uninspired a choice as could possibly be made for the most 'odious and thankless' job in the realm. Cavendish wasted little time in accepting this morsel of nepotism and arrived in Dublin, with Spencer, on the morning of 6 May. His official induction was scheduled for the afternoon and he spent the morning with the Under Secretary, Thomas Burke, at Dublin Castle, which served as the headquarters of the British administration in Ireland. Had he looked out of the narrow window, beyond the smartly dressed guards at the gate, he would have seen Mullett's pub across the way.

Cavendish's arrival in Dublin, as the harbinger of peace, was marked by an eruption of celebration, shrill whistles, booming military bands and the joyful songs of ordinary people. He immediately fell in love with this Georgian city and its extrovert people who were as ready to laugh as furiously put up their fists. He would, however, not have had time, on that first day, to witness the dreadful poverty that existed side-by-side with the elegance that captivated him. He would have heard the scrape of a fiddle and the clatter of cartwheels on cobblestones as great drays pulled loads of Guinness barrels through the streets. But he would not live to observe the swirls at the bopping Star of Erin Dancehall; nor smell the mephitic stench of side-streets where one overflowing lavatory and a single tap served the entire community; and he would be saved from stumbling across slavering boys and their flame-haired colleens, away from the intrusive light cast by gas lamps, breathlessly losing their virginity against the walls of begrimed alleyways.

It was a beautiful warm evening, later, on that first day, as Cavendish strolled along the Liffey Quays toward his official residence in Phoenix Park. As he lingered at the entrance to the park, soaking up his surroundings, he would not have failed to see the towering Wellington Obelix or soaring Phoenix Monument from which that great bird rose from its pyre. He would have heard the man grinding a tuneless barrel-organ; been delighted in the floral shower of brilliant hues; and savoured the scents of hawthorn and nightstock as he was serenaded by a thrush. Up ahead he caught sight of Burke and hurried to catch up. He did not notice the seven waiting men, who had received excellent intelligence regarding their victim's movements, lolling on the verge. Nor did he take in the two jaunting getaway cars of Kavanagh and the gnarled 'Skin-The-Goat' waiting to whisk the assassins away.

Cavendish joined Burke a short way from the gate lodge of the Under Secretary's estate and the pair proceeded deep in conversation. Up ahead the seven men casually ambled toward the couple in a three-three-one formation. The front three were to pass their victims and turn so that Cavendish and Burke would be surrounded. Kavanagh removed the nosebag from his horse and prepared for a quick getaway. When Cavendish and Burke were surrounded, the muscular, mash-nosed Joe Brady and the youthful Tim Kelly unsheathed their blades. Brady struck first as the sun set behind the church spires and huddled rooftops. He swiftly buried the blade three times into Burke and, as the Under Secretary's legs melted beneath him, grabbed a fistful of his hair, pulled his head back and slit his throat as his eyes rolled back in their sockets. Kelly plunged his blade in Cavendish's shoulder and, as the Chief Secretary sank screaming to his knees, nearly severed the ineffective arm he raised to fend off the next blow. As Cavendish lay back on the grass, blood gurgling from his wounds, Kelly bent down and gutted him. The assassins, their deed over in seconds, sprang onto the two getaway vehicles and swiftly headed off in different directions.

The following day, black-rimmed cards were sent to newspaper offices triumphantly claiming responsibility for the Invincibles and promising more. The infamous police of the notorious G Division of the Dublin Metropolitan Police swung into action to pursue the assassins and anyone they thought may be involved. At the other end of the spectrum, the *Irishman* sang that 'against [England] any weapons are lawful' and that the assassination of Cavendish was ' ... the most popular murder since Talbot was shot in Dublin'. The desired damage to Anglo-Irish relations was immediately achieved, but, for the Invincibles, this was to be their defining moment. They were hunted with such ferocity that their leaders fled to America and the chiefs of the Dublin Invincibles were rounded up. The police investigation was made easier when one of the Dublin leaders, James Carey, turned super-informer in return for amnesty and passage to South Africa as a protected witness.

Quinlan would not have played a role in Cavendish's assassination. He was, however, a Fenian and possibly an Invincible and the leadership had an assignment for him and another Irish nationalist, O'Donnell. Neither belonged to the Dublin Invincibles or would be recognised by Carey, whose evidence had sent five of the Dublin leaders to the gallows and another three into periods of long penal servitude. He, under no circumstances, was to survive such treachery. Quinlan and O'Donnell, probably with false identities, were delegated to ensure that.

Carey, big and flabby, with an enormous bragging mouth, was not hard to track and monitor even though he had been issued a new identity. When he boarded the *Melrose Castle* bound for Cape Town and Durban, Quinlan and O'Donnell boarded as well. On the lower decks Carey playing cards and smoking cigars was at his boastful best. As the ship steamed into Cape Town, on a clear and gusty day, it hooted a warning to a passing fishing boat. It was the cacophonous moment that O'Donnell had waited for and he shot the unsuspecting Carey at close range. The crack, however, was heard by many and O'Donnell was quickly overpowered and taken into custody to await his return to London, where he was tried and executed. The tall, open-faced Jimmy Quinlan, with whiskers and elevated cheekbones, disembarked.

5

DAMPHOOL CRONJE

*Go back, Cronje, you juggins, and take your
    damphool Boers,
We've other things to think of than those
    useless shells of yours,
And when you get the blues again and failure
    makes you howl
I would recommend another dose, from Doctor
    Baden-Powell.*
        MAFEKING MAIL No. 19, 27 NOVEMBER 1899

Baden-Powell, as Quinlan was led off to prison, inspected the Town Guard in the Market Square and gave a short speech: 'All you have to do is to sit tight and when the time comes to shoot straight ... Take my word for it, if you act like I fully expect you will act, the Boers will never enter Mafeking.' He closed this pep-talk to the sweaty, dusty and tired men by calling for three cheers for the Queen. Colonel Vyvyan followed by bellowing for three cheers for Baden-Powell.

The opening phase of the Siege of Mafeking is hailed as one of the greatest defensive feats of all time. This stage was to last for five weeks and cost the Boers any chance of victory in the war. That the Boers swallowed the bait prepared for them was a stroke of genius by Baden-Powell and an immeasurable tactical blunder on the part of General Piet Cronje – the 'Old Fox'. After this phase, things are not as clear cut.

In September 1899, Commandant-General Piet Joubert, the South African Republic's Commander-in-Chief, appointed Cronje as General for the Western Front. Arthur Conan Doyle described the bearded Cronje as a 'hard swarthy man, quiet of manner, fierce of soul, with a reputation among a nation of resolute men for unsurpassed resolution.' The stubborn, grizzled Cronje, a tough-as-an-ox pioneer who had survived the Great Trek, was highly regarded amongst rank and file Boers. Neither Joubert nor De la Rey shared this opinion, but considering Cronje's reputation, decided it was prudent to give him a high profile command with De la Rey appointed as his Second-in-Command to exercise control over him.

Cronje has been pilloried for directing approximately one-fifth of the Boer forces to Mafeking at a time when they had their best strategic advantage. Cronje's intention was to overrun Mafeking and then veer south toward Kimberley. However, he was loath to risk the lives of his forces in a frontal attack on Baden-Powell's trenches and machine guns. For this he has been accused of cowardice. Nothing could be further from the truth.

Cronje was hamstrung by Kruger and a Boer defensive attitude. While it is true that Cronje probably suffered from a siege mentality – a reputation earned in the First South African War when he wasted an entire Boer commando besieging a small British force – he was under conflicting orders to take bold action whilst exercising extreme caution. Though the instructions were not explicit, it is generally accepted that Boer commanders were advised that they should avoid situations where the casualties would be higher than 50. It has been suggested that had De la Rey been in command he would have taken Mafeking in a few hours. On the contrary, De la Rey advised Cronje to avoid the place and head south immediately. The mistake Cronje made was to scoff that this recommendation was premature and counter with his belief that Mafeking, at little cost, could be taken if a modicum of patience was exercised.

To surround Mafeking, Cronje positioned himself and the Potchefstroom and Lichtenburg commandos to the south-west with two guns. General Snyman was placed, also with two guns, at McMullen's farm to the east with the Zeerust, Marico and Worlmaransstad burghers. General Steenkamp, with the Rustenburg commando, was sent to Signal Hill to the north-east with one gun. A laager, with two guns, was situated at Game Tree to the north-west with two guns. Finally, a laager, to the south, was sited at Jackal Tree with one gun.

Irrespective, the Boer circle of investment was porous, with wide gaps in their lines which were neither guarded nor regularly patrolled. This allowed a good deal of movement through Boer positions. Further, problems were apparent in the laagers from the outset. Abraham Stafleu, a Dutch teacher who shortly before the war began teaching at a school in the western Transvaal and, at the outbreak of the war, joined Snyman as a non-official member of the Red Cross, wrote in his diary: 'The officials needed to perform the necessary tasks had not yet been appointed and there was no clear line of demarcation between the functions of the various officers. Already there were a disturbing number of cases of dysentery. The newly appointed Laager Commandant made it his duty to look to the provision of clothes and blankets. Many burghers had only been able to bring one blanket with them on their horses and some were so poor as to be practically shoeless.'

> *This is our lot if we live so long and labour unto the end —*
> *That we outlive the impatient years and the much too patient*
>   *friend:*
> *And because we know we have breath in our mouth and*
>   *think we have thought in our head,*
> *We shall assume we are alive, whereas we are really dead.*
>   KIPLING, 'THE OLD MEN'

Baden-Powell intended to follow a policy of aggressive defence. He was convinced that if he gave the Boers regular 'hard kicks' they would treat the town with circumspection. On 13 October, the fierce afternoon sun warping the air, *Firefly* returned from reconnoitring to the north. Captain Williams of the British South Africa Police (BSAP) reported that he had found puzzled Boers examining the debris and the hole in the ground caused by the exploding dynamite trucks. He also brought back with him the second casualty of the siege, again a Barolong scout. Tom Hayes, the Principal Medical Officer, remarked in his diary: 'A native was brought (in) ... suffering from concussion of the brain caused by the dynamite explosion. He died before I saw him. I held a post mortem. Instructions were passed around for everyone to go to sleep prepared for action.'

Sleep, that night, could not have been easy. Every available man not on patrol had been sent forward and their horses led back into town. Some manned the trenches and the remainder lay in the open veld. The imagined threat, in the blue-smeared moonlit veld, strained taut nerves. A breeze, from the west, carried with it noises that were amplified in the minds of the expectant protectors. Two BSAP troops that did manage to get some sleep were surprised by a Boer patrol and captured. Then, as the first grey of daylight tinted the sky, a tattoo of rifle shots was heard to the north-east in the arc between the railway line and the Ramatlhabama road.

Just before dawn, on Saturday 14 October, Captain Lord Charles Cavendish-Bentinck, on patrol with a squadron of the Protectorate Regiment to 'try and get a chance at the enemy', smelt the sharp aroma of coffee and wood-smoke. Bentinck had split the squadron into smaller patrols and had about 60 men with him. He gave the command to halt, dismount and proceed on foot to a slight rise, Signal Hill, where a flicker of light could be seen against the still dark sky. As they crept up the rise Boer voices could be heard. Bentinck gave his men the range and posted himself on the flank. 'Give 'em beans!' he shouted as he fired a single shot that thwacked into the bank at the far side of the hollow. The surprised Boers scrambled up as two volleys were fired at them.

Bentinck had grossly underestimated the number of Boers in the vicinity and soon found himself in a battle with 500 of the enemy. A corporal, a kilometre away in one of the patrols that had been split off, observed that Bentinck was in grave danger of being surrounded. The corporal, in one of the only instances of sense to be displayed that morning, decided to rush back to Mafeking to alert Baden-Powell rather than render assistance to his commanding officer.

Within a half hour, an armoured train, under the command of Williams with 50 BSAP troops, was proceeding up the line, puffing hard and clicking over the metal joints. The Boers transferred their attention to the train, which allowed Bentinck to retreat. Williams and his troop, from the train, opened fire with rifles, two maxims and the 1-pounder Hotchkiss of Lieutenant Kenneth Murchison. The Boers, strafed and scythed from the train, were forced to move back and take cover. Behind them, from higher ground, a quick firing Krupp, a Maxim and a 1-pounder Vickers fired on the train which was soon shrouded in dust, smoke and escaping steam. Mauser bullets smashed into its steel sides or whined away over the veld. Inside the racket was deafening. Neilly of the *Pall Mall Gazette* reported that the troops 'closed in their cab, were almost deafened by the noise of action and the hammering of the enemy's bullets against the steel armour.' Stafleu, with the Boers, grumbled ' . . . .we were unfortunate in not having steel tipped ammunition in the Maxim to use against the armoured train although the Mauser bullets worked well.'

Sounds of battle carried clearly to Mafeking and anxious townspeople gathered in Market Square. The fear that the town was about to be sacked momentarily took secondary importance as a commotion swept through the assemblage. A Dutch woman screamed that soon 'every English throat would be cut'; another shouted gleefully that the streets 'would run with English blood deep enough to wash her doorstep.' Baden-Powell restored order by having the two arrested and dragged off to jail.

Baden-Powell then made the first of a number of mistakes that he would make that day. He decided to send Captain Fitzclarence with 50 members of the Protectorate Regiment to support Williams. Lieutenant Brady, also of the Protectorate Regiment, was to act as backup to Fitzclarence. They were ordered to ride to the train, 'to assist and if necessary draw off the enemy and relieve the crew of the armoured train.'

Firtzclarence's party dismounted short of the train and left their horses behind a cluster of abandoned Barolong huts. As Fitzclarence advanced the Boers fell back. Spurred on by the ease with which the Boers were being driven off, he sped up. The Boers, unbeknown to Fitzclarence, were sucking him into a trap. They were manoeuvring in such a way that Fitzclarence was brought between them and the train thus cutting off the fire from Williams, who feared hitting British soldiers. The Boers were now able to concentrate their fire on Fitzclarence. Particularly effective were Boer snipers concealed in the branches of trees scattered round the Boer position. First to fall, shot through their heads, were two Irish cousins, Corporals Parland and Walshe. As Fitzclarence pushed up Signal Hill, a gauze of blue gun smoke hovering in the blistering heat, a party of Boers drifted south to circle his right flank and surround him. Baden-Powell was informed by field telephone of the impending disaster.

Baden-Powell, who had heard the firing from the train suddenly stop, assumed it had been taken out by a Boer shell. Rather than confirm this on the field telephone that had just conveyed the news of Fitzclarence, he decided to risk even more of his force. Baillie, the war correspondent of *The Morning Post*, remarked: 'The strain on Colonel Baden Powell and the headquarters' staff must indeed have been great. For four hours they were anxiously waiting. Reports were not favourable, and they knew that a disaster to this small force risked the whole defence as there was literally not another man to send to their support.' Baillie, a retired cavalry officer, volunteered to cycle to the battlefield to try and get a message to

Fitzclarence to retire. Bentinck was ordered to ride with his men to cover the withdrawal.

Baillie soon ran into trouble as the Boers spotted the sun glinting off the handlebars. Only the hard riding of Bentinck saved him. Bentinck, with support from Murchison and the Hotchkiss, was then able to drive off the Boers flanking Fitzclarence and save him. By noon the armoured train was steaming back with some of the wounded in the care of Major Anderson. At the field hospital – the air heavy with chemical smells, the buzz of flies and the sweet, sticky odour of blood – Angus Hamilton, war correspondent for *The Times*, reported that one man, 'with extraordinary coolness in seeing the nature of his wounds, which were seven, exclaimed that it still might be possible for him to enjoy the functions of a married man.' Others, their faces clouded with horror and their uniforms spattered with blood, rolled round, beating at their wounds. An engine and a passenger coach, flying a Red Cross flag, were dispatched to bring back any other wounded still lying on Signal Hill. This train came under Boer fire and was forced to return – prompting Baden-Powell to send Cronje a letter of protest under a flag of truce.

Angus Hamilton, in his report, wrote: 'The action of Captain Fitzclarence in endeavouring to meet the Boer commando was one of those inopportune acts of gallantry where loss, should the fight be successful, is overlooked. Stafleu, in his diary, commented ' . . . the English were shooting far too high. In the beginning of the fight two of our men were killed, one Engel who was shot in the head and Ockert Oosthuizen who was killed when the bolt of his rifle was shot off and tore open his insides. There were also two badly wounded men who had legs shot off.' He added that members of the Rustenburg commando had been accused of cowardice. Later, after surveying the battlefield, he wrote: 'The battlefield yielded up six rifles. Veldcornet Jan Louw went to see . . . [the] battlefield. In the pockets of the dead he found papers that revealed their identity. It was very sad. One dead soldier had a letter from his betrothed in which she questioned why he should have taken up arms against the Boers and not rather have concentrated on his farming which was going well. She was always living in fear for him. Veldcornet Louw took the address of the woman and was to send a short letter about the soldier's participation in his final battle and to express their sorrow at the outcome. Louw gave orders that the bodies were not to be disturbed, but it was afterwards discovered that the finger of one of the bodies had been cut off in order to steal a ring.'

Bentinck, for his hasty decision to get into a scrap without assessing the extent of his opponent, and Fitzclarence have been criticised for their foolhardy actions. This is unfair, as they were carrying out Baden-Powell's explicit and aggressive wishes which proved that while he was a brilliant defender, he was an atrocious attacker. This was demonstrated time and again whenever he resorted to 'hard kicks'. Even though the Boer casualties were heavier, the risks for Baden-Powell were inestimably higher and, moreover, wasted precious ammunition. The one advantage Baden-Powell got from this action was the disheartening effect it exercised on the Boers. 'The Boers held off, and did not molest the town until 11 days later, during which time the defences were greatly strengthened,' wrote Major Alexander (Alick) Godley of the Royal Dublin Fusiliers, who was selected by Wolseley for Baden-Powell. If Baden-Powell is to be criticised then Cronje ought to be crucified for allowing an opportunity to go begging. Godley summed this up by stating: 'Had the Boers pushed home their attack in the first instance, nothing would have stopped them from riding straight into town.'

At noon on the following day, Sunday, an open landau flying a Red Cross flag and drawn by a fine pair of white horses approached the town. In the vehicle was Dr Pirow, Cronje's emissary. He was conducted through the defence lines and directed to Dixon's Hotel where Baden-Powell met him and invited the Boer to join him for lunch.

Pirow, claiming that most Boers had never seen a Red Cross flag before, apologised for firing on the train Baden-Powell had sent to collect casualties. He assured Baden-Powell it would not happen again and added that stretcher bearers and ambulances could visit the scene of yesterday's fighting unhindered. Baden-Powell acknowledged the apology in a note to Cronje which he sent with a case of whiskey. From Pirow, Baden-Powell also learnt that additional artillery was being brought from Pretoria and that Cronje, fearful of Baden-Powell's dummy defences, intended to bombard the town into submission.

These matters, however, were side issues. It had been suspected that the deeply religious Boers would not fight on the Sabbath. Over lunch Pirow presented Baden-Powell with a proposal, which he readily accepted, that Sundays be regarded as a day of peace. Other than for isolated instances, this surreal meshing of Christian faith and warfare was to be honoured throughout the siege. On that first Sunday afternoon, the residents attended church services, sang rousing hymns and prayed for deliverance as the brass-band of the Bechuanaland Rifles entertained the town with a flourish of trumpets and a clash of cymbals on the Recreation Ground.

The train returned to Signal Hill, above which vultures circled, to collect the dead while Baden-Powell rode round the perimeter checking the defences. On his return he gave orders, for the following day, that women and children be sent to the Women's Laager, which would fly a Red Cross flag, and that bunkers and dug-outs be improved to protect the garrison from shelling. That evening, the air cool and silken as the horizon was flamed by the setting sun, the dead cousins were brought back to Mafeking to be sewn into canvas bags. They were buried that night by the Catholic Priest, Father Ogle. The moon had risen and the night was haunted by a piercing solitary bugle sounding the Last Post as Ada Cock, a resident of Mafeking, concluded her diary entry for the day with the observation that 'there seems but small chance for us.'

Baden-Powell, not as pessimistic and well aware that the Boers could take Mafeking at any moment, was confident that they were not going to risk the bold stroke necessary to do so. Admitting they were going to shell the town showed they were not intending, in the short-term at least, to storm Mafeking. He had thus achieved his first objective of drawing off and holding Boer forces from the main theatre of the war.

But, in those first few days, Baden-Powell was not the cool, calm and collected commander of myth. By day, dressed in khaki shirt and shorts and wearing the pinched Stetson he would make famous, Baden-Powell would spend many hours in his lookout surveying Boer lines through his Zeiss fieldglasses. When not here, he would visit the ill and wounded in the hospital, or plot ways to confuse the Boers who appeared to be, and were, gullible. Godley commented that Baden-Powell was 'fussed and worried ... We have all worked our best and he is rather crabbing our show – says the horses do not look well – how on earth could they? And that the regiment is not fit to take the field. He appears to expect us to work like a trained cavalry regiment.' Baden-Powell also put enormous pressure on the beefy, red-faced Charles Hore, who Godley described as 'a nice old thing who mistook his vocation and ought to be a comfortable old farmer.'

In the afternoons, for an hour or two, he would read, sketch, write letters, update his Staff Diary or compose encouragements for his men. This one appears to have been inspired by Fitzclarence and Bentinck:

Bluff the enemy with show of force as much as you like,
but don't let yourself get too far out of touch with
your own side without orders, lest you draw them on into
difficulties in their endeavour to support you. ... Do not always
wait for orders, if you see the situation demands action.
Don't be afraid to act for fear of making a mistake − 'a
Man who never made a mistake never made anything.' If you find
you have made a mistake, carry it through nevertheless with energy.
Pluck and dash have often changed a mistake into a success.

By night he would slip on a pair of gym shoes and tour the defences. He claimed that he crawled through the moonlit veld reconnoitring enemy positions. 'Once,' he boasted, 'having crept up a donga to look at a Boer fort, I was seen by the enemy, and they came out to capture me. I at once signalled to imaginary friends in the donga below me, and the Boers ran back into their fort.' There is strong evidence, particularly with regard to the fiasco of Game Tree on Boxing Day, that these nocturnal reconnaissance excursions were nothing other than a figment of a fertile imagination. When he did sleep, he slept lying back in an easy chair or on a camp mattress − protected by a barricade of biscuit tins − on the veranda of his office. Baillie wrote: 'I always know he is there, as I pass, when I see a pair of boots sticking out.'

The picture painted of Baden-Powell is of an isolated, impenetrable man. Yet, the legend is completely different. Neilly reported: 'None that I have met could beat Baden-Powell in the matter of alertness and sleeplessness. From cockcrow till nightfall he was at it.' And when he was 'at it' he was supposedly walking with his running gait and whistling the opening chorus from the *Belle of New York*. One moment he was pacifying anxious townsfolk with instructions to emulate Brer Fox and 'lie low and say nuffin' and, the next, disappearing silently into the blackness of night to terrify the Boers. Baden-Powell partly supplied the reason for this conflicting image: 'Luckily my early play acting instincts come in useful, and though my mind was in my boots at times with anxiety − I was able to maintain a grin to reassure those anxious appealing eyes that mutely asked at every turn "Is it all right?" "Are you sure we can go on?"'

Baden-Powell did most to foster the legend of himself at Mafeking. Every utterance and action was formulated to hit the right note with the gallery and each sequence timed to excite the admiration of his audience −

the British public. His achievement in holding up a force six times greater than his, while his peers were being humiliated, was not enough. While nothing can be taken from his accomplishment, he exaggerated the number of Boers facing him from 6 000 to 12 000 and vastly over-reported their casualties. This was performed in a tone of casual heroics that made light of his difficulties. England was dazzled.

And the war correspondents, though not fooled, toed the line. They were warned by Baden-Powell at the outset that no criticism of his actions or conduct during the siege would be tolerated. Angus Hamilton tried to sneak a report out of Mafeking that had not been passed by the censor. Baden-Powell found out and instructed the editor of *The Times*, George Buckle, to fire him – which, to his eternal disgrace, he did. It was only after much grovelling that Hamilton was reinstated and his press credentials restored. The seasoned reporters, however, sensed the story of a lifetime in the making and they were not going to do anything to spoil it.

Sol Plaatje provided many of these correspondents with secretarial and translation services. Vere Stent, editor of the *Pretoria News*, recalls their first meeting:

> One fine morning I became aware of a very smart, sprucely dressed young native standing to attention before me.
>
> "Well?" said I.
>
> "I hear you need a secretary-typist, sir," he answered.
>
> "Well, so I do. Is your master one?"
>
> "I haven't a master," said Plaatje, with a faint smile.
>
> BRIAN WILLAN, SOL PLAATJE: A BIOGRAPHY

The first shell fell on Mafeking at 9.30 am on Monday, 16 October 1899. Thirty thousand more, in excess of 150 tonnes, would shake the town before the siege was lifted. It was not the picnic many have claimed.

High lust and froward bearing,
*   Proud heart, rebellious brow –*
Deaf ear and soul uncaring,
*   We seek Thy mercy now!*
The sinner that forswore Thee,

The fool that passed Thee by,
Our times are known before Thee —
Lord, grant us strength to die!
KIPLING, 'HYMN BEFORE ACTION'

Stafleu, in his diary, wrote: 'From the north we had a beautiful view of the town. The sun shone brightly on the many white houses, in between which the tops of cypress trees could be seen. In the morning light many window frames glistened. There was a deadly silence. It was as if the dominating thought was that we would have to destroy or doom this happy town to grief. The first cannon shots from our side were fired, and from here on the only thought was to win or die.'

Tom Hayes, in his diary, recalled: 'At 9.00 am we buried Corpl Jones, who died of his wounds last night. Just as the service was finished the Boers fired their first shot. I got on the roof of our house, with the glasses, and could see them on Signal Hill, about 3½ miles off. The next shot came harmlessly overhead: it sounded like the wind humming through very tense telegraph wiring, then a shell burst about 50 yards from Victoria Hospital. I saw Colonel Vyvyan, and we discussed the advisability of moving the wounded and women there, but gave it up as we shortly expected shelling from all sides. While on the roof I saw a shell explode beside some twenty natives, who were watching operations from a truck. There was a good deal of confusion among some women in the Railway Camp, so I got on my horse and ordered them to the Laager. The poor people were so terrified that they were afraid to leave their houses, but a shell came through the roof, of one, and exploded inside, soon made them take my advice. The shells came thick and the people had to lie low ... They now opened from a heavier gun — a Krupp quick firing — with more powerful shells. One exploded in Riesle's Hotel, breaking the window and part of the wall. In the intervals of firing, we amused ourselves with running out and picking up fragments of shells.'

Baden-Powell was near the Recreation Ground when the first shell came with a whishing rush of air and exploded with a great flash. A wild-eyed girl, on a bicycle, nearly rode into him as the grey smoke, smelling of high explosives, blew across the road.

'Young lady,' admonished Baden-Powell, 'you had better go home and get under cover. The Boers are beginning to shell us.'

'Oh!' she responded. 'Are those shells? May I stay and look at them?'

Later, everyone boasted 'how they dodged the shells and how brave they were.' Godley, noting Baden-Powell's calmness under fire, praised him for the manner in which he steadied the town's frayed nerves: '[It was] splendid to see him, just as one or two shells burst in the Market Square, sitting in a chair with his staff all round him dictating messages as cool as a cucumber.' For the rest, their brags were mere bravado. On that first morning of shelling, the NCO in charge of the police office rushed for refuge to Riesle's cellar; Charles Bell threw himself in a well; Weil took refuge under the railway bridge; Miss Becker, a resident, was hysterical; and others bolted in terror for the river bed.

The shelling continued for four hours, then suddenly stopped. A man, with four white handkerchiefs tied together as a flag of truce, was seen approaching. The flag was carried by an Englishman, Everitt, who was fighting for the Boers. As with Pirow, he was brought to Market Square where Baden-Powell waited for him. A large milling crowd had gathered and Baden-Powell had already affixed a notice to the hotel wall:

Killed: one hen.
Wounded: one yellow dog.
Smashed: one hotel window.

Everitt handed Baden-Powell a note from Snyman. Baden-Powell read it loud. It demanded the immediate surrender of the town 'to avoid further bloodshed.' Baden-Powell feigned amazement and looked round the uplifted faces of the tittering audience, 'When?' he asked. 'When will the bloodshed start?' The only blood spilt that day, in fact, was on the Boer side. Stafleu concluded his diary entry for the day with 'Mr Visser from Pretoria who arrived to fight alongside his friends from the Marico district, shot off three of his fingers whilst climbing onto his horse.'

Filson Young was awe-struck when he viewed the town after the siege. 'Thirty thousand shells! I have been in the neighbourhood of about a hundred bursting shells, and every burst will be a memory for a lifetime; but thirty thousand! The heart stops at the thought.' He concluded: 'I am not exaggerating when I say what by far the greater number of the houses in the town had been struck by shells, and that very nearly all had been struck either by shells or bullets ... As one passed house after house, one with a gaping hole in its side, another with the chimneys overthrown, another with the whole wall stove in, none with windows completely glazed, all bearing some marks of assault — as this panorama of destruction unfolded itself one marvelled that anyone should have lived throughout the siege.'

'I dread anything that reminds me of that ghastly time, I really dread it,' shuddered Lord Cecil years later.

The initial terror of the shelling was exacerbated by reports of a wagon, drawn by 20 oxen, that was transporting to Mafeking a 94-pound French Creusot Siege Gun. No one in the town had seen one before, but all knew its fearsome reputation. The gun — known as 'Grietje' to the Boers and christened 'Old Creaky' by the residents — was positioned to the south at Jackal Tree Hill on a specially constructed platform. At 10 am on 24 October, a lookout on Cannon Kopje reported that the gun barrel was being elevated and pointed. The alarm jangled through the town as confused residents dashed screaming for shelter. A half hour later there was a boom, followed by a screeching rush overhead like the passing of an express train and a thudding explosion. Silence. Then a little eternity of four minutes. And a repeat.

Not a day passed, other than Sundays, that shrapnel, common shells and minor projectiles did not pound the town like a pestle. 'They make life hell,' lamented Angus Hamilton. Some shells were filled with phosphorous compounds, others had messages attached to them. They came from all points of the compass, sporadically or in concentrated bombardments that lasted six hours. When these missiles hit the ground they either exploded and dispersed a shower of dust, steel, splinters and stones as sharp as arrowheads or did a demon dance as they scudded, for up to 2,5 kilometres, before exploding. The smoky air was redolent with the acrid aroma of explosives and hot, burnt dust.

'Divine services. No thunder. Haikonna [no] terror; and I have therefore got ample opportunity to sit down and think before I jot down anything about my experiences of the past week,' wrote Plaatje during the peace of the second Sunday of the investment. 'I have discovered nearly everything about war and find that artillery in war is of no use. The Boers seem to have started hostilities, the whole of their reliance leaning on the strength and number of their cannons — and they are now surely discovering their mistake. I do not think they will have more pluck to do anything better than what they did on Wednesday and we can therefore expect that they will either go away or settle round us until the troops arrive.'

Commentators wonder at the relatively few casualties from the shelling, particularly amongst the white residents. Because the Boer lines were forced to remain a few kilometres from town, most firing was done blind and was thus inaccurate. Nor, from that distance, could they make out which trenches were manned by troops and which by dummies. The major reason, however, was that the sandy soil absorbed much of the shock and the single-storey buildings, other than the convent, were constructed from clay bricks and mud which minimised the danger of collapsing buildings and exploding stone. Thus, if residents took shelter, the risk of harm could be reduced.

There is an old Colonel called Hore,
Whose dugout's the best in the Corps,
When the shells fly about
We shout 'Hell, look out!'
And we see the old beggar no more.
TIM JEAL, BADEN-POWELL

In the white town immense energy went into the construction of bomb-proof shelters. Black labourers, particularly from amongst the Shangaan refugees from the mines, were rounded up and set to work to construct these bunkers for their allies. Because of the nature of the clayey soil it was not necessary to reinforce or support the sides of these havens. The essential element was the roof which consisted of a steel cover, corrugated iron, a metre of sand on the steel covered by tarpaulin. Every available steel rail was carted from the well-stocked railway depot and girders, bridging material and corrugated iron were commandeered. Historians have, unkindly, attributed the greater number of fatalities amongst the black residents of Mahikeng to either a lack of purpose for not excavating bunkers or a passive fatalism. The truth is that Baden-Powell made no steel or iron available to them to construct effective shelters and, worse, took from them whatever they had to construct bunkers in the white town.

But, nonetheless, there was capricious and shocking peril. Angus Hamilton reported the deadly effects of one bombardment: 'As the shell rebounded from the ground leaving a hole many feet long ... it [came] in contact with a native before it wrecked the apothecary's store. Mingled with the fragments of glass and the contents of the shop were shreds of cloth and infinitesimal strips of flesh, while the entire environment was splashed with blood. The poor native had lost an arm, a foot lay a few yards from him, and his other leg was hanging by a few shreds of skin ... The ruin of the building had scarcely been realised, and the vapour of the chemicals from the shell mingling with the scattered perfumes of the shop – when a second shell screaming its passage through the air hurled itself with a terrible velocity against the other window of the same building. Five men standing in the interior of the building miraculously escaped, but a corporal, who had gone from the scene of the death of the native to get a "pick-me-up" from the adjoining bar at Riesle's Hotel was blown to pieces. In such a manner does the death toll pile itself up – with the impending slowness of a juggernaut and the haunting persistency of fate. If these were the actual numbers of the killed upon this date, there were also two who were wounded, one of whom has since died, thus giving to one day a terrible trio.'

William Hayes, a doctor and brother of Tom, recounted in his diary: 'A shell fell in front of Lennon's shop yesterday. It got a nigger and dispersed the most of him in different directions. His cap with part of his head in it and a foot were found on the verandah floor, whilst kaffir dogs finished the rest of him which was in small pieces.' Sol Plaatje, in his diary, wrote: '[A shell] entered the sitting room at Riesle's new Mafeking Hotel and played havoc with the furniture. Mrs Graham, who was shot at the Women's Laager was in the hospital and progressing favourably: a fragment of a shell that burst near the Recreation Ground entered the hospital and frightened her so much that she broke one of her blood vessels and died in consequence. She was a young widow and leaves three little chickens to fight life's battle without parents.'

By a system of lookouts who would observe the guns when they fired coupled with the ringing of alarms, most white residents were able to get to a bunker before a shell reached the town. The psychological effect and carelessness were of greater concern. *The Mafeking Mail* reported that Creaky's 'unpleasant belch would twang its woeful discord on the harpstrings of our nerves.' Cecil was writing a report in Dixon's Hotel when a shell dropped down the chimney and burst behind the mantelpiece. It wrecked the panelled room and killed a waiter. His mental health, already poor from news of the death of his mother and antics of his wife, suffered a further setback. Others took to alcohol abuse while some, like Hore, became increasingly sickly.

Added to the wail of shells and their explosions was the quieter, but deadlier, whine and hiss of bullets fired by Boer snipers. Plaatje humorously recounted what it was like: 'I was roaming along the river at 12 o'clock with David yesterday when we were disgusted by the incessant sounds and clappering of Mausers to the north of the town: and all of a sudden four or five "booms" from the armoured train quenched their metal. It was like a member of the Payne family silencing a boisterous crowd with the prelude of a selection she is going to give on the violin. When their beastly fire "shut up" the Maxim began to play: it was like listening to the Kimberley R.C. Choir with their organ, rendering one of their mellifluous carols on Christmas eve; and its charm could justly be compared with that of the Jubilee Singers ... '

But the sickening aria of the Mausers would soon start again, sometimes at rates of 100 rounds per minute. Plaatje, a few days later, wrote: 'After I left Mr Mahlelebe yesterday ... Mauser bullets were just like hail on the main road to our village. I had just left the fence when one flew close to my cap with a "ping" — giving me such a fright as to cause me to sit down on the footpath. Someone behind me exclaimed that I was nearly killed and I looked round to see who my sympathiser was. When I did so another screeched through his legs with a "whiz-z-z-z-" and dropped between the two of us. I continued my journey in company with this man, during which I heard a screech and a tap behind my ear: it was a Mauser bullet and as there can be no question about a fellow's death when it enters his brain through the lobe, I knew at the moment that I had been transmitted from this temporary life on to eternity ... I was dead! Dead, to rise no more. A few seconds elapsed after which I found myself scanning the bullet between my fingers and thumb, to realise that it was a horsefly.'

Some had miraculous escapes. A man, Nelson, was hit in the temple and the bullet exited the other side without further damage, while a canary was transported intact, in its cage, by a bouncing shell and deposited in the adjoining street. These incidents were, however, the exception. William Hayes wrote in his diary of a man who was shot: 'It entered him between the 10th and 11th ribs, then must have pierced the liver downwards and backwards and striking the *fascia lumborum* must have glanced along injuring the kidney and leaving a wound of exit just above the iliac crest about 2 inches from the posterior superior spine.' Doctors operated while Mauser bullets pinged through the hospital windows and roof; Captain Girdwood, the Assistant Commissariat Officer, threw his arms in the air and fell from his bicycle saddle as a mortal bullet entered his stomach; and Mrs Poulton, hit in the neck, slipped quietly from her chair as she poured coffee for her husband.

Humans were not the only casualties. Tom Hayes mourned: 'The unfortunate horses had been badly knocked about and for some time after the fighting stopped, men were busy shooting those who could not recover. I have read about horses screaming when shot but none of ours made any noise, except a deep sob or groan when mortally wounded.'

' ... today was Sunday. What, Sunday? (HA! HA!)', wrote Plaatje gleefully. 'The usual Holy holiday ... This is the Lords day?' And how the Lord used it. If Boer fire was not enough, the besieged suffered from smallpox, dysentery, leprosy and a host of other sicknesses which attended one of the wettest and hottest summers on record. Tom Hayes wrote, on being informed by Bell of a suspected case of smallpox in Mahikeng: 'I visited him and found it to be so. Had him isolated then and there under a tree near the BSA Police Camp. The place is surrounded by yellow flags and two white men with loaded rifles on guard. I told him he would be shot if he strayed away from the limits set out by the yellow flags ... [In] the Laager in the afternoon [I] found most of the children suffering from opthalmia: they are all very crowded and miserable.' On another occasion he reported: 'The hospital is full, many are dysentery cases.' To round off the horror Stafleu moaned: 'A plague of locusts darkened the sky in some places. The locusts ate everything in sight. When the locusts had gone the flies continued to make life a misery.' Baden-Powell, to his mother, enthused brightly, 'Everything in the garden is lovely.'

It would be unnatural to expect the residents and garrison not to get used to the hardship, shelling and constant fire. Tom Hayes wrote: 'One redoubt I visited had rigged up a stuffed man and put him on a fence. The Boers fired about 50 rounds from a one pound Hotchkiss and finally shot off one of his legs, much to the delight of our boys, who were smoking in the trenches and enjoying the fun.' On another occasion a guard stopped three small boys who were leaving the town while shelling was at its heaviest.

'Here! Here! Where are you going?' shouted the sentry. 'Please sir, we're going fishing,' they chorused.

Baden-Powell noted the ways in which residents reacted to the onslaught: 'People take the shelling in different ways, according to their temperament. Some run like hares, others fling themselves flat, others just hunch their shoulders, and one there is who merely takes a passing but critical interest in them; when a shell bursts within ten feet of him he merely growls "what a rotten bursting charge!"'

Of Baden-Powell's reactions, Vere Stent recorded a conversation he was having with him: 'A shell whistled overhead and landed in the market place. I hoped the Colonel would take cover but he didn't, he only went on talking. A second shell sang a little nearer and raised clouds of dust not two hundred yards away. The Colonel closed the book which he had been reading, and, marking the place, rose quickly, whistling to himself, as is his habit, and as a third shell wrecked a couple of outstanding buildings, said, "You had better come inside." I needed no second invitation.' While this was happening the post office monkey would clamber from his perch and hide under a biscuit tin; Bell's dog would dive into a dugout; and other dogs would playfully scamper after flying shrapnel.

And, as the bombardment became commonplace, so carelessness became a serious danger. A boy playing marbles during shelling was blown to bits by a direct hit. A man in a party of four drunken souls was killed in a hail of bullets when they marched on the Boer lines. Smith, a refugee from Johannesburg, died while helping Gerans, the wagon maker, and Green dismantle an unexploded 94-pound shell. Green lost a leg and Gerans had his 'fingers very much blown about.' Plaatje passed the scene a few moments later, '[I] looked and saw things mighty gloomy in the ... shop: grown-up folks screaming in the dark smoke like piccaninies [boys] ... while old Gerans could be seen walking about in front of the shop, his face as black as that of a corner man in McAdoo's Vaudevilles' (an American Negro troupe who visited Kimberley in 1898).

Cronje positioned himself to the south of the town for a very good reason. He assumed, as this was 'a white man's war', that the southern entrance through the black *stadt* to Mafeking would be Baden-Powell's Achilles heel. 'At the time of the investment,' commented Plaatje, 'General Cronje sent verbal messages to the chief advising him not to mix himself and his people in a white man's quarrel. This view of General Cronje's was, at the beginning of the siege, in accord with local white sentiment. The European inhabitants of the besieged town had a repugnance to the idea of armed Natives shooting at a white enemy; but the businesslike method of General Cronje in effecting the investment had a sobering effect upon the whole of the beleaguered garrison; the Creusot especially thundered some sense into them and completely altered their views.'

Cronje calculated that after laying the garrison to waste with shells, he could feint a southern attack while the bulk of his troops entered the white town from the north-east. After heavy shelling on 25 October — over 300 fell on the town in the morning — Boers could be observed massing in the trembling, burning distance to the south of Cannon Kopje. They began their advance just after noon. Seven hundred and fifty metres from the *stadt* Captain Marsh and his squadron opened fire with support from a Maxim and a seven-pounder from well-concealed positions. The fire was so intense that the Boers were soon retreating. The group attacking from the north-east had been faring better but, on hearing of the withdrawal in the south also fell back. Baden-Powell once again showed himself a defensive genius. But, it was not British Pluck that saved the day — it was the Tshidi-Barolong.

Chief Wessels of the Barolong had at first refused to assist Baden-Powell in the defence of Mafeking until the Tshidi were armed by the British. Baden-Powell, at the outbreak of hostilities, to bolster his defences, issued 500 Tshidi warriors with Snider rifles and other ancient blunderbusses and promised Wessels that if the Tshidi assisted him they would be allocated land at the end of the siege. Stafleu noted in his diary: 'It appears from available evidence that [Wessels], a kaffir chief, has chosen the side of the English.' Captain Marsh's men, who so fiercely defended the town, were 400 of these armed Tshidi tribesmen. 'The Barolong youth had its baptism of fire on October 25, 1899,' wrote Plaatje, 'when General Cronje tried to storm the garrison by effecting an entry through the native village. He poured a deafening hail of nickel into the native village. The natives who were concealed behind the outer walls of the *stadt* waited with their rifles in the loopholes, according to Captain Marsh's instructions, till the Boer were quite near to them, then returned the fire with satisfactory results.' The remaining hundred armed Tshidi were in the frontlines, with the Cape Police defending the north-east.

The town would have fallen on 25 October but for the heroism of the black residents. That is how it would be for the rest of the investment. Siege diaries are specific on this issue, that historians and commentators have chosen to ignore direct Tshidi involvement is a disgrace. Tom Hayes wrote: 'At length [the Boers] came within long range of Cannon Kopje, which opened on them. This checked their advance for a time but they crept on towards our east. The natives in our stadt are very steady [and] not a man fired till the Boers had advanced to within 1000 yards, when they let them have it and some empty saddles told their own tale. In the meantime a great fusillade broke out on our east and I found that it was our pickets coming in – two Cape Police and their natives. One of the Cape Police saddles turned under his horse's belly, as he tried to mount, and he had to cut it loose: then one of the native scouts fell off his horse; a Cape Policeman stopped and two natives came to get him up: at this group there was a perfect fusillade and a storm of bullets, but they got him mounted and brought him in alright.'

There are other recorded instances of Tshidi and black involvement in the opening weeks of the siege. Plaatje recorded: 'On Friday [27 October 1899] morning Teacher Samson [Barnabas Samson] and 15 others crept along the river until they were close to a party of Boers, who were busy sniping the [Fingo] location from an ambush. They killed eight of them and wounded several; they were all going to return without a hitch – but they advanced to discern the dead men, and Samson received a slight wound on the shoulder.'

'Yesterday [28 October]', he continued, '22 Fingoes went out to the brickfields, which may be said to be exactly on "disputed territory": they took shelter among the bricks and killed several of them, which vexed the latter to such an extent that they fetched one of their 7-pounders.'

So incensed was Cronje that he sent Baden-Powell a note of protest: 'It is understood that you have armed Bastards, Fingoes and Barolongs against us. In this you have committed an enormous act of wickedness ... the end of which no man can foresee! You have created a new departure in South African history. It has hitherto been a cardinal point in South African ethics ... to view with horror the idea of arming black against white ... reconsider the matter, even if it cost you the loss of Mafeking to disarm your blacks and thereby act the part of a white man in a white man's war.'

Baden-Powell, in his reply, stated: 'As regards the natives now taking part in the defence of Mafeking. They have only taken up arms in defence of their homes and cattle, which you have already attempted to shell and to raid.' Despite all the evidence to the contrary this lie of Baden-Powell's is accepted by historians as the extent, other than for scouting and cattle raiding, of Barolong involvement throughout the siege. There appears only one explanation. Again the cult of Baden-Powell. His supporters, to embellish and magnify the myth, have found it necessary to concentrate their attention on the small British forces, while focusing on Baden-Powell. His detractors, to tear down the legend, do the same.

The essential difference is that the former elevate the siege to a pivotal event in the South African War, while the latter, to deflate Baden-Powell, write it off as a non-event. The fact is that the siege was the crucial event of the opening weeks of the war; it was Baden-Powell's defensive genius and foresight and Tshidi bravery that made it possible. That the Tshidi have not been accorded a place in history for their critical efforts to save South Africa until reinforcements arrived is a serious failure on the part of historians and an unjust insult to the role of the black and coloured defenders of the town. In fact, if reticence was displayed, it was by the British. Plaatje wrote, on 6 November, 'Twenty Barolong under Paul went to accompany 80 whites, who went to annoy the burghers of the laar down the river. More than 80 volunteered to go but on learning that they were not going to fetch the Dutch cannon which causes a great deal of annoyance from the west, all but the twenty got disgusted and declined to proceed on an errand with such trifling design.' The following day 20 Barolong tried to capture the gun, 'despite any European orders to the contrary', and would have succeeded but for the Boers rushing reinforcements to defend it.

Of the records regarding Tshidi involvement that of Plaatje should be regarded as unrivalled because of the extent of his personal involvement. He played a crucial intermediary role between the black inhabitants and the British authorities because of his linguistic talents. He translated intelligence gathered by the black scouts and, later, black guerrillas. The importance of this role cannot be underestimated because Baden-Powell's incoming intelligence was based almost entirely on these reports. Moreover, he was responsible for translating and communicating orders and issuing passes to black runners and scouts. It is thus clear that he would have intimate knowledge of Barolong involvement and what was happening outside the Mafeking lines.

On 26 October Cronje again resorted to crushing the town with shells. To support his bombardment he ordered Commandant Louw to dig in, to the east, in a position from where Mauser fire could be concentrated on Market Square. Baden-Powell decided that his second 'hard kick' of the siege would be directed at Louw's position that night. It was also agreed, as it was believed that the Boers were terrified of bayonets, that the 64-man party under Fitzclarence would attack Louw with fixed bayonets and not rifle fire. In the moon's pallid glow the group moved across the veld, the only sounds carried on the gentle breeze that of the drone of Boer voices. They swarmed into the trench. From Mafeking – the air lit briefly by orange muzzle flashes – shrieks, the dull pop of Mausers and muffled screams could be heard. Stafleu recalled: 'The English attacked the laager in the night. I was petrified having been awoken by the attack. One burgher was so scared that he could not fire his rifle. Hans Snyman, the veldcornet, skilfully rallied his men shouting out that they were not to panic as the Lord Jesus was their General and would protect them.'

'Luckily,' he continued, 'the greatest part of the trench was covered with corrugated iron which protected the burghers against bayonet thrusts. One ... narrowly missed being bayoneted in his tent and rushed outside where he shot his attacker. He also shot a second attacker who lived a short time whilst making a ghastly groaning noise. He begged for water and was given it, then he called out for his mother and Jesus, crying "Oh Lord! Oh Lord!" before he died.'

Fitzclarence was forced to retreat, only to be caught in the crossfire between the Boers and Cape Police before making it back to Mafeking. Six British troops were killed and many wounded. Baden-Powell claimed over 40 Boers killed and many more wounded. A story was put about as to how the Boers had begged for mercy as they were stuck like pigs: 'You must not stick me, you must not stick me,' they are supposed to have cried. Only one Boer, in fact, was killed – mortally wounded by a stray bullet from his own side.

The following morning, Stafleu, walking amongst the British dead noted: 'One was on his back with his arms in the air, an open mouth and wild eyes, his skull cracked open, and another lay with gaping wounds to his chest and legs.' Lieutenant Swinburne angrily commented: 'A mistake for a little force like ours, as we cannot afford to lose the men.' For his supposed gallantry – he claimed he killed four Boers with his sword – Fitzclarence received the Victoria Cross.

On the evening of 30 October, Stafleu enthused, 'The sunset was beautiful, everywhere the burghers stood in groups on the wall of the fort and stared, enjoying the wonderful and beautiful mix of colours.' At the same time a messenger was sent by Cronje with a warning to

Baden-Powell to surrender as he intended to take the town on the morrow. Tom Hayes wrote in his diary on 31 October: 'Cronje true to his threat that he would wipe us out today, began an attack at daylight on all sides. The heaviest fighting was near Cannon Kopje' which was manned by Colonel Walford, a garrison of 50 BSA Police and a number of Tshidi residents.

Cannon Kopje is a red, broken, rocky outcrop. The old, crumbling, circular fort built 15 years before was demolished before the siege and an open rampart constructed in its place. Maxims were positioned on either end with the 7-pounder in the centre. Alongside was a lookout tower manned by a German soldier of fortune, Baron von Dankberg, who had joined the British. Against this position ranged 2 000 Boers, 'Creaky' and two guns. A cottony mist still hung above the Molope, behind Cannon Kopje, as the first shot was fired.

In the lookout a piece of shrapnel tore through Von Dankberg's coat and shattered the telescope in his hand. Sniper bullets plucked at his clothing but he remained at his post, sending down information as the battle reached a climax. Not so lucky were eight defenders below who were killed in the action. Plaatje, who watched the Boers advance on Cannon Kopje, noted that the fortifications looked ragged as a consequence of incessant Boer shelling: 'All of a sudden there came volley after volley from the ... fort and we could see [Boers] fall when the Maxim began to play; some dead, some wounded and some presumably to wait until dark. Their officers, who were mounted behind them and urging them on, were – with one exception – the first to run and at 9 o'clock they hoisted the Red Cross.' The exception, among the Boer officers, was a Scandinavian, Captain Johannes Flygare, who was incensed at Boer cowardice in wanting to fight from behind rocks and not take to the field. Stafleu concurred: 'General Koos Snyman said that he was forced to whip some burghers to make them fight.'

Captain the Honourable D Marsham, Angus Hamilton reported, was struck by a bullet while rendering assistance to one of his men. 'As he attempted to do this a rifle bullet passed through his chest, and a moment later he was dead just as a second bullet passed through his shoulder. It was as fine a death as any soldier could perhaps have chosen.'

Yet, neither Marsham nor any of the other defenders received the Victoria Cross for their actions in a defence which certainly saved Mafeking and were among the bravest deeds of British soldiers during the siege. Nor is official mention made of the role played by the Tshidi in repulsing this Boer attack which was to prove the last direct assault on the town for six months. Tom Hayes, who was at the Molopo bridge, 'saw six natives creep up to within 500 yards of the enemy; and hold in check 50 Boers, who were blazing away.'

The day after the battle of Cannon Kopje the residents of Mafeking were presented with the first edition of their own newspaper that was sponsored by the war correspondents and fully supported by Baden-Powell, who was worried about the white residents becoming depressed:

MAFEKING MAIL
Issued daily, shells permitting.
Terms 1/- per week payable in advance.

The good-natured George Whales of the *Cape Press* was to be its editor and Ernest Parslow, of the *Daily Chronicle*, the deputy. Baden-Powell, who felt that a newspaper would lift the gloom of isolation, issued only one provision — there was to be no criticism of his conduct or of operations and of that he would be the sole judge. This censorship was to be a major headache for the editor as even mildly critical articles were muzzled, such as one titled 'The Steed Stewing and Burgoo Boiling Establishment' about the contents of the soup manufactured in the soup kitchens.

Most issues of the single-sheet newspaper were filled with virulently anti-Boer comment. It also gazetted appointments and promotions, reported news brought in by runners, announced sports fixtures for Sundays, published letters to the editor and carried articles of general interest to the residents. Life was not easy for those involved in its printing as they were subject to frequent interruptions and calls to arms, as were all members of the press corps or Town Guard. Once, while Whales was at his desk, a 94-pound shell entered one wall, passed through his office and exploded in the adjoining house. By the end of the siege there were 11 bullet holes in the wall behind his chair and a piece of shrapnel imbedded in it.

The newspaper had hardly hit the streets on 1 November than a scoop occurred that would have been a sensation anywhere.

Shocking occurrence in the market square last night
Special Correspondent Dead

Last night Mr Ernest G. Parslow the special correspondent of the London Chronicle and South African news was killed by a revolver shot while standing in the lobby of Dixon's Hotel. Lieutenant Kenneth Murchison, whose name it will be remembered was mentioned in Colonel Baden-Powell's General Orders of Tuesday last (Cannon Kopje) as having so ably assisted in compelling the Boers to retire by shots from a 7-pounder taken out at Ellis's Corner, has been arrested on the capital charge. The event has caused a most profound sensation as both the accused and the deceased were greatly esteemed.

Murchison was a two-metre tall gunnery officer who had been a major in the Royal Artillery in India before being forced into retirement because of his highly volatile personality. He was exceptionally skilled and talented, but those who knew him had often complained that they thought him insane because of his hair-trigger temper and persecution mania. He had rejoined the British Army as a lieutenant on half pay.

It is not known what caused the argument that resulted in the incident, the details of which were reported in the *Mafeking Mail*. Parslow and Murchison had dined together at Riesle's Hotel and left at 10 pm and entered Dixon's Hotel arguing furiously.

'You are no gentleman,' Parslow accused. Then he challenged Murchison to a fight outside.

Murchison told Parslow to go away and called him a 'stinker.' Parslow, enraged, challenged Murchison to a duel in Market Square. He added that if Murchison did not accept he 'was no man'. Murchison turned away to leave but Parslow persisted. Then, a revolver cracked and a bullet, which drove fragments of his skull deep into his brain, hit Parslow in the middle of his forehead. He gave a hollow groan and pitched forward.

'My God! It's an accident,' shouted the distressed and dazed Murchison. 'The revolver went off accidentally.'

'What have I done? What's this for?' asked Murchison, later, as the revolver was removed from him and he was placed in handcuffs by the arresting officer.

'You are charged with shooting a man', replied the officer.

'That's right, old boy. He brought it on himself,' stated Murchison as he was led to prison.

He was sentenced to death.

Plaatje lamented the incident: 'My dear friend Mr E.G. Parslow was murdered by Lieutenant Murchison ... The murder has not only deprived me of a good friend but it has wrecked me financially. He paid for my little assistance so liberally that I never felt the price of foodstuffs that reigned here since the commencement of the siege. The cause of the murder is incomprehensible but the reasons are hardly tangible.'

The case of Murchison brings to light growing interpersonal strife within the town that would often acrimoniously spill over. William Hayes noted in his diary: 'A native I was going to operate on today wanted it done without chloroform. I gave him a prod of the knife and settled the matter. They are awfully plucky devils and give no trouble.' The following day, bubbling with indignation, he commented: 'Stent sent me a letter to say that we were in the habit of doing operations at the hospital without chloroform or ether. It is a rotten thing to say. He says he will put it in print, as he has native evidence to prove it. I put up a notice warning him off the premises at the hospital and all other "war" correspondents with him.'

In the first few days of November, Creaky was moved to higher ground on the south-east. On 4 November, the Boers, realising Baden-Powell had not placed an obstacle on the railway line, pushed a trainload of dynamite toward the town from the north, hoping it would explode in the railway yard. It did not make it all the way, stopping alongside the cemetery. Angus Hamilton reported: 'It was night, and the town was just about to rest, when it was shaken to its foundations by a most deafening roar; sand and stones, fragments of trees came down as hail from the skies, the whole place being lighted with a livid glow of blood-red flame. After it there came silence, broken here and there ... by the shouts and shrieks of a town in the confusion of a panic.' The following evening, on the Recreation Ground, the town, in response, celebrated Guy Fawkes. The Boers, who had been notified, sat on their defences to watch the fun.

Baden-Powell, on 7 November, again indulged in a 'hard kick' and had to be rescued by the Tshidi once more. He ordered that Godley, with 90 men, two 7-pounders and a Hotchkiss, be removed from an armoured train to attack a laager to the south-west which he believed threatened the southern defences. The Boers were scattered by Godley but a column came rushing from Cronje's laager and would have cut Godley off had not the Barolong, with accurate fire, been able to hold the Boers off long enough for Godley to return to safety.

But for persistent shelling and mausering, little happened the following week. Then, on 15 November, during the season's first heavy rain, Pearson, an American despatch rider for Reuters, entered the town. He reported that Ladysmith and Kimberley were also besieged and that General Lord Methuen was marching on Kimberley. He added that Boers were waiting for Methuen at Modder River and that Mafeking would probably have to delay hope of relief. This news led to rationing being instituted by Baden-Powell for the first time.

Cronje, at the same time, received orders to head south to join the forces waiting for Methuen. *The Times History of the War in South Africa* commented: 'At last, after he had been sitting in front of Mafeking for five weeks, the absurdity of wasting nearly a third (sic) of the two Republics available forces on the capture of one small town became obvious.' Cronje and his men, a month later, would inflict a terrible humiliation on Methuen at Magersfontein. Cronje, however, would be captured at Paardeberg later in the war and be exiled to St Helena. After the war he joined the American circus of Frank Ellis.

The news of Cronje's departure with 4 000 Boers and half a dozen guns was joyously greeted in the town. Residents sat on their roofs watching the dwindling cloud of curling dust to the south. Scouts brought in news that Snyman, with the Marico, Rustenburg and Lichtenburg commandos, had been left in charge of the 2 000 remaining Boers. Baden-Powell had achieved his objective and many of the young men in the town urged him to end the siege now, break out and join Plumer. He was having none of it. The military phase of the siege was at an end, the 'sit down' psychological phase now began.

From this time Baden-Powell has been accused of doing everything possible to extend the siege. The evidence certainly suggests this to be true. Even his supporters accept this, but point to the fact that he was trying to lure Boer forces back to Mafeking. In this he would be singularly unsuccessful as Snyman's forces would continue to dwindle to as few as 800 before swelling to 1 400. However, as a psychological battle the balance of the siege was invaluable to the war effort and, for Britain's cause, it was better that he remain holed up in Mafeking. The reverse effect on Boer morale would have been immeasurable. The question is, at what cost was this advantage achieved? But first, an interlude.

6

DEATH OF A PIGEON

For a bird of the air shall carry the voice,
And that which has wings shall tell the matter.
ECCLESIASTES 10:20

In the early dawn of 12 October 1899 as Nesbit's train was being ambushed at Kraaipan, Lady Sarah opened the door to the veranda of the Frasers' house at Setlagole, where she had proceeded on her orders to leave Mafeking before the siege. The wind had dropped completely, but the morning was bitterly cold. The loafers whom she had seen lounging outside the store the previous day were huddled in blankets and straining their eyes, in the pink light of dawn, toward the stutter of gunfire from Kraaipan. In this ramshackle trading post 70 kilometres south of Mafeking, Lady Sarah would have been keenly aware that she had been ousted from the hub of things, and her frustration at being removed from the action was to mount in the weeks to come.

'Before long,' recounted Lady Sarah, 'a mounted kaffir rode wildly up, and proceeded, with many gesticulations, to impart information in his own tongue. His story took some time, but at last a farmer turned round and told me the engagement had been with the armoured train, as we anticipated, and that the latter had "fallen down" [as the kaffir expressed it].'

Deciding it was unsafe to remain at Setlagole, she instructed the cart driver to inspan the mules while she returned to her room to pack. The Frasers advised her to head for Mosita, a small mud-and-stone hutted Tswana village 40 kilometres to the west, where she was assured she would be made welcome by Mr Keeley, the local magistrate. Soon, she and the long-suffering Metalka were again jolting across the countryside to the accompaniment of a singing whip and the cussing of the driver. 'I found myself listening to his varying epithets with stupefied curiosity,' commented Lady Sarah. 'During that four hour drive we only met two natives and one huge herd of cattle, which were being driven by mounted kaffirs, armed with rifles, to Mosita, our destination, where it was hoped they would be out of the way of marauding Boers. At last we reached the native stadt of Mosita, where our appearance created great excitement. Crowds of swarthy men and youths rushed out to question our driver as to news. The latter waxed eloquent in words and gestures, imitating even the noise of the big gun, which seemed to produce great enthusiasm among these simple folk. ... In the distance we could see the glimmering blue waters of a huge dam, beyond which was the farm and homestead of Keeley.'

Lady Sarah was warmly received by the anxious Mrs Keeley, a round-faced woman in her mid-thirties with five small children and another well on the way. She was extremely worried about her husband, who was in Mafeking on business and had been ordered by Baden-Powell to remain in the town and assist in its defence. 'At last,' sighed Lady Sarah, 'I had found someone who was more to be pitied than myself. She, on the other hand, told me our arrival was a godsend to her, as it took her thoughts off her troubles.' Mrs Keeley would not long regard Lady Sarah's appearance as a blessing. Though Lady Sarah recollected her stay with the Keeleys as the 'bright spot of those dark weeks,' the Keeleys, according to Brian Roberts in his book *Churchills in Africa*, recalled her with anything but affection. This would become obvious later when, as a prisoner of the Boers, an indiscretion by Lady Sarah led to the arrest of Mr Keeley.

Mrs Keeley was not just concerned for her husband. Her family was amongst the few white English families in the sparsely populated district. The local Dutch farmers had professed loyalty to the Crown, but once hostilities commenced fathers and sons crossed the border to join the Boers. Before these rebels departed, however, they instructed their wives and daughters to look out for the safety of Mrs Keeley. Many of them visited Mrs Keeley, who was renowned for her knowledge of medicine, home cures and elementary dosing and she, apparently, saw nothing inappropriate in a British citizen keeping the enemy in the prime of health. The curious situation thus existed that the neighbourhood women cared for each other while their men fought on opposing sides.

That evening, the light ebbing, the air silken and the shadows grown long, Lady Sarah took a relaxing walk round the dam. In these peaceful surrounds it appeared incredible that a short distance away people were dying in war. In the distance she caught sight of the herd of cattle she had seen earlier as they were driven toward the dam. 'It was curious to see the whole herd, some five or six hundred beasts, break into a clumsy canter, and, with a bellowing noise, dash helter-skelter to the water – big oxen with huge branching horns, meek-eyed cows, young bullocks and tiny calves, all joining in the rush for a welcome drink after a long hot day on the veldt.'

The ensuing weeks were crammed with boredom. The only book Lady Sarah had to read was Du Maurier's *Trilby*, which she read over and over, each time empathising with the heroine's lament, 'The days are so long, and there are so many of them.' So interminably tedious was her stay that she was reduced to Biblical uttering, 'The evening and the morning were the sixth day.' News, also, was scarce until she received a letter from Gordon, her husband, regarding the situation in Mafeking. The idea dawned on Sarah that if messages could be smuggled out of Mafeking then the reverse was also possible. From the Tswana of Mosita she selected 'a trusty old nigger', Boaz, to carry messages in a cartridge case to and from the town. His fee, for this dangerous journey, was three pounds each way.

With the arrival of her first note Baden-Powell saw an opportunity to use her as a message depot. 'She acted as the chief medium,' reported Angus Hamilton, 'by which Baden-Powell managed to get his despatches through to the government in Cape Town.' The information she sent to Mafeking, however, was based on rumour so often incorrect. Her report that Vryburg was taken by the Boers without a shot being fired was correct, while the gossip that Bechuanaland had been annexed by Kruger was not. The messages she received were taken by runners to the nearest telegraph point.

She sent regular messages to Mafeking, even if she had no news, 'to uplift the residents spirits'. In many of these letters she commented on the wilful ignorance of the Boers. In one she claimed that the Boers fancied that Joseph Chamberlain was the manufacturer of Chamberlain's Cough Syrup, which was sold in the Cape Colony. In another she recounted the story of an old burgher and his wife sitting on their veranda on a Sunday afternoon. The old man, on seeing a minister riding toward the house, fetched his Bible and randomly opened it. The clergyman, on arrival, climbed the steps to the porch and peered over the man's shoulder.

'Ah! I see you are reading in the Holy Book – the death of Christ,' exclaimed the priest.

'Alle machter! Is he dead indeed?' blurted the woman. Turning to her husband, she admonished, 'You see, Jan, you will never buy a newspaper, so we never know what goes on in the world.'

Mr Keeley returned to Mosita in early November, having been allowed to leave Mafeking to defend his family. He was able to tell Lady Sarah of everything that had occurred in the town up to the death of Parslow. The tall, handsome, highly respected Keeley took an instant dislike to his guest. Her taloned manner, certainly, was annoying. But, it was her unhelpfulness that was most irritating. While concentrating her mind on higher issues she ignored the everyday domestic problems facing the Keeleys. Only once did she help. Mr Keeley was beating locusts off his vegetable patch and needed someone to continue while he lit his pipe. Lady Sarah was the only person in the vicinity and she took over this chore for the minute or so required. One London newspaper, overwhelmingly out of step with its peers which continually fawned over the adventures of Winston Churchill and his aunt, commented dryly, it is 'all very well but we commiserate with her poor maid.' They should have mentioned the Keeleys as well.

With money running short to pay Boaz and boredom straining her to breaking point, she decided to undertake a trip to Vryburg. The information she was sending Mafeking was trifling and she wanted to enter Vryburg to see if she could gather more worthy news. But, first, it was necessary to test the water.

She lent her horse, Dop, to a young Boer neighbour, Brevel, who wished to drive some cattle to Vryburg to sell them. In return for the use of the animal she gave him a cheque to cash, some letters to post and a note addressed to the magistrate requesting newspapers and information. If, she thought, he could openly deal with the British and their institutions without arousing the suspicion of the Boer occupiers, then she could safely visit the town as well. A few days later she was surprised when Brevel returned with her money and a depressing response from the English magistrate whose office had been seized and who was about to leave Vryburg as he had been ordered out. The letters had not been accepted by the Post Office because they bore the stamps of the Cape Colony and not those of the South African Republic. Should she stamp them correctly, the letters could be posted.

Brevel, however, related rumours that were rife in Vryburg. He informed Keeley that Boers were planning to wreak vengeance on any who supported the British. He also told them that Kruger had entered Bulawayo and was preparing a triumphal march south and that Ladysmith and Kimberley had fallen. 'No matter how miserable people in England were then,' declared Lady Sarah, strengthening her resolve, 'they will never realise fully what it meant to pass those black months in the midst of a Dutch population; one felt oneself indeed alone amongst foes. Smarting under irritation and annoyance, I decided to go myself to Vryburg – Dutch town though it had become – and see if I could not ascertain the truth of these various reports, which I feared might filter into Mafeking and depress the garrison.' She ended by noting that Mr Keeley approved of her going and hastily facilitated the arrangements.

Word was put out that Lady Sarah was going to Vryburg to consult a dentist. Mr Keeley arranged for Arthur Coleman, a younger brother of Mrs Keeley who was fluent in Dutch, to accompany her. 'I was much excited,' she noted, 'at the prospect of visiting the Boer headquarters in that part of the country, and seeing with my own eyes the Transvaal flag flying in the town of a British colony. Therefore I thought nothing of undertaking a sixty miles' drive in broiling heat and along a villainous road.'

The trip was uneventful. Along the way they passed farm after deserted farm. The ugly farm houses, built of rough brick, stone and mud, were unpainted, with small windows punched through without regard for symmetry. A few kilometres from Vryburg they caught sight of about 30 Boers – the first time she had seen the enemy since the war began – but the Boers ignored them and circled away. As they descended into the basin, where the neat town was laid out, they could see the white tents of the Boer laager beyond and the railway to the east. Her initial impression of Vryburg was that it was a town 'which looked as if it had gone for a walk and got lost.'

In the shop-lined main street they stopped outside the Court House, almost hidden in trees, above which a Vierkleur hung limply. In the grounds guards stood and lounged about. Another group studied a notice, translated for her by Coleman, affixed to a tree:

WAR NEWS
Latest Reports

Price 3d   Vryburg, Oct. 31, 1899

Mafeking Speechless with Terror

Kimberley Trembles

40 English Soldiers Desert to Join our Ranks

It appears by telegram received this morning that the Burghers started firing on Mafeking with the big cannon.
The Town is on fire and is full of smoke.

At the Central Hotel, also in the main street, they were received by an incredulous manager – a greying Englishman who warned them not to disclose who they were because a new Boer magistrate had taken office that morning. Strict regulations regarding people leaving or entering the town were being imposed with immediate effect and all the town's provisions had been commandeered by the Boers, who had issued notes of credit to be paid after the war. He also gave her news of some British victories in Natal and complained of the Boer habit of over-reporting British casualties.

That afternoon she visited three of the recuperating soldiers who had been wounded at Kraaipan. They praised the Boers for their kind treatment but moaned that the doctors were rough and that there were no anaesthetics or pain relievers available. Later, from the hotel, she observed the Boers milling about. 'I admitted to myself that they sat their horses well and that their rifle seemed a familiar friend, but when you have seen one you have seen them all. I never could have imagined so many men absolutely alike: all had long straggling beards, old felt hats, shabby clothes and some evil-looking countenances. Most of these I saw were men of from forty to fifty years of age, but there were also a few sickly-looking youths, who certainly did not look bold warriors. These had not arrived at the dignity of a beard, but, instead cultivated feeble whiskers.' Boer women though, she concluded, were the most fearsome; 'they urge their husbands in the districts to go and join the commandos, and their language was cruel and blood thirsty.'

The hotel manager informed her that the new magistrate had forbidden anyone to leave without a pass – documents which were issued only under exceptional circumstances. She instructed Coleman to pretend he was a Dutch farmer who had entered the town with his sister to buy provisions and urgently needed to get back to his farm. Surprisingly, passes was issued without hesitation. Fearing permission might be retracted, they decided to leave at daybreak. That night the hotel manager lent her a shabby old ulster, a sailor hat and a woollen shawl with which to disguise herself.

Before sunrise Lady Sarah was woken and she dressed quickly. She put on the sailor's hat, around which she twined the shawl. Her identity concealed, they were ready to go. The sun, enormous and red, was just rising as they reached the newly erected check-point. Coleman informed the Boer sentries that 'his sister' was suffering from toothache and unable to speak. Within a few minutes they were back on the road to Mosita, and melancholy boredom.

At Mosita she became increasingly depressed. Her trip to Vryburg had reawoken her curiosity and thirst for adventure. She argued continuously with Keeley and took her temper out on his wife. Within the district rumours about her presence circulated. One was that she was a daughter of Queen Victoria sent to spy on her rebellious subjects, another had her as the wife of Baden-Powell. In mid-November, to the unrestrained joy of the Keeleys, she informed them that she intended playing a greater role in the war and was returning to Setlagole.

Things were certainly more exciting at Setlagole than they had been at Mosita. The Frasers were so bellicosely patriotic that they continually attracted Boer patrols. Then, two days after her arrival, Pearson, the Reuters representative, stopped on his way to Mafeking. That Sunday she accompanied him to view the wrecked train at Kraaipan. While he took photographs she clambered over the rocks. 'There was not much to see, after all — merely a pilot armoured engine, firmly embedded its whole length in the gravel. Next to this, an ordinary locomotive, still on the rails, riddled on one side with bullets, and on the other displaying a gaping aperture into the boiler, which told its own tale. Then came the armoured truck that I had seen leaving Mafeking so trim and so smart, but now battered with shot; and lastly another truck, which had been carrying the guns. This had been pushed back into a culvert, and presented a dilapidated appearance, with its front wheels in the air. The whole spectacle was forlorn and eerie ... [and] as silent as the grave. Swarms of locusts were alone in possession, and under the engine and carriages the earth was a dark brown moving mass, with the stream of these jumping, creeping things.' Her curiosity satisfied, she persuaded Pearson that it was time to return.

After a few days, Pearson returned from Mafeking. He showed her a basket of carrier pigeons and persuaded her that this was the swiftest and safest way for her to communicate with Mafeking. She was delighted that old Boaz's expensive and slow service could now be dispensed with. Pearson, to demonstrate the effectiveness of these birds, penned a cheerful note to Baden-Powell on the situation at Setlagole, which he ended with 'Lady Sarah Wilson is here doing good work as an intelligence officer.' He then selected a white pigeon that he assured her had won many prizes, attached the note to the bird's leg and released it. The bird rose, uncertain at first as it fluttered round, then, finding its direction, disappeared.

The pigeon could not have done worse. Not only did it land in a Boer laager, but it chose Snyman's headquarters at McMullen's farm to perch on. A keen-eyed Boer, Dietrich, seeing the message canister clipped to its leg, shot it and took the message in to the General. Two days later a patrol, led by Dietrich, arrived at Setlagole.

The first Lady Sarah knew that Boers had arrived at Setlagole was when she entered the dining-room. An exceedingly short American relative of the Frasers, with an axe in his hand, was frantically taking up the floorboards. Watching him was a particularly tall and big-boned Englishman who was a friend of the American's. Both were noted for their jingoism and bravado. Lady Sarah inquired what they were doing.

'We are going to hide, Lady Sarah,' bawled the trembling American. 'The Boers are on the premises.'

She informed the pair they would suffocate in the unventilated hold. The small man, axe still in hand, gibbered, 'I will not go to fight; I am an American. I will not be put in the front rank to be shot by the English, or made to dig trenches.'

She lectured the pair on bravery and informed them that the Boers would be unlikely to press-gang the services of two such cowardly specimens. She then sat down for lunch. Through the green venetian blinds she was able to watch the Boers looting the store. They had demanded coffee and many tins of salmon and sardines. Of these delicacies they seemed particularly fond, eating the latter with their fingers, after which they drank the oil, mixed for choice with golden syrup. After their repast they fitted themselves out in clothes and luxuries

114

... This amusement finished, they proceeded to practice shooting, setting bottles at a distance of about 50 yards.'

As the commandeered brandy took effect the shooting became wilder. Earlier, bottles had erupted as the Boers took aim and fired. Later, as the Mausers sprang in their hands, only puffs of dust danced in acclaim of their efforts. Toward evening, as the horizon was flamed by the setting sun, the drunken Dietrich tried to explain to Fraser that God Almighty had ensured that the pigeon land on Snyman's roof and that they were awaiting the arrival of Veldcornet De Kocker, who would issue orders with regard to Lady Sarah's fate. Fraser informed Lady Sarah about the pigeon and told her what he knew of De Kocker, a convicted sheep-stealer.

The pompous, middle-aged De Kocker arrived in a cloud of pluming dust at 9 o'clock the following morning. In the living room he read a printed proclamation to the residents of Setlagole: 'This country now being part of the Transvaal, the residents must within seven days leave their homes or enrol themselves as burghers.' Lady Sarah requested a pass to enter Mafeking so that she could join her husband. He informed her that it was not in his power to do so but he would arrange a pass for her through Snyman — who had just taken command of the Mafeking forces — whom he was sure would give her permission. Leaving Dietrich to guard her, he departed.

That evening, as the sun dropped low and the dusty air was red and golden, she received a note from Snyman refusing her permission to enter Mafeking and instructing her to remain at Setlagole. He had not reckoned on the fury of a lady who greatly resented her eviction from the town only to have it confirmed by the enemy. She decided to confront Snyman. Ordering Vellum to inspan her cart she, with Vellum and her driver, headed for De Kocker's laager to secure the pass to get her to McMullen's farm.

They made good time along the sandy road, hammered by a sun that quivered in the blue sky. There was a great bustle of activity as lookouts spotted their approach. De Kocker, who walked as if he had a saddle between his legs, came to meet her and ordered her to descend as the cart was outspanned outside his house. 'I now saw the interior of a typical Dutch house, with the family at home. The [wife] came forward with hand outstretched in the awkward Boer fashion. I had to go through this performance in perfect silence with about seven or eight children of various ages, a grown-up daughter, and eight or ten men, most of whom followed us into a poky little room for the whole family. Although past ten o'clock, the remains of breakfast were still on the table, and were not appetising to look at ... I meanwhile studied the room and its furniture, which was of the poorest description; the chairs mostly lacked legs or backs, and the floor was of mud, which perhaps was just as well, as they all spat on it in the intervals of talk and emptied on to it the remains of whatever they were drinking. After a short while a black girl came in with a basin of water, with which she proceeded to plentifully sprinkle the floor, utterly disregarding our dresses and feet. Seeing all the women tuck their feet under their knees, I followed their example, until this improvised water-cart had finished its work.'

A pass was issued to get her to Snyman's laager and eight kilometres from Mafeking they crested a rise and saw the shimmering town before her. They passed where Cronje's laager had been and saw vultures picking the remains of horses and cattle that had either died or been slaughtered. She considered making a dash for the *stadt* and Mafeking, but Vellum would not hear of it as he told her they would be shot by snipers concealed in the bush. They turned off the road and immediately came upon a Boer outpost, whose occupants were as startled to see an English lady as she was to see them. Lady Sarah and her party were ordered to wait until sundown, when a relieving guard would arrive. As the fierce sun began to wane she spotted the formidable relief guard approaching. 'The men were mostly of middle age, all with the inevitable grizzly beard, and their rifles, gripped familiarly, were resting on the saddle-bow; nearly all had two bandoleers apiece, which gave them the appearance of being armed to the teeth – a more determined-looking band cannot be imagined. The horses of these burghers were well bred and in good condition, and, although their clothes were threadbare, they seemed cheerful enough, smoking their pipes and cracking their jokes.'

The relieved guards, the barrels of their rifles glinting in the setting sun, then escorted her to Snyman's headquarters, where a crowd of some two to three hundred armed Boers had assembled to catch a glimpse of the 'spy' mentioned in the note. A Boer, Snyman's secretary, who spoke English fluently, came out of the house when he heard the commotion. She thrust a letter, in which she demanded an immediate interview with Snyman, into the hapless man's hand. He quickly returned to inform her that the General would see her at once.

Inside the house, in a dark and dusty room, she found herself facing two bearded, hunched old men seated on a bench. They were introduced to her as General Snyman and Commandant Botha. The high cheekboned, grey-suited Koos 'Hammerkop' Snyman, with deep ragged age lines across his face, was the most stolid, supine and incompetent of the Boer generals. Little did Lady Sarah know, at that meeting, that the Boers under Snyman were on the verge of mutiny because of the depressing effect the failure to take Mafeking was having on morale.

'The General Koos Snyman reminds me of a medieval despot', complained Abraham Stafleu in his diary. Of the Boer officers he was as scathing: 'I am disappointed in the Boer officers, they live far away in the "Grand Hotel" [McMullen's Farm], abandoning their men and relying on juniors for reports, rather than going to see for themselves. They also hold constant war councils which achieve nothing.' Stafleu also recounted that when Boer supplies arrived at Mafeking the General and his officers always helped themselves first. 'Honesty has long disappeared as a national trait from amongst the Boers and their officials,' he claimed. Snyman's burghers, during the siege, would continually petition their officers to be released to join other commandos. Many others simply packed their bags and left of their own accord.

Snyman, on hearing Lady Sarah's request to enter Mafeking, lost his temper. Taken aback, she suggested that he exchange her for a Mrs Delport, whom she had been informed was in the Women's Laager and wished to leave Mafeking. He refused outright, a decision that would drive him to distraction over the next few weeks. It suddenly dawned on Lady Sarah that she was to be held as a prisoner of war. It never occurred to her that the Boers would do anything but her bidding. She resolved, as she was led off to the shabby field hospital where she was to be held, that she would make their lives unbearable until they relented.

At the hospital she was shown into a tiny fly-infested room crammed with a blood-stained operating table, a medicine chest, broken sofa and, in the corner, a dilapidated washstand. The walls were peppered with bullet holes and the rough floor boards cracked and loose. Wafting through the smashed windows were the wail of a harmonica and the odours of human excreta. Abraham Stafleu was disgusted by the lack of hygiene in the Boer camps: 'Through laziness, the Boers failed to provide latrines for their men and the space around their fort was becoming unhygienic. It was difficult to avoid walking in the waste and I was forced to put Bluegum oil under my nose to be able to breathe.'

Lady Sarah was stripped and searched by two Dutch nurses while the Boers pored over her possessions in an adjoining room. While she was dressing, a messenger arrived to inform her that Snyman had decided to exchange her, not for Delport, but for a convicted horse-thief, Petrus Viljoen, who was languishing in the Mafeking jail. On 2 December she wrote Gordon a letter: 'I am at the laager. General Snyman will not give me a pass unless Colonel Baden-Powell will exchange me for a Mr Petrus Viljoen. I am sure this is impossible, so I do not ask him formally. I am in a great fix ... ' While she was writing this, Snyman was sending a telegram to Pretoria: 'What shall I now do with Lady Sarah Wilson? Please answer speedily. In my opinion she is an important spy.'

The following day, a Sunday and day of rest, she wandered about the hospital. It was a hot, gusty day and she heard singing emanating from the back of a tiny house. 'It is difficult to conceive anything so grotesque as some Dutch singing is. Imagine a doleful wail of many voices, shrill treble and deep bass, all on one note, now swelling in volume, now almost dying away, sung with a certain meter, and presumably with soul-stirring words, but with no attempt to keep together or any pretensions to an air of any kind, and you will have an idea of a Dutch chant or hymn. This noise – for it cannot be called a harmony – might equally well be produced by a howling party of dogs and cats.'

She received a reply to her letter from Gordon shortly after the congregation trooped from the service. 'My dear Sarah, I am delighted to hear you are being well treated, but very sorry to have to tell you that Colonel Baden-Powell finds it impossible to hand over Petrus Viljoen in exchange for you, as he was convicted of horse-stealing before the war. I fail to see in what way it can benefit your captors to keep you a prisoner. Luckily for them, it is not the custom of the English to make prisoners of war of women.'

Two days later she received a letter from Baden-Powell:

December 5, 1899

Dear Lady Sarah,

I am so distressed about you. You must have been having an awful time of it, and I can't help feeling very much to blame; but I had hoped to save you the unpleasantness of the siege.

However, I trust now that your troubles are nearly over at last, and that General Snyman will pass you in here.

We are all very well, and really rather enjoying it all.

I wrote last night asking for you to be exchanged for Mrs Delport, but had no answer, so have written again today, and sincerely hope it will be all right.

Hope you are well, in spite of your troubles.

Yours sincerely

R. Baden-Powell

Unknown to Lady Sarah, Baden-Powell had broached the subject of a possible exchange with Mrs Delport, who flatly refused to entertain the idea.

At the field hospital Snyman's cowering secretary, who conveyed the news that an exchange for anyone other than Viljoen would not be countenanced, was on the receiving end of a Lady Sarah tantrum. Her temper was not improved by Snyman's remark that if the exchange for Viljoen were not agreed she would be sent to Pretoria where she could find a 'pleasant ladies' society'. She informed the unfortunate man that she had no intention of going to Pretoria, unless they took her by force. She also threatened to give Snyman no peace until she received a satisfactory reply. With that, she stormed through the hospital, speaking her mind freely to the engrossed nurses and patients. Then, as her storm became a tempest, she spotted a female German doctor. 'It was the first of her species I had come across,' stormed Lady Sarah, as she focused her fury on the hapless Teuton who, as a professional woman, represented a coming order that was anathema to her. She could accept the Boer women who arrived at the laager to view the shelling of Mafeking and who delighted in being able to fire a Mauser into the town – but never those who sought to revolutionise the position of women.

So vicious was her onslaught on the medic that Lady Sarah's guards were doubled to protect others she may single out. Snyman was beginning to panic: 'Please, please,' he begged in a telegraph to Pretoria, 'send me at once your decision concerning Lady Sarah Wilson. She is most unwilling to stay here any longer.' Matters were no less farcical in Mafeking, where Baden-Powell was now holding a lottery amongst Boer women to see if any wished to be exchanged. None did.

The pressure from within Mafeking on Baden-Powell was enormous. The residents did not wish him to relent because Viljoen, the son of the pioneer hunter Jan Viljoen, knew the town well and would be invaluable to Snyman. On the other hand, Cecil, the British Prime Minister Lord Salisbury's son, insisted that the exchange be made otherwise he would involve his father in the matter. Baden-Powell, against his better judgement, decided to accept the terms. This, however, was not the end of the matter. Viljoen refused to leave prison.

While Baden-Powell was ordering the reluctant prisoner to accept his freedom, Lady Sarah's mules were doing all they could to maintain theirs. 'A vexatious delay occurred from the intractability of the mules,' she huffed. 'Which persistently refused to allow themselves to be caught.' The war was temporarily forgotten as Snyman urged all available men to round up these stubborn beasts. It is said that when the mules were finally inspanned and Lady Sarah had departed, he dropped to his knees and gave thanks to the Almighty.

Two kilometres from Mafeking Lady Sarah passed the dejected Viljoen being transported to the Boer lines. As she triumphantly entered the Mafeking soiree she received an extraordinary welcome as cheering soldiers, waving their smashers in the air, poured from the trenches. 'From the first redoubt,' she recalls, 'Colonel Baden-Powell and Lord Edward Cecil ran out to greet me, and the men in the trench gave three English cheers, which were good to hear; but no time had to be lost in getting under cover, and I drove straight to Mr Weil's house.

The *Mafeking Mail*, in its editorial, commented: 'We are sure we represent the whole of Mafeking when we offer the most hearty congratulations to Capt. Wilson and Lady Sarah Wilson on her ladyship's safe arrival in our tight little garrison, after her experiences with the Boers.' The warmest welcome, however, came from the Boers as Baden-Powell's and the residents fears were realised. Abraham Stafleu was present when Viljoen arrived at the laager and noted that 'he was able to provide the Boers with a detailed report of conditions in Mafeking. Viljoen was also able to point out to the crews of the guns where and when to shoot to best effect.'

Within five minutes of her arrival, more accurate shelling was throwing death and gravel everywhere. Tom Hayes noted: 'Another 94-pounder burst in Market Square ...; it killed a gunner, a piece went through his brain, also a native, blowing off his left arm, right leg and half his pelvis.' These were not the only casualties. Plaatje wrote; 'I have never before realised how keenly that I am walking of the brink of the grave. It is really shocking, while still meditating how one of your fellow creatures met his fate at the shell of the Dutch cannon, that many more had their legs and [backs] shattered somewhere; and it is an abominable death to be hacked up by a 94-pounder.'

7

BE PREPARED! ZING-A-ZING! BOM! BOM!

Star of wisdom, child of gladness,
Tell him all your troubles.
Mary's boy has banished sadness,
Why be sorrowful now?

JOHN GLYNN

'Baden-Powell made us die of laughing.'

ALICK GODLEY

Lady Sarah's first order of business was to have a bunker excavated, in front of Weil's house, that would befit a Churchill. Hers, reached by wooden steps, was panelled with white painted pine and decorated with African spears and a large Union Jack. 'It much resembles the cabin of a yacht,' she remarked. 'A triumph in its line.' It was launched with a dinner party and it came to depict the style of Britons under the most appalling conditions. British magazines published photographs of her and the bunker in numerous features. Fashion spreads had her posing at the entrance in a summer dress, mounting the steps in a khaki creation or reclining on the sandbags in an outfit more suited to Henley.

But, for most, these havens were dark, claustrophobic and dingy – the only light that of sunshine glinted through the opening. In the morning the residents scuttled into them like bugs and in the evening, begrimed with sweat and dust, they would emerge squinting in the glare. By day they were the fertile breeding ground for boredom and apathy.

122

Contrary to Baden-Powell's fears before the siege that Lady Sarah would hog his limelight, he found in her a leading lady perfectly in sync with himself. Shortly he was praising her as a remarkable woman whose influence on the 'morale of the defenders is immense'. 'Colonel Baden-Powell,' she gushed in response, 'has inspired all ranks with confidence; while never sparing himself, and seemingly never to take any rest, he has made the timid feel they can repose with confidence, and the pugnacious that no opportunity will be lost to strike when the occasion offers.'

Lady Sarah, on her release by the Boers, was quick to tell the reporters who flocked to interview her of the low morale among the Boers and the mutinous state of many burghers. Based on this, Baden-Powell drafted a letter to the Boers:

NOTICE
TO THE BURGHERS OF THE Z.A.R. AT PRESENT
UNDER ARMS NEAR MAFEKING.

From the officer commanding Her Majesty's Forces, Mafeking.

Burghers, I address you in this matter because I have only recently learned how you are being intentionally kept in the dark by your officers and your Government newspapers as to what is really happening in other parts of South Africa. As officer commanding Her Majesty's troops on this border, I think it right to point out to you clearly the inevitable result of your remaining any longer in arms against Great Britain.

You are all aware that the present war was caused by the invasion of British territory by your forces, and as most of you know, without justifiable reason.

Your leaders do not tell you that so far your forces have met with what is only the advanced guard of the British force, and that circumstances have changed within the past week; the main body of the British is now arriving daily by thousands from England, Canada, India and Australia, and is about to advance through your country. In a few weeks, the South African Republic will be in the hands of the

English; no sacrifice of life on your part can stop it. The question now put to yourselves before it is, is this: is it worth while losing your lives in a vain attempt to stop their invasion or to take a town beyond your borders which, if taken, would be of no use to you? (And I may tell you that Mafeking cannot be taken by sitting down and looking at it, for we have ample supplies for several months to come.)

The *Staat Artillery* have done us very little damage, and we are now well protected with forts and mines. Your presence here, or elsewhere, under arms, cannot stop the British advancing into your country.

Your leaders and newspapers are also trying to make you believe that some foreign continental powers are likely to intervene on your behalf against England. This is not in keeping with their pretence that your side is going to be victorious, nor is it in accordance with the fact. The S.A.R. having declared war and taken the offensive, cannot claim intervention on its behalf. And were it not so, the German emperor is at present in England, and fully in sympathy with us; the American Government have warned others of their intervention on the side of England should any other nation interfere; France has large interests in the gold fields identical with those of England; Italy is entirely in accord with us; and Russia sees no cause to interfere.

Your leaders have caused the destruction of farms in this country and have fired on women and children, and our men are becoming hard to restrain in consequence. Your leaders have also caused invasion of Kaffir territory, and looting of their cattle, and have thus induced them to rise, and in their turn to invade your country, and to kill your burghers. As one white man to another, I warned General Cronje on the 14th November that this would occur, and yesterday I heard that more Kaffirs are rising, and are contemplating similar moves; and I have warned Snyman accordingly. Thus great bloodshed and destruction of farms threaten you on all sides, and I wish to offer you a chance of avoiding it. To this end my advice to you is to return without delay to your homes and there remain peacefully until the war is over. Those of you who do this before the 14th instant will be as far as possible protected, as regards yourselves, your families, and property, from confiscations, looting, and other penalties to which those who remain under arms may be subjected when invasion takes place.

Our secret agents will communicate to me the names of those who do and of those who do not avail themselves, before the 13th instant, of the terms now being offered.

To ensure their property being respected, all the men of a family must be present at home when the troops arrive and be prepared to hand over a rifle and 150 pounds of ammunition each.

The above terms do not apply to officers or to members of *Staats Artillery*, who may surrender as prisoners-of-war at any time; nor do they apply to rebels from British territory or others against whom there may be other charges. It is probable that my force will shortly take the offensive.

To those who, after this warning, defer their submission till too late, I can offer no promise, and they will only have themselves to blame for any injury or loss of property that they or their families may afterwards suffer.

(Sgd.) R.S.S. BADEN-POWELL,
Colonel

Mafeking, 10th December, 1899

Snyman responded indignantly that Baden-Powell was childish.

History is correct in deriding Snyman. Whereas Cronje had shown some aggression, his successor was content to passively sit back and bomb and starve Mafeking into submission. But, as Baden-Powell teased, 'Mafeking cannot be taken by sitting down and looking at it.' Yet, Snyman deserves some sympathy. He is pilloried for not doing more to achieve what Cronje could not do with three times the force against defences that were not as secure as when he took command. Further, Baden-Powell's defenders have continually been understated by British historians, who exclude the Barolong forces at his disposal. At times, Baden-Powell's defenders outnumbered the besiegers. And, while Baden-Powell was preserving his British troops in trenches, he fought a successful secret war of attrition behind the Boer lines that created more headaches for Snyman than anything else during the siege.

Angus Hamilton, war correspondent for *The Times*, was of the opinion that the success of the Barolong cattle raiders, whom Baden-Powell called 'cattle-thieves', in stealing Boer cattle should have conferred 'upon them a unique value in the garrison.' He described how a raid was conducted: 'they approach as near to the grazing cattle as discretion permits, marking down when twilight appears the position of these beasts that can be readily detached from the mob. Then, when darkness is complete, they crawl up, divested of their clothes, crawling upon hands and knees, until they have completely surrounded their prey. Then quietly, and as rapidly as circumstances will allow them, each man "gets a move on" his particular beast, so that in a very short space of time some ten or twenty cattle are unconsciously leaving the main herd. When the raiders have drawn out of earshot of the Boer lines they urge on their captives, running behind them and on either side of them, but without making any noise whatsoever.'

Under the title 'Our Beef Providers', an article appeared in the *Mafeking Mail* on the cattle rustlers. 'The appearance of some under-cut, juicy and succulent, on certain breakfast tables made us curious in this time of siege as to its origin. We learned it was "Native" beef, and the following account, which we prefer to give in its own picturesque language, is interesting in connection with the subject of our meat supply.' The account was written by Sol Plaatje:

Mathakgong, the leader of 'the expedition of 10th', whose loot was captured by the enemy a fortnight ago, said he would not have a quiet night until that fiasco had been blotted out; so on Friday he took four men with him to go and make another trial. Yesterday he and his companions were coming in with what appeared to be a span (12 head) of oxen they had captured close to Batho-Batho, near Maritzani, at 5 pm. They brought them down safely until they reached the Magogo Valley, where the Boers fired at them. The Boers first of all fired from their right and before they had time to reply another volley came from their left. They replied calmly, four men went to the right (where the heaviest fire was) and one to the left. The Boers soon shut up but not until they had wounded two oxen. One fell amongst the Boers and one just outside our advance trench, and ten came in safely.

Night after last (Saturday) 12 armed Barolong left our advance trench, south of the Stadt, to go and annoy the Boers. They crossed their line without being observed and were only fired at on their return. As soon as they returned their fire the Boers ran back to their trench and were silent for the night.

The theft of cattle had a devastating effect on Boer morale as they were constantly fearful about what was happening at home. Abraham Stafleu noted: 'For this reason many burghers were constantly away on leave, but the leave was too short to do anything substantial for their families and long enough to damage military operations. There was no structure set up to handle the granting of leave. The veldcornet was given the task of allocating leave – which made his job very difficult and open to charges of unfairness. Too many just left without asking for leave.'

But stealing cattle, important as the job may be for a besieged town, was not the rustlers' main task. This, alluded to in Plaatje's article, was to act as guerrilla fighters. Mathakgong was the true hero of Mafeking, his raids each netting up to 50 cattle while he also harassed and killed Boers. Plaatje wrote in his diary: 'The little skirmishes had with the Boers outside have had a great effect among the latter … Mathakgong's name is a household word on every farm. The cattle have been centralised and strong guards put over them. They are strongly encamped in trenches surrounding the cattle fence, and they are just ready to give him a cordial reception. They say he has killed many Boers at their farms during last month, including women and children.' Plaatje noted after another raid by Mathakgong: 'On Saturday evening they attacked his [a Boer by the name of "Barwise"] farm, drove the Boers, servants, dogs, etc., out of the homestead and then took the cattle. They wanted to get hold of the calves but when they opened the kraal (during the heat of the fire) the calves jumped out the back and followed their running owners.'

In desperation Snyman gave an order that any black found leaving or entering Mafeking was to be shot. Abraham Stafleu reported 'he wanted to see no more captured blacks. They must be executed on the spot. A number of the officers attempted to oppose this order saying that it was tantamount to murder but Snyman would not relent.' He backed up this

127

order with a letter of protest to Baden-Powell who responded in the manner he had done to Cronje.

Mafeking, 8th Dec., 1899

To General Snyman,
  near Mafeking

Sir, – I beg to thank you for having handed over Lady Sarah Wilson in exchange for the convict P. Viljoen.

At the same time, I beg to point out that I have only consented to the exchange under protest, as being contrary to the custom of civilised warfare.

In treating this lady as a prisoner-of-war, as well as in various other acts, you have in the present campaign, altered the usual conditions of war. This is a very serious matter; and I do not know whether it has the sanction of General Joubert or not, but I warn you of the consequences.

The war was at first, and would remain, as far as Her Majesty's troops are concerned, a war between one Government and another; but you are making it one of people against people in which women are considered as belligerents. I warn you that the consequence of this may shortly be very serious to your own people and you yourself will be to blame for anything that may happen.

Regarding your complaint as to your being attacked by Natives I beg to refer you to my letter dated 14th November, addressed to your predecessor, General Cronje. In this letter I went out of my way, as one white man to another, to warn you that the Natives are becoming extremely incensed at your stealing their cattle, and the wanton burning of their kraals; they argued that the war lay only between our two nations, and that the quarrel had nothing to do with themselves, and they had remained neutral in consequence, excepting in the case of the Mafeking Baralongs, who had to defend their homes in consequence of your unjustifiable invasion. Nevertheless, you thought fit to carry on cattle thefts and raids against them, and you are now beginning to feel the consequences; and, as I told you, I could not be responsible. And I fear from what I have just heard by wireless telegraph that the Natives are contemplating further operations should your forces continue to remain within or on the borders of their territories. Before the commencement of the war the High Commissioner issued stringent orders to all Natives that they were to remain quiet and not to take up arms unless their territory were invaded (in which case, of course, they had a perfect right to defend themselves) ...

While of the subject of Natives please do not suppose that I am ignorant of what you have been doing with regard to seeking the assistance of armed natives, nor of the use of the Natives by you in the destruction of the railway line south of Mafeking. However, having done my duty in briefly giving you warning on these points, I do not propose to further discuss them by letter.

> I have the honour to be,
> Sir,
> Your obedient servant,
> R.S.S. BADEN-POWELL, Col.

The raids, far from stopping, intensified after Snyman's order. But when rustlers were caught retribution was swift and savage. Stafleu recounted that 'The burghers of Groot-Marico captured two cattle thieves with 10 head of cattle. They told the Boers that it was very easy to take cattle into Mafeking because there was too great a distance between the laager and the lookout. They were sentenced to death and four burghers were chosen and carried out the sentence. The general gave Veldcornet Arie Oberholzer a severe reprimand for taking the thieves prisoner and not carrying out the sentence on the spot.' On another occasion he noted 'another cattle thief was captured at Rooigrond and shot close to town and left unburied as a warning.' The Boers were far from happy with the brutality of Snyman toward blacks and one even went so far as to write to President Kruger, who responded 'that the shooting of prisoners, especially those caught driving cattle was an atrocity and was to be stopped immediately.'

Snyman ignored the order. Shortly after, a group of 33 rustlers were surrounded in the bush near Rooigrond. The burghers sent back to the laager for a maxim, herded the raiders together and mowed down all but

129

one. Snyman sent a letter of protest to Baden-Powell, who lied in his reply, 'I know nothing of the 32 men, they were certainly not under my orders, or as far as I was aware of my officers.' This betrayal was doubly so when it is considered that the black residents of Mafeking were not allowed to share this stolen beef — it was reserved for the whites of the garrison.

The immense danger faced by the cattle rustlers was slight in comparison to that faced by Baden-Powell's scouts and native runners, known as 'kaffirgrams.' Seldom armed, they were castrated or shot as spies if captured by the Boers and flogged by the British if they did not carry out their orders to the letter. Major Dennison, at Kuruman, who would receive notes from Baden-Powell, reported 'Several of the native runners were shot in cold blood by the Boers, many of whom take a delight in putting natives up in the road and coolly shooting them down. The shedding of native blood is not counted as murder by many of them; on the contrary, they talk and laugh over the deed, describing the fear and agony of the poor sufferer with jeers and laughter.' Had it not been for these men, Baden-Powell would have had little contact with the outside world or reliable information to work with.

Part of the reason Snyman was so ineffectual was because Baden-Powell managed to continually push his forward trenches out. The further Snyman was pushed from Mafeking, the less accurate became the shelling and the more porous his extended lines. The Shangaan trench diggers, under heavy fire, excavated these lines often as close as 50 metres from the Boers. Also, to the south-west, the Barolong continually pushed outward, eventually taking Fort Cronje, which ensured adequate grazing for the garrison cattle and livestock. With the forward trenches manned by the Black Watch and the holding of the most dangerous area, the Brickfields, by the Fingo and Cape Boys the town was effectively being defended and fed by the residents of colour.

In Mafeking, the latest addition to the garrison, Lady Sarah, was quickly initiated into the incessant bombardment. Soon after the completion of her bunker she was playing cards with Goold-Adams when she remarked of a shell, 'How near that sounds'. It landed a metre away and she and her guest momentarily vanished in a cloud of dust and gravel. But, for her, like the rest of the civilians, it was the Mauser bullets that were the most terrifying. 'It was practically impossible to walk from one building to another without being shot at,' she commented. She added, after a near miss, 'For a moment I thought I was killed, but my trembling limbs and chattering teeth soon convinced me to the contrary.'

'The siege of Mafeking is no joke,' she reported to *The Daily Mail*. 'Death is ever present with us, a stern reality. Do we but cross the street we cannot tell whether we shall not be suddenly struck down from an unexpected quarter or maimed for life, and this in spite of prudence and precautions. For in a siege of this duration one cannot live an entirely underground existence; business and duties must be gone through with, although it sometimes staggers me to see how unconcernedly men walk about the streets whistling and joking in the intervals of shelling, to note the clang, clang of the blacksmith's anvil, close to my bomb proof, before even the noise of explosion has died away – and to watch the happy unconcern of the black boys, whose lively chatter is wholly undisturbed by these terrible missiles.'

However, Snyman's gunners had fallen into a routine that soon became second nature to the residents. The shell firing was so punctual that many set their watches by it. A salvo would be hurled into the town starting at 4.30 am, known as 'reveille', which would last until breakfast. At noon the town would be bombarded for an hour, then again from 4.30 to 5 pm The most pleasant part of the day now followed. Lady Sarah recalled a typical evening: 'Then night would gradually fall on the scene, sometimes made almost as light as day by a glorious African moon ... The half-hour between sundown and moonrise, or twilight and inky blackness, as the case happened to be, according to the season or the weather, was about the pleasantest time of the whole day. As a rule it was a peaceful interval as regards shelling. Herds of mules were driven along the dusty streets to be watered; cattle and goats returned from the veld, where they had been grazing in close proximity to the town, as far as possible out of sight; foot-passengers, amongst them many women, scurried along the side-walks closely skirting the house. Then, when daylight had completely faded, all took shelter,' to await Creaky's 'good-night' boom which came between 8 and 9 pm.

But for Lady Sarah the worst of the day came soon after because she hated the night. 'There was something very eerie in the long nights for after the fall of darkness no lights were allowed for fear of drawing fire. Occasionally the intense quiet would be broken by a volley from the enemy ... lasting for ten minutes, and then dropping to single shots fired at intervals . . . I would peep out on the mysterious moonlit veld – until at length would come the blessed daylight.'

The bunkers and the system of alarm bells minimised the dangers in the white town. In reality, the greater external threat was from the elements. The season was particularly stormy, with one deluge, in early December, especially memorable. At noon, a black, thunderous cauldron of clouds built up from the south. Soon a high wind was breaking trees and tearing birds' nests from high branches. Lightning flashed and the dread cries of animals were carried ahead by the howling gale. The wind that ripped doors from their hinges and chased dust devils down the wide streets was infused with the smell of rain. Old Tshidi tribesmen, who had looked up at the clouds and sniffed at them and held wet fingers up to sense the wind, claimed they had never experienced anything like it. By 2 pm the clouds had rolled over the town and the first drop of rain was followed by a cloudburst of 200 millimetres in little over an hour.

The *Mafeking Mail*, in its report, commented: 'More damage to property was done by the storm than the Boers could ever accomplish in their "storming". Rations were destroyed, kits washed away, and in one case a man was nearly drowned, or smothered in the mud. He slipped in, fortunately feet downwards, and had not two of his companions been near him and promptly "hauled him back again" he would have been done for. At the hospital redan the underground kitchen was flooded with six feet of water, the dinner beef spoiled and various little "extras" the men had subscribed to buy, were lost. The Women's Laager trench was an underground canal. The sisters were washed out from their bomb-proof (one nearly drowned) and the Cape Police had an hour's diving in the seven feet deep coffee coloured pool for Maxim ammunition.'

Captain Fitzclarence, who was up the river with a sniping party, nearly got washed away by the swollen river. A drunken volunteer in the cemetery almost drowned when he fell into a freshly dug grave from which he could not get out and, in the Women's Laager, the bedridden – their beds made from boxes – shrieked in terror as they floated round the trenches as if on gondolas. When it was over brandy was rushed to the sodden men in the look-outs and black labourers were ordered to bale out bunkers and trenches. The next morning, the humidity insufferable, the Boers unleashed a heavy bombardment and Mausering of the town as residents tried to dry clothing in the sun and recover possessions imbedded in the rapidly drying soil.

132

Horrific as the situation was, the greatest problem remained the boredom, which was increasingly tinged with despondency as the realisation dawned that the prospects of a speedy relief was remote. Nerves were more frayed, tempers shortened and carelessness endemic. It was one of these incautious acts — a marble-playing boy being killed by a shell after the alarm sounded — that contributed to the founding of the Boy Scouts.

> *These are our regulations —*
> *There's just one law for the Scout*
> *And the first and the last, and the present and the past*
> *And the future and the perfect is 'Look Out!'*
> *I, thou and he, look out!*
> *We, ye and they, look out!*
> *Though you didn't or you wouldn't*
> *Or you hadn't or you couldn't;*
> *You jolly well must look out!*
> KIPLING, BOY SCOUTS PATROL SONG

Baden-Powell recalled what Burnham had told him of boys in Bulawayo being put to use to keep them out of mischief and to release men for duty in the defence works. A Cadet Corps, for boys between the ages of nine and 15, was formed under the command of Lord Edward Cecil and a drunk, Lieutenant Ronald Moncreiffe. Captain Goodyear's son, Warner, was given the rank of Cadet Sergeant-Major. Before being given regular duties, the boys were taught drill and discipline.

No aspect of Baden-Powell's life is more shrouded in myth than the founding of the Boy Scouts and the role played by the Siege of Mafeking in the formulation of the idea. And no person was more active in perpetuating this legend than Baden-Powell himself. Much of the lie was necessary, later, to counter allegations that he plagiarised the concept of the Boy Scouts from Ernest Seton, an American woodcrafter. While it is true that Baden-Powell would have been unlikely to have pursued the idea of a youth movement had it not been for the siege, it is equally correct that the Mafeking Cadet Corps did not play a major role in either the defence or in his thinking at the time. The latter claim is perfectly obvious from the fact that he placed the Cadet Corps in the care of the two men, after Hore, that he despised the most. The Corps was as much a scheme to get this pair out of his hair as it was to put the boys of the town to some use.

It was only much later that Baden-Powell would refer to the Cadet Corps as the Mafeking Boy Scouts. And it was only when the storm threatened to swamp him that he credited the Corps as the precursor to the founding of the movement. What the Cadet Corps did was to lay a seed in his mind that would germinate later. 'The possibility of putting responsibility onto boys and treating them seriously was brought to the proof in Mafeking with the corps of boys raised by Lord Edward Cecil there in 1899 and led me to go into it further.'

Whether he stole the blueprint for the Boy Scouts from someone else or not is a matter for debate. What is clear is that even before Ashanti he was concerned with the training of British soldiers, the quality of these soldiers and the problems of getting the youth of Britain's slums off the streets. It could not have escaped his attention that once the boys of Mafeking were trained and given responsibility they became happy, useful citizens. It was only a small step from this to realise that by harnessing boys to an ideal, they could easily be shaped into future soldiers. Baden-Powell concluded long before he met Seton that by inculcating boys with the concept of character, honour, duty, loyalty, health and manliness they would automatically become good citizens. It was no accident that these notions were also the basis for his perfect soldier.

'If I were to form the highest ideal for my country,' he wrote, 'it would be this – that it should be a nation of which the manhood was exclusively composed of men who have been, or were, Boy Scouts, and were trained in the Boy Scout theory. Such a nation would be the honour of mankind. It would be the greatest moral force the world has ever known.' The proof of the pudding was in the eating because the Balilla, Mussolini's youth movement, was based on the Boy Scouts and so too, indirectly, were the Hitler Jugend.

The call of the pack all over the world is 'We'll do our best'; so when your cubmaster comes into the circle you can chuck up your chin and, all together, you howl out – making each word a long yowl: 'A-ka-la! – We-e-e-ell do-o-o-o ou-u-u-r BEST.' Yell the word 'best' sharp and loud and short and all together.

BADEN-POWELL

134

Dressed in forage caps or smasher hats and yellow puggarees, the boys of Mafeking were soon doing their duty for God and the Queen. Mounted on mules, until these were needed for the pot, then bicycles, these boys provided a much needed boost to the town's auxiliary services.

Baden-Powell's fear was the despondency which threatened to unravel his carefully engineered siege from within. He planned to occupy the Boers at the town for as long as possible, but had not psychologically prepared the residents for a lengthy siege. It required that he do something very quickly before the unimagined public relations triumph of Mafeking turned sour.

The despair in the town was palpable. Most residents had lost a loved one or a close friend, the evidence of which was in a cemetery filling with white crosses. Mr Urry, the Standard Bank manager, avoided the hospital because the 'groans and shrieks of the dying are too terrible to hear.' Those who had lost limbs or part of their faces were there for all to see and their tales of treatment without adequate anaesthetic or pain relief was sufficient to rob even the hardiest soul of sleep. Dysentery persisted in the unhygienic surrounds and typhoid, quickly isolated, struck in the Women's Laager. Heavy rainstorms and oppressive humidity were the ideal conditions for mosquitoes to multiply and fleas to flourish in the wrecked homes and dank, airless and unhealthy bunkers. And, as hope of relief faded, so news filtered through of British disaster-atop-calamity in the rest of the country.

> It was our fault, and our very great fault, and not the judgement
>   of Heaven.
> We made an army in our own image, on an island nine by
>   seven,
> Which faithfully mirrored its maker's ideals, equipment, and
>   mental attitude —
> And so we got our lesson: and we ought to accept it with
>   gratitude.
>   KIPLING, 'THE LESSON'

In the trenches, the problems, though obvious, were as debilitating. Cavalry troops, who were supposed to be mobile, manned the defences and peered motionless along the blue barrels of their weapons for long hours at a distant enemy. Frazzled by the sun by day, soaked in the evening and damp by night; they slept with the nightmare visions of the pain imprinted in rigor mortis on the faces of dead friends. Stiff, bored and unfit, they often longed for the excitement of action.

Baden-Powell gave them sport and entertainment instead. He decided that Sundays, with their freedom from shelling, would not only be days of respite but filled with fun and activity. A well-drilled troop of lancers, in early December, with lances manufactured in the railway workshop, heralded the panacea with a medieval parade. Sports, played on the recreation ground to the accompaniment of the Regimental Band followed. At first the sports were mainly mounted activities. Baden-Powell, in the handicapped polo tournaments, in which he participated, would give his side 'verbal assistance delivered increasingly in stentorian tones.' As the horses became soup, so mounted games gave way to soccer and cricket. The *Mafeking Mail* built up all the sports by publicising fixtures and reporting on the results on the Monday.

Each Sunday the dark facts of the past week were brushed aside by such diversions as horse shows, bicycle races and mule team driving competitions.

RECREATION GROUND
VARIETY ENTERTAINMENT
by the
CAPE POLICE and BECHUANALAND RIFLES
to be followed by a
WIDE WORLD SHOW

HIDDEN HOLLOW
VARIETY ENTERTAINMENT
by the
PROTECTORATE REGT. and THE B.S.A. POLICE

Committee decides best performance and prizes awarded

WIDE WORLD SHOW

The Grand Siege Driving-competition
One prize for the most original turn-out
One prize for the lady passenger in the vehicle that wins the race.
The race consists of driving a vehicle round a circular course while the band plays. When the halt sounds, the vehicle that is nearest to

the winning post wins the race. Drivers choose their own pace, but may not stop till the halt sounds. Any kind of vehicle, any kind of animal or team, but each vehicle must be provided with some sort of alarm, such as horn or whistle, etc., which must be kept sounding during the race.

Shops and banks opened for business and the recently introduced rationing orders were relaxed on Sundays. Mr Minchin, the attorney, won a prize for his foal at an Agricultural Produce Show; Sergeant Brady's son won first prize in the Siege Baby Show; boys from the Cadet Corps were pitted in competitions for accurate and efficient delivery of letters; and a bizarre cooking competition was organised between the chefs of Dixon's and Riesle's Hotel to demonstrate to the Boers the terrible privations of the siege on the town:

DIXON'S	RIESLE'S
Soup	Brunois Sauce
Gravy	Entrees
Entrees	Lobster Croquettes and Anchovy Butter
Fillet of Beef	Compote of Giblets & Mushrooms
Braised Ox-Tongue	Forced Ox-Heart, York Ham & Peas
Poultry	Poultry
Roast Fowl and Bread Sauce	Roast Fowl
Stuffed Roast Duck	Ham
Joints	Joints
Roast Beef Roast	Sirloin of Beef & Yorkshire Pudding
Roast Mutton	Roast Leg of Mutton
Roast Lamb & Mint Sauce	Roast Pork
Roast Veal, Corned Beef, Carrots	Corned brisket
Vegetables	Side of Lamb & Green Peas
Baked & Boiled Potatoes	Vegetables
Green Peas	Green Peas, New Potatoes Vegetable Marrow
Sweets	Sweets
Current Pudding, Custard	Plum pudding & Brandy Sauce
Tea, cheese & Coffee	Tea, cheese & Coffee

The Boers, at first, fumbled over their Bibles in indignation at the sacrilege. But, they too were bored and soon they were using the truce day to meet with old friends from the town as they walked in the veld or created amusements of their own.

Baden-Powell, the showman, was in paradise. He appeared at one gymkhana as a ringmaster – dressed in tails, white bow tie and clown's hat – swishing a ribbon whip 10 metres long. And, when not playing the fool, he served tea to the townspeople from the travelling wagon. His favourite, though, was the Sunday night concert at the Masonic Hall. 'Colonel Baden-Powell is one of the best fellows going,' wrote trooper Alfred Spurling. 'He sings comic songs, and had a lot of sketches at a exhibition which was held the other day.'

After the 'Irish Jubilee Song' by Mr Adams, 'The Promised Land' by Mr Cooper, 'The Hottentot Dance' by Corporal Curry and a ventriloquism sketch by Mr Lees, appeared the star. Baden-Powell, one moment, was the impossibly moustachioed 'Signor Paderewski', next he was playing the piano with his toes and emitting falsetto shrieks. He was a Cockney, 'The Regimental Sergeant-Major' and 'Mr Personally-conducted Look' in the sketch 'Mafeking to Mayfair'.

So popular, initially, were these diversions that many took to endangering their safety by partaking in them outside of Sundays. A football match, between Troops and Town, on a Wednesday afternoon, nearly turned into a disaster when a 94-pounder bounced through and crashed into the Town Office. Private Footman was not so lucky. He ignored the alarm bell while strumming a banjo and rehearsing 'Gone are the days' for the Christie Minstrel show and a shell blew him to bits.

Baden-Powell, with the help of the *Mafeking Mail*, enhanced the distractions by converting minor stories into major news events. While these certainly softened the nightmare and lifted morale, they did wonders for Baden-Powell's persona at home. One of these stories was the discovery by Godley, who had been riding one morning past Mr Rowland's farm, that one of the gate posts was the barrel of a 16-pounder ship's gun dated 1770 on the barrel. It was refurbished by Connolly and a carriage built for it by Gerans. Christened 'Lord Nelson', it fired a solid shot the size of a cricket ball. While the cannon was used through the rest of the siege, its only success appears its maiden delivery – Godley wrote 'it bumped down the road exactly like a cricket ball ... and one old Boer tried to field it with disastrous results to himself.'

It never occurred to Baden-Powell that the black residents may also be stressed and in need of a pick-me-up. Life did, however, carry on in Mahikeng. Plaatje, on Sundays would attend a church service in the morning, ride his horse Whiskey, visit friends or go for a walk. Lady Sarah reminisced: 'These natives always displayed the most astonishing sang-froid. One day we saw a funny scene on the occasion of a Kaffir wedding, when the bridegroom was most correctly attired in morning-dress and an old top-hat. Over his frock-coat he wore his bandoleer, and carried a rifle on his shoulder; the bride, swathed in a long white veil from head to foot, walked by his side, and was followed by two young ladies in festive array, while the procession was brought up by more niggers, armed, like the bridegroom, to the teeth.'

Myrrh is mine, its bitter perfume
breathes a life of gathering gloom;
sorrowing, sighing, bleeding, dying,
sealed in the stone-cold tomb.

JOHN HENRY HOPKINS, FROM THE CELEBRATION HYMNAL

Christmas Day was celebrated in Mafeking on Sunday 24 December as it was uncertain whether the Boers would shell Mafeking as usual the following day. The town was not bombarded on Christmas Day so the event was celebrated over two days. No other occasion demonstrated the obscene disparity between black and white Mafeking than Christmas 1899 — it was an ominous sign of things to come.

Plaatje was ill those two days. He was becoming increasingly depressed and this was affecting his health. 'Christmas Day. I am not yet able to turn out,' he lamented on 24 December. 'I remember my low state with an afflicted sense. To think that this is the second Christmas of my wedded life and I have to spend it, like the first one, so very, very far away from the one I love above all: it is becoming too big and I wish I could drive the thought from my mind. Still I remember last year when I spent three lengthy, solitary days in old Mrs Diamond's [Mrs Lesoane, the mother of Diamond Lesoane] beautiful garden and she fed me with the first issue of her fructuous grove's fruits and greenery. I told her how happy we would both be if my kind little wife, whom she very much longed to see, was with us; we were consoled, however, by the knowledge that she was on that day presenting my first-born to his saviour under a magnificent Christmas Tree somewhere, and that she would sooner or later bring us our little darling boy who would positively be the happiness of our hearts next Christmas (today) in the same garden, the cultivation of our aged lady friend. But here I am today so very far from having that expectation of our calming meditations fulfilled. I am not even graced with as little as a congratulatory missive from both of them, but am nailed to a sick-bed with very poor attention – worst of all surrounded by Boers. I had expected a ready-dressed chicken from my friend Merko as I have developed a dire hatred for all other food, and was almost starving when David came from him with two. Hence I discovered that despite my mental tribulations, I was not absolutely friendless.'

Food restrictions were lifted in the white town for the two days of Christmas. On 24 December, despite the grilling heat, Lady Sarah hosted a luncheon for guests that received the following invitation: 'Lady Sarah Wilson requests the pleasure of . . . 's company to lunch on Christmas Day at 1.30 at her Bombproof. Mr Weil hopes to provide a fat turkey.' Baden-Powell was one of the guests and the turkey, together with a traditional plum pudding, had made a magical appearance from Weil's store. At the commencement of the siege all provisions were commandeered by the military authorities. The most blatant transgressor of these regulations was the man, Ben Weil, in whose care the stores were placed.

That afternoon the children, both British and Boer, of the besieged town were hosted by Lady Sarah at a tea party. These 'poor little white-faced things' were brought shrieking and cheering from the Women's Laager in gaily decorated turn-outs driven by the officers of the Protectorate Regiment. Weil again managed to find ingredients that had been 'overlooked' for the cakes and pies that were baked. At the party the 250 children each received a Christmas cracker and a gift from Lady Sarah as the nurses and nuns sang Christmas carols. The leftovers were loaded on a cart and taken to the *stadt* to be shared amongst the Tshidi children.

Hail the heaven-born Prince of peace!
Hail the Son of Righteousness!
Light and Life to all he brings
risen with healing in his wings;
mild he lays his glory by,
born that man no more may die,

born to raise the sons of earth,
born to give them second birth.

CHARLES WESLEY AND OTHERS

Christmas day in Mafeking and the Boer Laager began much the same way – most went to church. Abraham Stafleu did not attend the church service in the Boer laager but could hear Snyman, as part of the sermon, urging the Boers, whom he claimed stood alone, to take inspiration from God to fight the good fight. In a temper Stafleu confronted Snyman and pointed out to him the contribution of Hollanders, Scandinavians, Germans, French, Russians, Irish and Italians to the Boer effort. 'During the heat of the argument,' fumed Stafleu, 'I accused the general of being so dumb that he knew nothing of the efforts of others – or he was merely completely thankless'. Snyman replied 'that a nation couldn't pray for every Jan, Piet and Klaas (Tom, Dick & Harry).'

It was more peaceful in Mafeking where the sounds of hymns and carols drifted from the churches. After the services the residents visited friends or took strolls along the shaded banks of the swollen Molopo River. Alcoholic beverages made an appearance from hidden stores and, in the packed bars, Queen Victoria was given three cheers. At Riesle's a magnificent feast was laid for residents.

May Christmas find you glad and well.
In spite of Kruger's Shot and Shell
****

DE MAFEKING HOTEL
British Bechuanaland
****

Riesle Proprietor
****

MENU

CHRISTMAS DAY 1899
Anchovy Croutons
Olives
***

Consommé Windsor
***

Oyster Patties
***

Smoked Calves Tongue
Giblet Pie
Tournedos Parisian
York Ham & Madeira Sauce
Fricassee of Veal
***

Roast Fowl and Bread Sauce
Boiled Fowl and Bacon
***

Joints
Baron of Beef & Yorkshire Pudding
Veal & Ham
Roast Side of Lamb & Green Peas
Suckling Pig & Apple Sauce
Roast Saddle of Mutton
Boiled Mutton and Capers
Boiled Bacon
Corned Beef
Tongue and Ham
***

Vegetables
Marrow, Green Peas
Baked and Boiled Potatoes
***

Xmas Pudding
Mince Pies
Sandringham Jellies
Victoria Sandwich

Dessert   Café Noir
***

RULE BRITTANIA

'We revelled in plenty' boasted Mr Riesle. In the refugee camp two had
already died of starvation.

Solomon Tshekisho Plaatje – Mafeking court interpreter, linguist and first secretary-general of the South African Native National Congress, the forerunner to the African National Congress.
(UNIVERSITY OF THE WITWATERSRAND, HISTORICAL PAPERS)

Sol Plaatje and Isaiah Bud-M'belle, both standing, with two unidentified friends or colleagues.
(University of the Witwatersrand, Historical Papers)

Elizabeth Plaatje – Sol Plaatje's wife.
(University of the Witwatersrand,
Historical Papers)

Olive Plaatje – Sol Plaatje's favourite
daughter, who died from the effects of the
1919 Spanish Flu.
(University of the Witwatersrand,
Historical Papers)

Black residents queue for rations in the British camp.
(MAFIKENG MUSEUM)

Shooting unlicensed dogs – these carcasses were added to the soup that was sold to black residents. (MAFIKENG MUSEUM)

Issuing rations in the *stadt*.
(MAFIKENG MUSEUM)

Residents enjoy a drink in the shattered Bradley's Hotel. (ELEANOR CASON)

The fishmongers shanty destroyed by a shell. (ELEANOR CASON)

Shell damage to the railway refreshment room. (MAFIKENG MUSEUM)

Rubbish strewn outside General Snyman's headquarters at McMullen's farm after it was abandoned at the end of the siege. (MAFIKENG MUSEUM)

A portrait of the interior of Baden-Powell's armoured train.
(UNIVERSITY OF THE WITWATERSRAND, HISTORICAL PAPERS)

The lookout at the armoured train.
(MAFIKENG MUSEUM)

The Women's Laager.
(MAFIKENG MUSEUM)

Baden-Powell surveying enemy positions.
(MAFIKENG MUSEUM)

Lieutenant Dunlop-Smith inspecting the horsemeat
that became an integral part of the town's diet. (MAFIKENG MUSEUM)

A portrait of a black 'runner' or messenger being run down by Boers.
(University of the Witwatersrand, Historical Papers)

An armed Tshidi-Barolong defender.
(University of the Witwatersrand, Historical Papers)

Armed blacks guard the convent. (Mafikeng Museum)

That evening, as dusk deepened, Lady Sarah was being escorted to her lodgings by Captain Ronald Vernon. 'I remember returning to my quarters,' she recalled, 'after the festivities, with this officer, and his telling me, in strict confidence, with eager anticipation, of a sortie that was to be made on the morrow, with the object of obtaining possession of the Boer Gun at Game Tree Fort.' It is unlikely that this was the first Lady Sarah had heard of the 'open secret' that was another of Baden-Powell's 'hard kicks'. So animated was Vernon that it is unlikely they heard the volley of shots behind them as Jim Mbala, suspected of being a spy, was executed by firing squad as the golden sun set on Christmas Day.

Baden-Powell in the legend is portrayed as a generous, compassionate, fair and wise leader. His lack of compassion toward black people is well documented. But, what is little recorded is his cruelty to those he disliked. He 'ballyragged' Hore continually and hounded Moncreiffe until he suffered a nervous breakdown, then jailed him. Nor was he fair. While six blacks were executed by firing squad, no white was. He upheld 115 sentences of flogging for blacks but commuted John Murphy's sentence of flogging because 'it was inappropriate to whip a white man.' For stealing food a starving black would be sentenced to 50 lashes for the first offence and death on the third. Black scouts who failed in their duties or whose information was proved incorrect were also flogged.

Baden-Powell, however, was not whipped for his scouting efforts. Angus Hamilton brilliantly captured the myth of Baden-Powell, the scout; in this *Boy's Own* piece of journalism for *The Times*:

His espionage excursions to the Boer lines have gained him an intimate and accurate idea of the value of the opposing forces and a mass of data by which he can immediately counteract the enemy's attack. He loves the night, and after his return from the hollows in the veldt, where he has kept so many anxious vigils, he lies awake hour after hour upon his camp mattress on the verandah, tracing out, in his mind, the various means and agencies by which he can forestall their move, which, unknown to them, he had personally watched. He is a silent man. In the noisy day he yearns for the noiseless night, in which he can slip in to the vistas of the veldt, an unobtrusive spectator of the mystic communion of tree with tree of twilight with darkness, of land with water, of early morn with fading night, with the music of the journeying winds to speak to him and to lull his thoughts. As he makes his way across our lines the watchful sentry strains his eyes a little more to keep the figure of the colonel before him, until the undulations of the veldt conceal his progress. He goes in the privacy of the night, when it is no longer a season of moonlight, when, although the stars are full, the night is dim. The breezes of the veldt are warm and gentle, impregnated with the fresh fragrances of the Molopo, although, as he walks with rapid, almost running, footsteps, leaving the black blur of the town for the arid and stony areas to the west, a new wind meets him, a wind that is clear and keen and dry, the wind of the wastes that wanders for ever over the monotonous sands of the desert. He goes on, never faltering, bending for a moment behind a clump of rocks, screening himself next behind some bushes, crawling upon his hands and knees. His head is low, his eyes gaze straight upon the camp of the enemy; in a little, he moves again, his inspection is over, and he either changes to a fresh point or startles some dozing sentry as he slips back into town.

It was on such information, gathered personally by Baden-Powell, that the decision was made to attack Game Tree on Boxing Day.

When first under fire an' you're wishful to duck,
Don't look nor take 'eed at the man that is struck,
Be thankful you're livin', and trust to your luck
* And march to your front like a soldier.*
*   Front, front, front like a soldier ...*
          KIPLING, 'THE YOUNG BRITISH SOLDIER'

The fort at Game Tree, a rocky knoll to the north of Mafeking with a tree perched on it, was chosen as a target because it was believed to be unmanned. The exercise was to boost morale and shake the lethargy from the troops. Occupied, it would be a death trap because there were 2,5 kilometres of open grassland to cover between Mafeking's outer defences and the thorn-scrub surrounded mound. On the brow, supposedly, was an open sand-bagged trench for 40 men with a bombproof shelter toward the rear. From Game Tree it was possible to see out, not in. Baden-Powell claimed he scouted the site on 23 December and reported it deserted.

It was a simple plan. The armoured train, under Williams, was to glide silently out of Mafeking at 3 am and take up a position 400 metres beyond Game Tree to cover the rear of the fort. The plan required the train to be in position before first light. Following the train was Vernon and a squadron of the Protectorate Regiment and Fitzclarence with another squadron. Their eastern flank was covered by a detachment of Bechuanaland Rifles commanded by Godley. To the south of the armoured train was a wheeled gun carriage under Major Panzera and a troop of Bechuanaland Rifles. In total 260 of the Garrison troops were involved in the operation. From their position, at first light, Williams would strafe the back of Game Tree while Panzera bombarded it from the front and covered Vernon's attacking squadron.

The night was calm with a light breeze from the north-west. The train, guided by two lookouts at the front who communicated via a mouthpiece, made its way quietly up the track. Eight hundred metres before their planned position the lookouts reported that a rail had been removed. To the left Game Tree was silhouetted against the starry sky rinsed with the light of the approaching day. Wisdom suggested they return to Mafeking. Vernon, however, decided to attack across the open ground without the cross fire cover from the train. He extended his men in a line and ordered them down in the long grass, waiting for Panzera's guns to open at first light at 4 am.

No-one bothered to inform Panzera of the problem or changed plans. The allotted time came and went and the only sounds to be heard were the chirping of waking birds. Panzera was puzzled that the train was not in position and held his fire. Nor could he see Vernon's troops sprawled in the grass. Time sped by as each group waited for the other. In the rear, Baden-Powell, appropriately at Fort Dummy, was frantically trying to get clarification.

After a half hour Panzera could wait no longer and opened fire. When 10 shells had been fired the train's whistle blasted the signal for Vernon to commence his attack. This was nowhere near sufficient bombardment, but the fort was supposed to be deserted so it was of no consequence. As the sun shoved its edge over the horizon so Vernon and his men rose from the grass only to come under murderous fire from Game Tree ahead of them. From behind, Creaky had been set to fire on their position as well. It still did not occur to anyone that they were entering a trap. The tall Vernon, his revolver drawn, staggered when the first bullet hit him. He got back to his feet and continued forward, though less certain. A second bullet hit him in the leg as he lunged up the slope and leapt into what was supposed to be an open trench but was covered by corrugated iron sheeting. The third bullet knocked him back down the rise and he gave a long bloody snore, stretched his legs and died. Even when a Maxim opened fire the squadron recklessly continued to sweep forward. Lieutenant Swinburne, who was with Fitzclarence, described his captain as 'like a hero in a silly woman's novel strolling about under fire, with the bullets spitting about all around him.' A bullet shattered Fitzclarence's thigh and he managed to drag himself to an anthill where he lit a cigarette. When Godley found the sense to stop this orchestra of terror and sound the retreat 24 lay dead, 23 were wounded and 3 captured. Troopers Ramsden and Martineau were awarded the Victoria Cross for bravery in assisting the injured.

Angus Hamilton, who reached the scene shortly after the retreat, reported: 'The heavy vapours from the shells still impregnated the air, and hanging loosely over the veld were masses of grey-black and brown-yellow smoke clouds. Boers on horseback and on foot were moving quickly in all directions ... the scene here was immensely pathetic and everywhere there were dead and dying men.' Hamilton also commented that while the majority of the Boers were sympathetic, some 'made attempts to rob the wounded and despoil the dead.' Tom Hayes who was on the train and remained to assist the dead and wounded noted: 'and a grim looking sight it was with their eyes staring straight open; some with their jaws blown off, others with fractured skulls and their brains scattered about.' Abraham Stafleu who watched the casualties being loaded onto the train recalled, 'Their blood oozed out of the wagon in a continuous stream.'

Plaatje is scathing in his diary: 'The Game Tree fiasco appears to be a heart rending burlesque. Never was such a wilful suicide committed by a community in our condition.'

Lady Sarah, shocked at what she saw, offered her services to the hospital. That evening, as she walked home, the 'Last Post' was wafting through the town. 'In the still atmosphere of a calm and beautiful evening, I knew that the last farewells were being said to the brave men who had gone to their last rest ... Of course Mafeking's losses on that Black Boxing Day were infinitesimal compared to those attending the terrible struggle going on in other parts of the country but, then, it must be remembered that not only was our garrison a very small one, but also that, when people are shut up together for months in a beleaguered town – a handful of Englishmen and women surrounded by enemies, with even spies in their midst – the feeling of comradeship and friendship is tremendously strengthened. Every individual was universally known, and therefore all the town felt they had lost their own friends, and mourned them as such.'

Game Tree was Baden-Powell's greatest blunder of the siege and the last of the 'hard kicks' that had all ended in disaster. Bell fumed, 'A fearful mistake was made ... all due to our not having carefully found out what we were going to attack ... lives had been thrown away for no purpose.'

Baden-Powell, in his report to Lord Roberts, claimed that his plans were betrayed to the Boers. There is no doubt of this. He claimed, however, that his intention in taking Game Tree was to extend the grazing to the north of the town and to open the way for relieving forces to enter Mafeking from that direction. Both claims are a ludicrous cover up. His assertion that he reconnoitred the site on 23 December is also laughable. Lieutenant Swinburne claims that the fort was a 'miniature Bastille' when they tried to storm it. The improvements could never have been undertaken in two days. A ditch had been dug in front, the ramparts raised to three metres and the trench, extended to accommodate 80 Boers, had been roofed in. Most damning was a black scout report on 25 December of increased activity at Game Tree. Baden-Powell, who was never forgiven by Vernon's mother, ended his report to Roberts with the statement that the debacle was a lesson for the Boers in that it was 'a brilliant example (of) the fatal results of storming a position.'

8

THE LONG GOODNIGHT

Man's inhumanity to man
Makes countless thousands mourn!
BURNS,' MAN WAS MADE TO MOURN'

The determined cheerful spirit of 1899 took a turn for the worse in 1900. As each message reached Mafeking informing Baden-Powell of further delays in the promised relief, so frustration and bitterness grew. Because a siege of this duration was never contemplated, the issue of supplies holding out became of greater and greater concern – and there is an unmistakable correlation between tightened rationing and mushrooming despair.

At the outset all livestock and essential stocks were commandeered and effectively belonged to the British military authorities. Price controls were introduced and the garrison supplies placed in the care of Weil under the command of Captains Ryan and Girdwood. Baden-Powell, in November, had estimated that food for the white garrison would last until the end of February and maize for the black residents until the end of December. It was assessed that there was plenty of red meat and fresh vegetables – grown largely in the market gardens along the Molopo. Shops were well stocked with necessities as well as luxuries and flour was sold side by side with pickled herring and pâté de foie gras.

Rationing was first instituted on 17 November, but, for whites, as Lady Sarah noted in December, this was hardly noticeable. Provisions 'at that early stage of the siege (were) as plentiful as ever, even the stock of Schweppes soda-water appearing inexhaustible. Besides this luxury, we had beautiful fresh tomatoes and young cabbages. The meat had resolved itself into beef, and beef only, but eggs helped out the menu, and the only non-existent delicacy was "fresh butter". This commodity existed in tins, but I must confess the sultry weather had anticipated the kitchen in that it usually appeared in the melted state.'

Baden-Powell wrote in his diary on 30 December 1899: 'Food reinspected: meat and groceries there are plenty ... and in going into meal I found that there is 60 days for both white and natives if my present system of rations for all is strictly adhered to.' But, messages were coming from Cape Town that relief could not be expected, at the earliest, before the end of May. There is no doubt that Baden-Powell was in a serious predicament and that stock taking and control were now the most important aspects of life in the beleaguered town. That rationing was necessary is beyond question. But, it was the discriminatory methods of distribution – of ensuring the white residents and British troops remained 'clean and plump' at the expense of the Tshidi-Barolong and black refugees – that raised queries and resulted in genocide.

> Time and Tide, they are both in a tale
>   'Woe to the weaker – woe!'
>   KIPLING, 'A DEPARTURE'

Baden-Powell's apologists have always pointed to the fact that he had little choice in the increasingly inhuman actions he pursued. Hogwash! That he contemplated sacrificing people based on the colour of their skin, particularly as it was this group that was effectively defending Mafeking, is obscene in itself. But an unexpected source provided a possible solution. Not only did he ignore it, he eliminated it because he was now concerned only with his growing personal stature and the implications of that for his career. It was essential, personally, for him to extend the siege as long as possible. The human costs of his efforts to keep Mafeking besieged, irrespective of the by-product boost it gave British morale, was, incalculably grotesque.

Chief Wessels advocated the mass arming of the Barolong to end the investment. At the time there was growing bitterness, particularly amongst the young Tshidi men, at the inability of Baden-Powell to resolve the matter when he had the means at his disposal. The word 'cowardice' cropped up more and more. At the end of December Thelesho Molema, a younger brother of Silas, agreed with Wessels when he wondered aloud to Plaatje 'why the authorities, seeing that the whites are afraid of the Boers, don't arm the Barolong as they would certainly go and rifle the "God-damned brutes away".'

The chief took action in late December and ordered tribespeople to refuse to work for the British or to act as runners. Wessels had wide support on this within his constituency but he lacked respect among the élite. Plaatje wrote. 'Wessels habitually parts with his 50 pounds after receiving his quarterly allowance. He would send several Cape Boys to buy some brandy for him. He would keep on sending one after the other and the last two or three would depart when the first had already returned, after which the old fellah would be so miserably under the exuberance of the damning drink as not to recognise the rest of them. Each of them would then pocket the 3/- and not bother about buying the brandy at all.'

The white authorities, with the support of the Barolong élite (including Plaatje), rather than heed Wessels decided to depose him for 'want of energy'. At a fiery meeting in the *stadt*, on 21 January, Baden-Powell and Bell held a meeting with the tribe where Plaatje acted as interpreter. Angus Hamilton reported that Wessels was placed on 'sick leave' and his duties transferred to two Barolong councillors: '[Wessels] told them in his amiable fashion that the English wished to make slaves of them, and that they would not be paid for any service which they rendered; nor would they be given any food, but left to starve when the critical moment came.' Wessels also warned his people that the British, if the food situation got worse, would expel the Tshidi from the town. It was as if he was peering into a crystal ball. One wonders if Plaatje would have made a different entry in his diary had Wessels been an esteemed leader: 'Things went on very smoothly until Wessels commenced to speak. He threw a different complexion on the otherwise excellent harmony which characterised the commencement of the proceedings. He misunderstood, misconstrued and misinterpreted every thing said and an undesirable scene ensued.' Once more the black élite were dazzled by British wile and missed a vital opportunity.

Chief Wessels had a premonition, which proved correct, when rationing was first introduced. The rationing then, though not life threatening, was discriminatory – in nutrition, quantity and variety – against the Barolong, and doubly so against the refugees. And, as stocks dwindled, distribution was tightened more for blacks than whites so that the gap between the two continually widened. Whites, though they grumbled about rationing before New Year, were not exposed to what blacks were already experiencing. It was reported, before December, that 'The kaffirs dig up dead horses and eat them, and sit picking on rubbish heaps. Some of them are starving.'

By the end of the siege blacks would receive 4 per cent of a white resident's total daily ration. Further, this allocation was inferior in quality as it consisted predominantly of indigestible rough grains – diverted from horse feed – and was deficient in protein and fresh vegetables. Moreover, blacks were not allowed to buy bread as flour and meal were considered 'white food'. The injustice of this is brutally evident when it is realised that most of the flour and meal reserved for the whites was commandeered at the beginning of the siege from the Barolong.

The inequity did not stop with the allocation of rations as they were not issued for free. Destitute whites who could not afford to buy their rations were provided theirs either on credit or via a special fund set up by the authorities. Credit facilities were not extended to blacks nor was the fund available to them. Considering that only 25 per cent of black residents had a family member employed during the siege makes the problem obvious. Historians have attempted to divert attention from this by claiming that blacks had access to land to continue growing crops while most whites did not. But, in reality, the continued shelling, the locust plague and the cutting off of blacks from their traditional lands by the Boer lines meant that no maize was able to be grown to supplement meagre rations.

Baden-Powell also employed devious ingenuity to make savings. He accused the Barolong of hoarding. His diary entry of 1 January stated: 'believe that large stores of grain hidden away in the *stadt*. Closed shop to see if there was any real want.' The shop was the store in the *stadt* from where grain was issued and by closing it he cut off essential supplies to the *stadt* – ostensibly to investigate whether deprivation would bring concealed stocks to the surface. But, Baden-Powell knew that Weil was the hoarder and that the wholesaler was profiteering. Baden-Powell entered in his diary: '[Weil's] stocks have been useful to us but his own duplicity has been a constant source of annoyance if not a danger.' Baden-Powell also suspected Weil of selling on the black market that flourished in Mafeking and of receiving stolen goods. By the end of the siege Weil had made a fortune from the investment. Baden-Powell took no action other than to have an 'unvarnished' talk with him, but, a black, caught hoarding even a sack of grain, could expect a prison sentence with seven days hard labour.

Bell eventually intervened and the store was re-opened, but efforts were doubled to sniff out concealed corn in the *stadt* and eliminate 'wastage'. As an example to the *stadt* it was decided to charge a group of Barolong women with wastage for making African beer. This gave Plaatje a glimpse of the chasm separating black and white culture. 'From a Serolong [Barolong cultural] point of view this whole jumble is more annoying than comforting. For this they [the military authorities] may be excused, as the arrangement is in the hands of young officers who know as little about Natives and their mode of living as they know about the man on the moon and his mode of living ... They do not know that kaffir beer to a common Morolong is "meat, vegetables and tea" rolled into one, and they can subsist entirely on it for a long time. If ever you wish to see the sense of the word economy, observe the kaffir beer by the amount of water poured into the corn to what is yielded.' Bell, again, was required to intercede. Though he managed to get the charges dropped, he was unsuccessful in convincing the British authorities that traditional beer was a saving.

The siege, by mid January, had endured for a 100 days. 'Houses are shattered,' reported Angus Hamilton, 'gaping holes in the walls and buildings, furrows in the roads, broken trees, wrecked telegraph poles, and that general appearance of destruction which marks the path of a cyclone are the outward and visible signs of the enemy's fire ... and, truth to tell, there is such glorious uncertainty about the date of our relief that it is perhaps possible that we may surpass the longest of historic sieges. At one time we confidently anticipated that the siege would be over in ten days. This, however, was in the days of our youth; since then we have learned wisdom, and eagerly seize opportunities of snapping up any unconsidered trifles in the way of bets which lay odds upon our being "out of the wood".'

As Barolong anger grew as a result of discrimination and their desperate situation, so the resentment of the whites increased. White residents were desperately unhappy about rationing; there were complaints from religious people about sport on Sundays; gripes that merchants were adulterating the sugar with sand and the coffee with meal; moans from patients that the hospital was overcrowded and the facilities inadequate; and accusations that military personnel were racketeering. Equally galling was the fact that the officers lived a life of luxury on 'gifts' from Ben Weil. Angus Hamilton reported: 'Mafeking at last is siege weary – and, oh, so hungry! It seems months since anyone had a meal which satisfied the pangs that gnaw all day … We are sick of it, so tired of the malaria, diphtheria and typhoid. We ask, when will the end be? And then we shrug our shoulders and begin to swear; for we have such sorrows in our midst … as would turn a saint to blasphemies!'

The whites were also offended by the manner in which the military authorities handled them. De Kock, Mafeking's leading attorney, was arrested for advising his clients, the merchants, that Baden-Powell had no legal rights to impound their stocks or interfere in their sale. The Town Guard, which included prominent citizens, were forced to take orders from junior officers and allotted the least interesting and most laborious tasks. Edward Ross, the local auctioneer, complained of continued 'kicks, sneers, arrogance and very little thanks'. Angus Hamilton picked up the growing air of bitterness: 'Those who were local merchants, men of peace, for the most part, with no very keen enthusiasm for martial glory, have seen the industry of a lifetime completely wrecked by the diffidence of the general staff and the unwillingness of the government to take such precautions as would have placed the town beyond the possibility of attack.' Baden-Powell noted in his diary 'that the townspeople are expressing themselves tired of the siege and of me, etc. they say … that I am asking for reinforcements not to be sent in order that I may gain kudos afterwards.'

Ross remarked of Baden-Powell, that 'there is always a future for him in the music hall'. However, even the diversionary activities, aimed at amusing the white citizens, were losing their lustre. Though crowds continued to be drawn to these events, they were lackadaisical. Angus Hamilton commented that Sundays had 'developed into a Sabbatarian charade in which we all assumed an active co-operation, and try to think we are having a giddy and even gushing time.' The jokes were stale, the sketches repetitive and the residents tired. 'Days roll into weeks and weeks into months,' sighed the busy Lady Sarah, 'but our life goes on here without much change or variation and yet there is a sort of change visible from the highest to the lowest. People are graver, there is a tired expression on most countenances, the women look paler, the children more pinched.' Another commented: 'Everybody, more or less, has the blues and is getting tired of it.'

The white residents blamed Baden-Powell for all their woes. This was not meanness, because the greatest accusation against him, and it encompassed all others, was that he was prolonging the siege for his own reputation. The townspeople were aware that Mafeking was 'making history' and they strongly suspected that their commander was revelling in it and extracting every ounce of glory for himself. Further, they believed he was minimising the dangers of their situation in his despatches and that this was the cause for the tardiness of the British in coming to their aid. This belief, that he was extending the siege, was widely held by the citizens, troops and the war correspondents. Neilly was hauled over the coals for trying to smuggle an uncensored letter to the *Pall Mall Gazette* in which he maintained that Baden-Powell was prolonging the siege as a 'promotion job'. Baden-Powell responded indignantly that he was totally unaware of, and unconcerned with, his growing fame and that Neilly was spreading 'barroom gossip'.

The enormously ambitious Baden-Powell, however, could hardly have failed to appreciate the potential the siege held for him. His sister wrote to him: 'Everyone is talking of you. You are the hero of the day … Your photo is in all the shops now.' Queen Victoria did not send him one, but two, telegrams: 'The Queen to Baden-Powell. I continue watching with confidence and admiration the patient and resolute defence which is so gallantly maintained under your ever resourceful command.'

Baden-Powell showed his hand with the issue of his famous 'Grousing Memorandum', which was printed in the *Mafeking Mail*. He could not risk all now and it contained an ominous threat to those who did not toe the line:

THE COLONEL ON 'GROUSING'

I hear that again wiseacres are busy in town, informing people as to what I am doing and what I am leaving undone. As their deductions are somewhat inaccurate I wish to state that the condition of affairs is in no way altered since my last general notice, which stated we must be prepared to remain besieged all that time. Indeed I hope that we may be free within the next fortnight or three weeks, but it would be folly on our part not to be prepared against possible unforeseen delays. Had we not been thus prepared in the first instance we should all have been prisoners in Pretoria by the beginning of January, and the Boers would now have been enjoying the use of our property in Mafeking.

I am, I suppose, the most anxious of anybody in Mafeking to see a relief column here and the siege at an end; all that can be done for our relief, from both north and south, is being done, but the moves of troops in the face of the enemy must necessarily be slow, and we have to sit in patience until they develop.

As regards the smallness of our rations, we could, of course, live well on full rations for a week or two and then give in to the 'women slaughterers' and let them take their vengeance on the town, whereas by limiting our amount of daily food we can make certain of outlasting all their efforts against us. The present ration, properly utilised, is a fairly full one as compared with those issued in other sieges — in fact I and my staff have, during the past few days, been living on a far smaller ration without any kind of extras to improve it — and we still live.

There are, by the way, two hints I should like to give for making small rations go further — hints derived from personal experience of previous hungry times — and these are: 1. To lump your rations together as much as possible for cooking, and not every man to have his little amount cooked separately. 2. To make the whole into a big thick stew, from which, even three quarter lbs. of ingredients per man, three good meals can be got per day.

It is just possible that we may have to take 2 ozs. off the bread stuffs, but otherwise our supplies will last well over the period indicated. It has been objected that we are feeding horses on oats, but the oats so used are a lot (of colonial oats) that have been found quite useless for making flour from for human consumption.

I am told that I keep back news from the public. This is not in accordance with facts, for I make a point of publishing all news of general interest as soon as possible after receipt, first by telephone, then by notices posted about, and lastly through Mr Whales, in the Mafeking Mail slips; I have no object whatever in keeping news back. Occasionally, of course, items of military information have to be kept quiet because, as we all know, their publication in Mafeking means their transmission within a few hours, to the enemy's camp.

Although it may have been somewhat out of my province, I have been writing to the High Commissioner as strongly as I could put them, the claims which the citizens and [white] refugees have for consideration in the matter of compensation, pressing for very early settlement on some more satisfactory basis than was the case on a former occasion. And there is no doubt that the good part they have borne in the defence of the place will add great force to their claims.

I have no feeling of doubt whatever that the large majority of the townspeople have sufficient confidence in me to know that I am working, as far as possible, for their good, but there are always busybodies in every assemblage to cavil at whatever is done, and I should just like to remind these gentlemen of the order issued early in the siege about 'grousing'.

I am always not only willing but anxious to personally hear any reasonable complaints or suggestions, and those who have them to make, need only bring their grievances to me to get what redress is in my power, but veiled hints and growlings cannot be permitted; at such times as these they are apt to put people 'on edge' and to alarm the ladies, and for these reasons they must be suppressed. 'Grousing' is generally the outcome of funk on the part of the individual who grouses, and I hope that every right-minded man who hears any of it will shut it up with an appropriate remark, or the toe of his boot. Cavillers should keep quiet until the siege is over and then they are welcome to write or talk until they are blue in the face.

By these remarks I do not wish for one instant to suggest that this 'grousing' is widespread. On the contrary the patience and loyal obedience of the main body of the inhabitants under the restrictions of martial law, form one of the conspicuous features of the siege. But there are a few individual grumblers – most of whom are known to me (as they will find when their claims for compensation come up for adjudication) – and it is these gentlemen that I desire to warn to keep quiet as otherwise I shall be ashamed if the fame of Mafeking and its heroic defence should be marred by any whisper among envious outsiders, that there was any want of harmony or unity of purpose among us.

R.S.S. BADEN-POWELL,
Colonel.

What the townspeople did not know was that Baden-Powell, the 'Hero of Mafeking', planned to abandon them if he believed he or his forces were in danger. He made secret contingency plans, if the situation required, to evacuate his forces to the west, taking all the garrison's ammunition and two days' rations with him. The town was to be left instructions to 'try and keep up appearances of the place being occupied for 2 to 3 days if possible', after which there was to be sent out a flag of truce. After the lengthy humiliation of the Boers, their reaction can only be shuddered at had this eventuality transpired.

But — with protest quelled, no immediate danger and his audience the Empire — now was not the time to think of abandoning the stage. He nearly sacrificed his Bulawayo force of Sir Herbert Plumer and 'The Boy', Kenneth McLaren, because of this. Plumer believed, wrongly, toward the end of March that a relieving force was on its way to Mafeking. Baden-Powell sent him a message to order him not to do anything as matters were not so desperate in the town as to warrant Plumer's joining with relieving forces.

Plumer, however, marched on the town on 30 March expecting Baden-Powell to assist him from within. Baden-Powell did nothing — even when Plumer was within 6 kilometres of Mafeking — other than launch a sham attack on Game Tree Fort. 'It looked like a review in the Phoenix Park, on a small scale,' snorted Tom Hayes. The Boers expected the worst. But, 'there were much fewer Englishmen than Boers had expected,' stated Abraham Stafleu. 'It was like a hunting trip, and shooting wild game.' Plumer lost 49 men — Baden-Powell none.

One of the wounded 'wild game' was 'The Boy'. Baden-Powell's little prince had been shot three times. He was informed that McLaren was dead and he rushed to the ambulance that brought the casualties only to find McLaren was not among them. He was then told there were fresh graves at the battlefield. Baden-Powell was beside himself with grief until, the following day, Snyman informed him that McLaren was a prisoner of the Boers and had received wounds to his stomach, back and leg. Baden-Powell wanted to rush to McLaren's side, but his officers restrained him. He, who had previously treated Snyman abruptly, now gushed as he begged his foe to release McLaren. Snyman refused. Baden-Powell sent Kruger a telegram requesting he overrule Synman. He received no reply. Baden-Powell contented himself by sending McLaren daily letters, cocoa, wine, a soft mattress, a silver hairbrush, books, eau-de-cologne, lemonade, stationery and money. Baden-Powell, enraged, ordered Plumer to make no further attempts to relieve Mafeking.

There is a reaper whose name is Death
LONGFELLOW

Any lingering doubts that Baden-Powell committed gross crimes against humanity are swept aside by his 'leave-or-starve' policy – a programme that would disgust even some of the Boer besiegers. Baden-Powell's apologists have either ignored the event or defend him by indicating that men such as Plaatje supported this action. Plaatje was in a difficult position. While a leader of his people, he was also employed by both the civil and military authorities. That he assisted in implementing the scheme is not in doubt, but he neither formulated the policy nor agreed with it. He was, in fact, appalled by the hardship it caused and huffed sarcastically 'The [British] would cause us to run over to the enemy and ask him for permission to settle outside peacefully and plough as usual.' Plaatje has also been criticised for supporting the rationing policy. This, again, is disingenuous because, sensibly, he supported rationing as essential – however, he was vociferously opposed to discriminatory rationing. Even though he was the only black resident to receive white rations, because of the importance of his position, he was deeply angered by the injustice he witnessed. On 24 January, when Baden-Powell issued the first proclamation that seriously affected rations to whites and further restricted those to blacks, Plaatje hissed, 'and white people are now going to buy food in rations and be compelled to buy small quantities, the same as blacks.'

The leave-or-starve policy is the event of the siege which has given historians the greater problems. Some, because the Boy Scout movement is so sensitive to His memory, have gone to enormous lengths to wish it away. The plan, however, was an aberrant, unspeakable act – a holocaust within a holocaust. The fact that it was not seemly, in a white man's war, to be rescued by a black tribe and, as a consequence, many died of starvation, is a crime for which the British must answer. Baden-Powell is not absolved – extending the siege for personal reasons and formulating policies he knew would be fatal for his black allies are offences for which he is directly responsible.

Neither, as has been claimed, was the leave-or-starve policy a scheme to rid Mafeking solely of the black refugees that were proving such a burden to the town's dwindling supplies. Nor was it a reaction to a message Baden-Powell received, in early February, that relief might be delayed until mid June. The lie of both these assertions is proved by the fact that Bell, at the January meeting with the Tshidi when Chief Wessels was deposed, raised the matter of the Barolong attempting to break out to relieve pressure on supplies. The truth is that though the black refugees suffered most from the leave-or-starve policy, as they were forced to leave, the Barolong were not exempt from its deadly consequences. And, the only reason it appears that Baden-Powell formulated this obscenity was to rid Mafeking of surplus blacks, keeping only the useful ones. It was thinking that had already gone into the Glen Grey Act in the Cape Colony, which sought to drive peasants and share-croppers from the land and turn them into wage labourers, and would later form a cornerstone of apartheid.

On 11 February Baden-Powell announced that grain would not be served to black refugees after 20 February, that they were to be banned from working and that passes to remain in Mafeking were to be issued them only in exceptional circumstances. 'I propose therefore to try and get all the refugees and foreign natives to leave the place by laying down stock through Colonel Plumer at Kanye and stopping the sale in the town,' he wrote. 'The amount thereby saved, eked out with occasional issues of meat, should keep the local Barolong and defence natives; the others could break out on stormy nights and make their way to Kanye.'

There are two reasons why the policy was a crime. As it was Snyman's intention to starve Mafeking into submission, he could hardly allow blacks to stream out of the town so that this eventuality could be delayed. Baden-Powell was well aware that Snyman would use all the means at his disposal to prevent even one person leaving. He cynically sent Snyman a letter of protest regarding Boer treatment of evictees. Snyman replied that the person sending these people to their death should not espouse their cause. Further, Baden-Powell claimed, correctly, that he had instructed Plumer to lay down provisions for these evacuees at Kanye in Bechuanaland. Most were so weakened, however, that they would have difficulty crossing a road, let alone making a considerable journey of 100 kilometres on foot.

Neilly, observing the black starvelings, wrote: 'I saw them fall down in the veld and lie where they had fallen, too weak to go on their way. The sufferers were mainly little boys – mere infants ranged from four or five upwards.' On another occasion he wrote: 'Hunger had them in its grip and many of them were black specks of living skeletons ... their ribs literally breaking their shrivelled skin.' Bell was also moved by the blacks who leaned over his garden wall and complained of hunger – 'at the same time the fact is demonstrated by the supplicant smiting with his hand the black empty leather bag which represents his stomach'. The magistrate also recalled that his yard was 'always filled with natives, who came in connection with their food supply: one man, a tall thin fellow, past fifty, when I was busy with other people about sunset, reclined on his back and proceeded to die of starvation.'

Baden-Powell, according to Neilly, informed the refugees 'that they could go over the lines in comparative safety.' 'The natives have been sent out in batches,' wrote a white resident. 'They are not armed and they have to walk through the Boer lines, at the risk of being shot. They must not return. It does seem hard lines. But of the two evils, the risk of being shot at is the simpler as it would mean starvation living here.'

The darkness of night swallowed these desperate skin-and-bone people long before the sounds of children crying in fear and the soothing voices of their frantic barefoot mothers died. This was the beginning of their ordeal. Refugee groups were sniped at, fired upon, stripped, flogged, tortured or had their throats cut by Boers who were ordered by Snyman to ensure no one left the town. A party of expelled women were stripped, flogged and ordered naked back to town; a group of 13 women were fired on at close range near Game Tree in an outrage where seven were killed and four severely wounded; and, two days later, nine out of a party of 11 were killed. And so it continued. Many who made it past the enemy lines were hunted by the Boers or lay down and died along the way. Chief Bathoen, a Tswana chief, sent humanitarian support and men to bring refugees to safety. Had he not done this the tragedy would have multiplied manyfold.

By the end of the siege most of the refugees had left and nearly half of the Barolong residents. Tshidi labourers who attempted to assist the remaining refugees by smuggling them into work parties were lectured, by Baden-Powell, on misplaced humanity. Angus Hamilton indignantly reported to The Times: 'There can be no doubt that the drastic principles of economy which Colonel Baden-Powell has been practising in these later days are opposed to ... the dignity and liberalism we profess, and which enter so much into the settlement of native questions in South Africa.' The article was spiked.

The most needy were being cast into the wilderness. The choice was simple — leave here or starve here. While this life-or-death decision was being contemplated, Baden-Powell was concentrating on the weighty issue of diverting the white residents' attention from their troubles with cycle sports:

WITH THE SANCTION OF THE COLONEL COMMANDING

CYCLE SPORTS
(postponed on account of conditions of the ground)
will be held at the
RECREATION GROUND
On
Sunday, February 18th
Commencing at 3.30pm

Lady Sarah Wilson has kindly consented
To distribute the prizes, which comprise:
Watches; a clock a most handsome hand-painted
"Wateau" fan; Silver Glove Buttoner;
Candlestick Mirror, Silver Mounted Pipes
Amber Cigarette Holders; Cigarette Cases; etc.

Referee: H.H. Major Goold-Adams
Judges: Major Godley; Capt. Cowan, Inspector Marsh
Handicaps: Lieut. Colonel Walford, Inspector Browne
Starter: C.G.H. Bell, Esq., C.C. & R.M.
Clerk of Course} To be appointed
Lap Scorer} on the Ground

The Totalisator
will be upon the Grounds
under charge of Sergt. Major Merry
***

By the kind permission of Capt. Cowan
the band of the Bechuanaland Rifles will
play during intervals.

As the effects of the famine on the black residents became more obvious by the day, so white citizens began to put pressure on Baden-Powell to alleviate their misery. Baden-Powell took a decision for which he has received misplaced praise. The most obvious solution, as his cavalry were sitting immobile in trenches and he intended no further 'hard kicks', was to convert horses into food. It occurred to him, probably from a suggestion from Lady Sarah, that the best cuts of the horses could be allocated to whites while the remainder could be used in the brewing of soup for blacks. But, again, he was being cynical because he planned to issue this watery soup as a substitute for rations — savings that could then bolster white provisions.

A foul-smelling horse-meat factory, fired by fuel made from cured dung and belching columns of black smoke, was established to the south-west of Mafeking. Baden-Powell related how the slaughtered horses were processed. 'When a horse was killed, his mane and tail was cut off and sent to the hospital for stuffing mattresses and pillows. His shoes went to the foundry for making shells. His skin, after having the hair scalded off, was boiled with his head and feet for many hours, chopped up small, and ... served up as "brawn". His flesh was taken from the bones and minced in a great mincing machine and from his inside were made skins into which the meat was crammed and each man received a sausage as his rations. The bones were then boiled into a rich soup, which was dealt at the different soup kitchens; and they were afterwards pounded up into powder with which to adulterate the flour.'

> Child as he was, he was desperate with hunger, and reckless with misery. He rose from the table; and advancing to the master, basin and spoon in hand, said somewhat alarmed at his own temerity —
>
> 'Please, sir, I want some more,'
>
> The master was a fat, healthy man; but he turned very pale. He gazed in stupefied astonishment on the small rebel for some seconds, and then clung to the copper. The assistants were paralysed with wonder; the boys with fear.
>
> 'What?' said the master at length, in a faint voice.
>
> 'Please, sir,' replied Oliver, 'I want some more.'
>
> CHARLES DICKENS, OLIVER TWIST

To the sweet sounds of the Regimental Band drifting pleasingly from the bandstand in the white town, the black starvelings were forced to purchase, from unsmiling matrons organised by Gordon and Lady Sarah, the festering broth from which grinning yellow-toothed heads could be seen squinting from the unctuous medley.

The ingredients of this 'horse' soup were supposed to be a secret and Baden-Powell censored an issue of the *Mafeking Mail* that commented on the abominable smell emanating from the horse-meat factory and the contents of the broth. And he should have been concerned because inside the factory was a nightmarish jamboree of sights and sounds. Horses were led onto the concrete floor and shot and, as they crumpled, they were struck twice with an axe to remove the head. The carcass, the legs still twitching, was then hung from a metal post and slit from one end to the other. The blue and yellow entrails, which writhed into a bucket, were then sorted and the waste tipped in the cauldron of soup. Alongside these dripping carcasses, which were then processed as Baden-Powell recalled, were the pink and sheeny undressed carcasses of dogs. The dogs that ended in the pot were *stadt*, or unlicensed, dogs. White residents were able to keep their pets if they bought a license, blacks could not as licenses were not issued them. Over 90 'unlicensed' dogs were shot for the soup. This 'rich', bountiful repast was enhanced with mules, chicken carcasses, locusts and husks.

There were three soup kitchens in the *stadt*, one in the Fingo Location and one in the refugee camp. Neilly reported 'Words could not portray the scenes of misery; five or six hundred human frameworks of both sexes and all ages ... dressed in ... tattered rags, standing in lines, each holding an old blackened can or beef tin, awaiting their turn to crawl painfully up to the soup kitchen where the food was distributed.'

The soup was not free. It cost 3d. a pint. Those that could not afford to buy the broth were supposed to be given it free. Plaatje contests this: 'Mr Bell issues free tickets to people without means and they always come to say that they do not get any soup although they had the ticket'. The British military coffers were swollen by over 3 000 pounds collected from these kitchens in the closing months of the siege.

The black residents were so hungry they foraged and fought on rubbish heaps and exhumed corpses of long dead animals from a pit outside the town. Neilly reported that blacks 'picked up meat-tins and licked them; they fed like outcast curs. They went farther than the mongrel. When a dog gets a bone he polishes it white and leaves it there. Day after day I heard outside my door continuous thumping sounds.

163

They were caused by the living skeletons who, having eaten all that was outside the bones, smashed them up with stones and devoured what marrow they could find. They looked for bones on the dustheaps, on the roads, everywhere.'

Some whites were shocked at the conditions of their black neighbours; others were concerned that blacks would steal their rations; most were terrified when a report of cannibalism circulated. Ada Cock would not let her children out of her sight: 'There were a lot of Shangaans under the trees here and they have been stealing my fowls. I have only nine left. They [the refugees] are dying of starvation. I don't know what they have been living on but the smell is something dreadful. They have been moved up to the empty Police Barracks and are killing and eating all the dogs they can get. Arthur says he believes they ate their dead chum as he was never carted away. Arthur is caretaker there and someone said he smelt human flesh roasting. It is quite dangerous to let the children run about by themselves. I don't know.' To protect white supplies, Baden-Powell instituted patrols in the town to shoot looters or those stealing food.

Plaatje, who stole Bell's grapes, was fortunate in that he dealt with the magistrate and not Baden-Powell.

> We have been testing to see if the Civil Commissioner's grapes are ripe; so far we have only been able to discover that they are sweet, but we cannot yet tell if they are ripe or green. There is, however, no likelihood of this being found out until there are no more grapes to taste!

> This morning I went round for another taste. I tried to pick only as much as necessary for tasting, when the whole bunch came down on my hand – rather a heavy weight. It weighed about three pound, but I was not the fool to replace it, although it was far too much more than I required ... just when I came in, I heard 'Do you know who always steals my grapes?'

> 'No.'

> 'To steal is no answer ... by Jove! It is you who always steals my grapes. Can't you fellows do without stealing?'

> I thought that the next question might be too unpleasant and I tried

to modify the flowing tide before it grew worse, so I began:

'I have only been eating ("eating" mind you and not "stealing") those in front of the stable, Sir.'

'I don't see why you should steal them even if they were at the back of the stable, for your father didn't steal any grapes.'

I successfully stemmed the tide when I interpolated: 'Well my father didn't work for the Magistrate.'

He turned around and went on with his business. He was still smiling when he eventually gave me the sweetest bunch in the garden!

SOL PLAATJE, MAFEKING DIARY

Charles Weir, the bank clerk, also showed humanity. He contended that his rations were more than sufficient and always spared some so that he may 'be able to satisfy some poor creature.'

Whites' rations, though more plentiful and nourishing, were only fractionally more appetising. The horse-meat butchery issued 500 kilograms of horse sausage daily, a delicacy reserved for whites. The plague of locusts also supplemented their diet. Taking a leaf from Baden-Powell's act, Lady Sarah sent a message to England: 'Breakfast today horse sausage. Lunch minced mule curried locusts. All well.' and, Private Sims achieved fame by recalling a recipe called 'sowens' − a porridge made from the husks of forage oats. It was filling and just palatable when seasoned with salt.

Baden-Powell again took stock in April and made this diary entry: 'Ap 20: Meat and meal stocks at present will last to June 12. But by forcing natives away ... we can get their share ... for whites.' Another wave of leave-or-starve rationing policies were instituted with the same deadly effects. Freed from the immediate worries of rations once more, Baden-Powell immersed himself in designing Mafeking's own one pound note − to be issued because the Standard Bank had run short of coins. His drawing depicted a Union Jack fluttering above three defenders with fixed bayonets, a young lady with child in arms and a cannon with a pyramid of spherical shells beside it. Once he had finished that, it was off to the photographic studio to sit for a portrait that would go onto the 'Siege

Stamp'. To his mother he wrote: 'My head on it. That, I think, is proof of our being an independent republic in Mafeking'. But it was lese-majesty, high treason in times of war, to depose the monarch from her rightful place. A murmur went round the town, already deeply suspicious of Baden-Powell, that this was the culmination of his autocracy.

A hasty cover-up was ordered. Soon the 'true' story appeared that ran something like this: Stamps were running short and Godley, Cecil and the Postmaster were discussing what to put on the beleaguered town's own issue. 'Oh B-P's head, of course!' Cecil is said to have exclaimed. The project was a special surprise for him and the trio kept it secret until they presented him with them. 'I don't like it,' he said, on being shown the stamps. Baden-Powell, sadly, had them withdrawn and reissued with a sketch of one of the Cadet Corps delivering letters on a bicycle.

In April the last rains fell and the oppressive heat lost its sting. The shelling also stopped as Creaky and the guns were needed elsewhere. The last shell, ironically, hit the Dutch church. The residents, finally, were free from their bunkers. During this temporary respite, Lady Sarah, concerned for those who had lost their homes and livelihood, wrote to her sister suggesting the possibility of a fund being established for the benefit of the residents of Mafeking. 'She implores me' wrote Georgina in an appeal letter, 'to take active measures to bring before the British public the destitute conditions of the nuns, refugees and civilians generally in Mafeking. She writes with authority, having witnessed the sufferings herself, and, indeed, having shared equally with them the anxieties and privations of this prolonged siege.' The response was immediate and soon the fund, waiting for the town to be relieved, stood at 29 000 pounds.

9

SOLD DOWN THE RIVER

Take up the White Man's burden —
Have done with childish days —
The lightly proffered laurel,
The easy, ungrudged praise.
Come now, to search your manhood
Through all the thankless years,
Cold, edged with dear-bought wisdom,
The judgement of your peers!
KIPLING, 'THE WHITE MAN'S BURDEN'

The bombardment stopped, the investment did not. Kruger wanted it over at all costs — Britain was not to have the moral victory. On 24 April his charismatic, impetuous grandson, Veldcornet Sarel Eloff, was sent with reinforcements, which included 40 French and German volunteers, to take Mafeking. The good-looking Eloff, a fervently nationalistic swaggerer with humorous blue eyes and square jaw, was a man from the Baden-Powell mould.

His first action was to send Baden-Powell a note challenging the garrison to a cricket match: 'To Colonel Baden-Powell. I see in the Bulawayo Chronicle that your men in Mafeking play cricket on Sundays and give concerts and balls on Sunday evenings. In case you would allow my men to join in the same it would be very agreeable to me ... Wishing you a pleasant day, I remain your obliging friend, S. Eloff'. Baden-Powell — put out by a competitor in the theatrical stakes — declined: 'Sir, I beg to thank you for your letter of yesterday ... I should like nothing better — after the match in which we are at present engaged is over. But just now

we are having our innings and have so far scored 200 days, not out ...
and we are having a very enjoyable game. I remain, yours truly, R.S.S.
Baden-Powell.'

Eloff, however, was not there to play games as he was planning a
melodramatic finale to the siege before Colonel Mahon's relieving force,
that was advancing from Kimberley, reached Mafeking. His plan was
simple: the *stadt* had always been Baden-Powell's blind spot and the black
defenders were angry and weakened by hunger. He would take a force to
the west and double back along the banks of the Molopo. Once he
entered the *stadt* he would signal Snyman, to the east, who would feint an
attack from that direction. Eloff, once inside the south-west defence lines,
would then only have the old mud-brick police headquarters to negotiate
before entering Mafeking. For him the only imponderable was the
reliability of Snyman. He did not reckon with the Tshidi saving Baden-
Powell once more.

Snyman was essential to Eloff's plan. He could probably take Mafeking
without Snyman's assistance, but never hold it. Persuading the general to
support him was not easy and a bitter argument ensued. Eloff was so
concerned about Snyman, that, when he finally assented, Eloff insisted
that he give his approval in writing. Eloff then left for his laager at Jackal
Tree and posted a message. 'We leave for Mafeking tonight. We shall
breakfast tomorrow at Dixon's Hotel.' So confident was he that he gave
an interview to the Reuters agent who was so impressed that he rushed
off to file the story before it happened. Premature headlines flashed round
the world: 'Fall of Mafeking − Fort after Fort captured − the whole town
in flames − Baden-Powell's despair.'

It was a fine, bitterly cold morning, with a westerly breeze, on 12 May,
when Eloff reached the westerly point of the Molopo, at 2 am, from
where he would commence his approach. With him were the 40 foreign
volunteers and 750 Boers of the Marico and Rustenburg commandos, of
which 500 were to stay back until the defences were penetrated. The
force dismounted, sent their horses back to Jackal Tree, crossed to the
north bank and waited for the brilliant full moon, that bathed the veld
silver, to begin setting before they moved. In pitch darkness they passed
between the two forts that made up the southern defences as they edged
along the river, using the nodular roots that twist in and out of the bank
as hand-holds. Shortly after 3.30 am the Boers reached the *stadt* and
scrambled up the river bank. The silhouette of the huts stood in relief

against the blue-black wall of night sky as Eloff struck a match, lit a tuft of grass and torched the thatch of the first hut he reached. This was the agreed signal for Snyman to commence his feint. But, the torching did not stop with this as Eloff believed that if he created panic in the *stadt* he could drive the frenzied mob ahead of him into Mafeking and sow confusion. Soon the sky was awash with fire as the Boers swept into Mahikeng.

Bedlam ensued as shrieking mothers picked up wailing children and fled toward Mafeking. From the east the crackle of gunfire could be heard as Snyman commenced his feint. Mafeking was woken as alarm bells rang out and frantic buglers called the defenders to their posts. Baden-Powell thought it another Boer demonstration and settled in for coffee. For Eloff, matters appeared to be running smoothly. The Barolong were stampeding as planned and his fears of Snyman had proved groundless. But, he was wrong. Behind him the Barolong men had let the Boers pass but then closed ranks — effectively cutting them off. And, to the east, unbeknown to Eloff, Snyman was only going through the motions as he desperately needed Eloff to fail because, if the upstart succeeded, his ineffectual command would be laid bare.

Nurse Craufurd, who lived to the west of Mafeking with her maid Elsie, woke with a start, peered out the window and saw the *stadt* in flames. She and Elsie hurriedly dressed and ran for the hospital. 'Shall I ever forget that run. Bullets seemed to come from all round, whizzing near us, and our legs seemed as if they would not move fast enough. Elsie fell, and I thought she was hit; but I helped her up. . . . As we ran I saw a crowd – a black mass of people it seemed, running from the *stadt* towards the BSAP fort. I nearly fell in the hospital; my legs were trembling so . . . After a little we heard cheering from the fort, and we were afraid to think what it could mean. Presently, we saw men looking in . . . As they came nearer and we saw them plainer, we said to each other they were Boers. As they passed us, we called out to them: "Who are you, and where are you going?" They said: "We are Republicans. The town is ours; your Colonel is a prisoner." Elsie threw up her hands, and began to cry and wail.'

Baden-Powell might well have become a prisoner had the Barolong not taken matters of defence in hand. They split Eloff's force in three, leaving him with 150 men to advance on the police barracks. A second group of Boers was cut off and surrounded in a kraal and the remainder either killed or forced toward the rocky outcrop that gave Mahikeng its name.

Barolong anger at the torching of their town spilled over and only Captain Marsh, under extreme personal danger, saved these trapped Boers' lives. 'At fearful personal risk [Captain Marsh] jumped amongst them and interposed himself between the cowering Boer and their would-be murderers', reported a witness.

Mafeking was still unaware of what was happening to the west. Soldiers in greatcoats stood around Market Square stamping their feet and blowing warmth into their fingers. Lady Sarah, who moved into Dixon's Hotel when the shelling of Mafeking stopped, recalled: 'All the previous week things had been much as usual: inferior food, and very little of it; divine weather; bridge in the afternoons; and one day exactly like another. In the early hours of the morning came the real event we had been expecting ever since the beginning of the siege — namely, a Boer attack under cover of darkness. The moon had just set, and it was pitch-dark. A fierce fusillade first began from the east, and when I opened the door onto the stoep the din was terrific, while swish, swish, came the bullets just beyond the canvas blinds, nailed to the edge of the verandah to keep off the sun ... The firing never abated, and I had a sort of idea that any moment a Dutchman would look in at the door ... In various stages of dishabille people were running round the house seeking for rifles, fowling-pieces, and even sticks, as weapons of defence. The Cockney waiter ... had dashed off to his redoubt, taking the keys of the house in his pocket, so no-one could get into the dining-room to have coffee, except through the kitchen window ... Hurried footsteps passed to and fro, dark lanterns flashed for an instant, intensifying the blackness, and all of a sudden the sound I had been waiting for added to the weird horror of the situation, an alarm bugle, winding out its tale ... followed by our tocsin, the deep-toned Roman Catholic Church bell, which was the signal that a general attack was in progress ... I went out to the front of the house facing the *stadt*, and therefore sheltered from the hail of bullets coming from the east ... Lurid light shot up into the sky in the direction where, snug and low by the Molopo River, lay the natives' habitation. Even then one did not realise what was burning, and someone said: "What a big grass fire!"'

The smell and crackle of burning thatch and wood permeated the air as Eloff made for the Police Fort and barracks from where he could control access to Mafeking. The Police Fort, which now served as Hore's headquarters, was a rectangular building constructed by General Sir Charles Warren 15 years previously. When the alarm bells had rung the troops stationed in the barracks had rushed for Market Square, leaving Hore, 21 men and Angus Hamilton who had spent the night there. Hore drew his men behind a wall but they were overrun as the first light of morning broke through the trees. One British trooper was killed in the brief skirmish and the rest captured.

At 6.30 am, Campbell, Baden-Powell's telephone operator, received a call from Hore's headquarters, from a man with a foreign accent, who informed him that the fort and Hore were captured. It finally dawned on Baden-Powell what was happening, but he was in a quandary. He had few troops to spare because, logically, he expected Snyman to attack from the east. He ordered Godley to the western defences to organise the few troops there and the Barolong defenders while he kept his main forces to the east of the town. Baden-Powell took the opportunity, before the expected attack came, to write a note to McLaren: 'Dear Boy. I hope you were not too disturbed by heavy firing in the night ... let me know if you want any clean pyjamas.'

Had Snyman attacked now it is unlikely Baden-Powell would have held Mafeking. The situation was so serious that prisoners, other than those charged with High Treason, were temporarily released to assist with defence works. For his bravery on this day Murchison had his death sentence commuted to life imprisonment. So alarmed was Weil that he managed to find some new rifles and a stock of ammunition in his stores, which had 'somehow' been overlooked, that were issued to anyone who could hold a gun.

Eloff, surrounded by Godley and his predominantly Barolong force, began his wait for his reinforcements and Snyman's attack, which never came. He realised that the 500 Boers he left up the Molopo were blocked, but remained confident throughout the day that Snyman would fulfil his side of the bargain. Nor was everything running smoothly in the barracks. Hore's own troops broke into the barrack stores and began looting. Incredibly, for a town supposedly suffering from shortages, were crates of whisky, wine, oranges, biscuits and tinned fruit and vegetables. Eloff's French soldiers, in particular, appreciated the stocks of wine. While one played the piano in the mess, another climbed onto the roof, waved a bottle of burgundy and shouted 'Fashoda est venge!' His heels skidded and he fell back dead, struck by a hail of bullets. The bottle of Burgundy, unscathed, was rescued by a connoisseur as it rolled from the roof.

As matters lurched out of control Eloff herded Hore's men into a room which became a fetid coop because one of the men was suffering from acute dysentery. Eloff visited the prisoners at regular intervals for a chat. 'He seemed to possess the complete mastery of the situation, his buoyant face was impressed with confidence of youth,' reported Angus Hamilton. 'He sat within the door on a case of Burgundy, his legs dangling, his accoutrements jingling, and the rowel of his spurs echoing the tick-tacking of the Mauser rifles'.

While the stand-off continued at the Police Fort, Lady Sarah went to assist at the hospital. Here one of the most enduring myths of the Boy Scouts, the legend of 'doing one's best', is supposed to have taken place. Baden-Powell, later, in fireside talks with scouts, would tell the story of young Hazelrigg who, he claimed, was shot near the heart when taking a message to Godley. He was bleeding to death when he reached the hospital. Lady Sarah consoled him by brushing his forehead with eau-de-Cologne. Just before he breathed his last he turned to her and sighed: 'Tell the Colonel, Lady Sarah, I did my best to give the message, but they got me first.' In reality, according to R. Urry, the manager of Standard Bank, poor Hazelrigg was shot in the groin and 'shrieked in a high treble voice for about five minutes before he died.'

The sun was gone and the gentle blue evening light was pierced with stars when Eloff finally decided to surrender. But, the telephone had been pulled from the wall and it was too dark for a white flag to be seen. Hore eventually managed to shout 'Cease fire! Cease fire!' to those surrounding the fort. Of Eloff's men, 60 were killed and 108 captured. The garrison lost 12 dead, mainly Barolong defenders. Tom Hayes commented that the Barolong had fought splendidly, driving the Boers out of Mafeking. Abraham Stafleu, convinced Snyman was a treacherous coward, wrote: 'Snyman is reported to have said, when Eloff captured the B.S.A.P. fort, that it wasn't necessary to send reinforcements to Eloff. They had the fort and tomorrow was another day.'

The Boer prisoners were taken to the Masonic Hall, which was to serve as their jail, and Eloff to Baden-Powell who was waiting for him in Market Square. 'Good evening, Eloff,' Baden-Powell greeted. 'You're just in time for dinner.' While they dined at Dixon's, Whales was writing the report of the day's events for the *Mafeking Mail*. Baden-Powell refused to allow him to print it because it referred to the Barolong involvement. Whales refused to retract the offending parts and the article was printed only after Baden-Powell left Mafeking.

Next morning, a steely autumn Sunday, Baden-Powell and Lady Sarah were joined at breakfast by Eloff and two officers – one German, the other French. During the meal Eloff cursed Snyman; the German requested that he be allowed to leave Mafeking as detention would land him in trouble with the German army from which he was on leave; and the Frenchman, who could not speak English, chatted 'about the African climate, the weather, and the Paris Exhibition.' 'It was', said Lady Sarah, 'one of the most curious meals at which I have ever assisted.' That evening a thanksgiving service was held in one of the churches – from which sonorous prayers and hearty songs issued through its pitted roof. 'We were rather mad,' explained one of the congregants, 'and it gave us a pleasant feeling to sing nice fighting psalms and hymns, because whichever way you look at it we are perfectly convinced out here that it is a righteous war.'

And there was cause for celebration: the end was in sight. 'As we near the end of the siege,' commented Lady Sarah, 'our conditions in the town are perhaps becoming more cheerful.' But, still, it was not over. Abraham Stafleu wrote that 'Word reached the Boer high command that Colonel Mahon and his relief column had reached Vryburg. Louis Botha with the support of President Kruger appointed Koos De la Rey to the position of head of operations on the western frontier. He arrived at Mafeking on 14 May, after Eloff's rout. De la Rey immediately left with a hundred men for Rietfontein to join up with General Liebenberg.'

The cannons roar was heard for miles,
    Around that little town,
Our Powell fought with might and main,
    For honour and renown.
The cruel Dutchmen thought they had,
    Fixed on bully beef,
But now let us sing the praises,
    'Of Mafekings relief.

And when the news was sent abroad,
    We gave a hearty shout,
For the brave men of Mafeking,
    Who kept old Kruger out.
They dined on horse flesh and locusts,
    'Twas our sad belief,

But now we know the news has come
  'Of Mafekings relief

Union Jacks were hoisted higher,
  For Powell's bravery
The shouting, singing, down the street,
  Showed Mafeking was free.
Now we must hunt old Kruger out,
  Whose caused a deal of grief,
The news we never shall forget.
  'Of Mafekings relief.

ERNEST HALL, 'THE RELIEF OF MAFEKING', A PATRIOTIC SONG

Much of Mahon's force of 1 100 — both Willoughby and White were amongst the officers — was made up of ex-members of Jameson's raiders who had done so much to cause the war and focus Boer attention on Mafeking. The Relief Column, at Setlagole, where Metalka joined them, moved west to avoid 600 Boers waiting at Koedoesrand on the main road to Mafeking. The Boers continued to snipe at their flanks and by the time they reached the Molopo, on 15 May, they had suffered 31 casualties. Plumer, with 800 men, joined Mahon at Massibi, 25 kilometres west of Mafeking. Waiting for them at Israel's Farm 15 kilometres further along the river, were De la Rey and Liebenberg with 2 000 Boers.

The residents of Mafeking sat on their roofs peering to the west on 16 May. They could hear the sounds of battle and see the banking cloud of dust. Knowing the column was facing De la Rey, most gave up hope and returned to the finals of the Siege Billiards Tournament. But, by sundown, Mahon had routed the Boers and broken through. He sent Major Karri Davis with an advance scout of Imperial Light Horse into Mafeking. At 7.00 pm Davis, with an ostrich plume in his hat, clattered into Market Square. 'Oh yes, I heard you were knocking about,' remarked a passer-by as Davis introduced himself.

Filson Young was with Colonel Peakman when they were confronted by a sentry at the outer defences who gave the rescuers a more spirited welcome.

'Halt! Who goes there?' shouted the guard.
'Friend!'
'Who are you?' he persisted.

'Colonel Peakman, in command of the Advance Guard of the Relief Column.'

'By jove, ain't I glad to see you, sir!'

AWA Pollock, of *The Times* and also with the Relief Column, remarked as they rode through the eerie moon-washed streets and observed the shattered housefronts throwing ragged black shadows: 'More damage was done in a single street in Mafeking than in the whole of Kimberley.' By the time the main body reached the town at 3.30 am, bringing with them wagons of food, on 17 May, the news had spread and a crowd singing 'Rule, Britannia' and 'Red, White and Blue' were waiting for them. Filson Young summed up the atmosphere: 'No art could describe the handshaking and the welcome and smiles on the faces of these tired-looking men; how they looked with rapt faces at us commonplace people from the outer world as though we were angels, how we all tried to speak at once, and only succeeded in gazing at each other and saying, "By Jove!" "Well I'm hanged!" and the like senseless expressions that sometimes mean much to Englishmen. One man tried to speak, then he swore; then he buried his face in his arms and sobbed.'

But, the man-of-the-hour was nowhere to be seen. His brother, Baden Baden-Powell, who was with Mahon, was nearly frantic. But all was well and he gave a great sigh when they found Impeesa — the wolf that never sleeps — fast asleep.

10

EXODUS

'I was so upset by the news ... that I went to bed with a headache.'
VIOLET CECIL ON BEING INFORMED OF THE RELIEF OF MAFEKING

How Britons, far and near, have watch'd the course
Of that grand stand, which they have grandly made
For Law and Liberty, for Right and Truth
Their eyes would soon be dry, their pallor cease,
And the bright glow, drawn from the consciousness
Of Duty bravely done, would gild their brows.
E GILBERT HIGHTON, 'THE SIEGE OF MAFEKING', A PATRIOTIC SONG

The first to leave Mafeking was Snyman. Mahon and Baden-Powell, as the sun grew warm and bright, undertook operations on the morning of 17 May to clear the Boers from round the town. 'It was a great sensation,' said Tom Hayes, 'After seven months shelling from the Boers, to be with our modern guns and see the enemy clearing like flies. Trench after trench full fled before the terrible aim of our shrapnel ... They had deserted most of their kit, lots of ammunition, cooking utensils and food. ... B.P. told Major Anderson, Willie [William Hayes] and myself to go over and take the hospital and any of our wounded that might be there ... Here we found Captain McLaren'. When they assisted The Boy out, Baden-Powell, on seeing his 'best friend in the world', broke down, flooded with emotion.

Abraham Stafleu, in his last diary entry, took up the story: 'The first bombs began to fall on McMullen "Grand Hotel" at 9.00 a.m. The burghers speedily abandoned their forts leaving everything just where it was. Some were only half dressed, without shoes or jackets which were left behind in their flight. Meal, sugar, coffee, rice, potatoes, clothes and ammunition were all left behind. For this bounty there was one man to thank, that same man that should have been awarded a Victoria Cross and the thanks of the English nation, and that was General Koos Snyman ... A laager was set up at Malmani and General De la Rey came to talk to the men. A group of Eloff's men informed the general about the circumstances surrounding the capture of their commandant and told De la Rey that they refused to fight any longer under Snyman. Even the burghers from his own district wanted nothing more to do with him. De la Rey was able to convince the Boers to continue fighting only when he placed them under his direct command ... This was the result of seven month's work. Under good and honest leadership the Boers could have defeated a far larger enemy. They were disorganised and demoralised under the leadership of a man who used his position to enrich himself and not to lead or manage.'

In Mafeking, the ordeal was over. The Relief Column, after clearing the Boers, officially entered the bunting-bedecked Market Square 217 days after the siege began. Following them, to wild cheering from the residents, were the defenders of Mafeking. Though the residents were 'giddy with relief', the atmosphere was pervaded by anti-climax. No part of the town was untouched by the lick of hell – iron roofs torn and twisted and flopping down, house corners crushed in and not a pane of glass anywhere, doors of empty houses drifted back and forth in the gentle breeze, hotels and shops a battered maze of splintered wood, the Mafeking railway sign aslant, Dixon's clock stopped at 2.39 by a piece of shrapnel and broken trunks of trees strewn in the rubble.

That evening a dinner of the last of the garrison's food was held and the remaining bottles of wine opened. On the Recreation Ground a bonfire was lit and the Queen's five-month-old Christmas chocolate distributed. 'God Save The Queen' rang out to the accompaniment of a banjo strummed by a boy and the wail of an accordion. 'The following day,' wrote Lady Sarah, 'The whole garrison turned out to attend a thanksgiving service in an open space close to the cemetery. They were drawn up in a three-sided square, which looked pathetically small ... then three volleys were fired over the graves of fallen comrades, and the "Last Post" was played by the buglers ... It was a simple ceremony but a very touching one.'

The sounds of the bugle had hardly died when the whining started. Particularly vociferous were Plumer's men, bitter that Baden-Powell had cheated them of glory. Plumer, they claimed, was a better officer who achieved more with less during the seven months. One of Plumer's officers noted wryly: 'To me the whole affair of the siege ... was an enigma. What in the world was the use of defending this wretched railway-siding and these tin-shanties? To burrow underground on the very first shot being fired ... seemed to me the strangest role ever played by a cavalry leader.' They certainly had a point because militarily there is no doubt that the neat, monocled Plumer contributed more and would have done even better had he not needed to worry about Baden-Powell in Mafeking.

Questions were also raised regarding Baden-Powell's near sacrifice of Plumer and his men, The Boy included. It is not clear whether this event contributed to the decline of their relationship over the years that followed. McLaren returned immediately to England to convalesce and in 1901 acted as Baden-Powell's London recruiting officer for the South African Constabulary. In 1907 he assisted Baden-Powell in organising the first Scout Camp at Brownsea Island, whereafter he became the Boy Scouts first manager, but he resigned a few months later. It appears that Baden-Powell was more eager to pursue the relationship but by 1912 it was in tatters and they did not see each other again.

Lady Sarah, her thirst for excitement not yet quenched, was next to leave. 'My eyes turned longingly towards the Transvaal and Pretoria,' she recalled. The region was still in enemy hands, but, she believed once Roberts reached Pretoria that would be the end of the war and she desperately wanted to witness his entry into Kruger's capital. 'Pretoria', she sighed, 'would be much more interesting than to trek to Kimberley, with Cape Town as the destination.' Her old friend, Mrs Godley, had returned from Bulawayo, and the two, with the incredibly resilient Metalka and Vellum, decided to undertake a journey most men would regard as insane. But she summed up her dilemma of staying in Mafeking on going to Pretoria, by stating that: 'This town, so long the theatre of excitement; then resumed by degrees the sleepy, even tenor of its ways.' It was no place for an adventurous soul.

On Sunday morning, 4 June 1900, the party packed their belongings in a Cape Cart and began the drive to Pretoria. 'It was a glorious day of blue skies and bright sun, with just enough breeze to prevent the noonday from being too hot,' she wrote of her farewell to the town. 'As we left Mafeking and its outworks behind, I had a curious feeling of regret and of gratitude to the gallant little town and its stout citizens: to the former for having been a haven in the midst of fierce storms during all these months; to the latter for their stout arms and brave hearts, which had warded off the outbursts of the same tempests, whose clouds had hung dark and lowering on our horizon since the previous October.'

'She will be quite the lioness when she returns to society,' hissed Thomasina Cowan cattily. But, women like Thomasina should thank Lady Sarah because, even though she opposed their liberation, she did much to romanticise the efforts of those fighting for the equality of women.

The citizens of Mafeking evacuated to safety before the siege poured back into the town that was slowly repairing the damage. 'We are now relieved and breathe the air of freedom once more,' wrote Bell in conclusion. 'The whole country is singing our praises, and Mafeking has made a name for itself, which will be recorded in history. Although we have suffered many hardships and troubles, we nevertheless all feel proud to think that each individual, both European and Native, has done his utmost to maintain the honour of the British Empire.'

But, the dark and lowering clouds were not lifted from Mafeking or Mahikeng. Mafeking, during the balance of the South African War, was to receive notoriety as the site of the first concentration camp for Boer women and children. It was the most 'deadly, deplorable and deficient' of all and, in a report on the camps, was singled out as having the 'most grossly culpable and negligent staff.'

Across the railway line the tribespeople in Mahikeng listened as muted tributes were paid to them for their bravery and resilience. They were, however, ordered to be disarmed, receiving a promise of continued British protection in return. But, this was not to be. On 12 January 1902 Boer forces crossed the border and attacked the defenceless *stadt* in revenge for its role in the siege. Canon Farmer, a missionary in the Transvaal, noted that when British forces marched on they left little protection behind and that blacks who had aided them were vulnerable to reprisal. Often, he wrote, blacks in these British 'controlled' districts were 'compelled to flee from the Boers [and] abandon most of their cattle and stuff. ... They look upon the kaffirs as dogs and the killing of them as hardly a crime.' The unarmed Barolong — without the promised protection from the resident British forces — watched helplessly as great damage was again inflicted on their property and livestock. In fact, more animals were lost, and more damage done, on that one night, than during the entire siege.

Angus Hamilton commented that 'In the history of these people there is not much in the consideration which we have shown them to justify their allegiance ... let us at least remember the debt of honour which we owe them.' The British could not even bring themselves to do this. Of the 29 000 pound Relief Fund raised in Britain by Lady Sarah's sister, Georgina, not one penny went to the Tshidi whose property and food were commandeered and looted; houses burnt and bombarded; and families killed, maimed and starved. Promised compensation was never forthcoming and the undertaking to provide the members of the 'Black Watch' with a farm was reneged on. Not one medal for bravery was awarded them and only a small plaque recording the services of the 'Black Watch' was affixed on the War Memorial erected to those who gave their lives in the defence of Mafeking.

But, the most disgraceful betrayal still awaited the Tshidi Barolong and this must surely represent one of the blackest episodes of the war. Baden-Powell told the Royal Commission on the War in 1903 that he had tried to make use of the Barolong during the siege 'but on the first attack on the town, they all ran away, so we did not rely on them at all.' In his official report he claimed he only made use of '300 armed cattle guards, watchmen and police' from the Tshidi. He also changed the name of the coloured Cape Boy Contingent to the Colonial Contingent and all the praise for the efforts of the Cape Boys went to the Colonial Contingent, which Baden-Powell omitted to tell anyone was made up of coloured troops. Algernon Hanbury-Tracy, Baden Powell's Intelligence Officer, tried to set matters right with regard the Cape Boys: 'It is quite impossible to describe the work done by these men under the most trying circumstances, but in stating that they were practically under one continuous rifle and shellfire for over six months, that they lived in the open all that time through the wet season, often with bad and insufficient food and scarcity of clothing, gives one some idea of what they suffered.'

With regard to Baden Powell's racist crimes, omissions, excesses and inhumanity perpetrated against black tribes, particularly the Tshidi-Barolong, his supporters often, as a last line of defence, use the 'context of the time' argument. There is no doubt that British imperialists and colonialists generally perceived themselves as superior and, in the 'context of the time', such beliefs were the norm rather than the

180

exception. But, care needs to be exercised where these ideas were translated into action, which, in the practice of governing pieces of far-flung empire, often resulted in the ignoring or the breaking of the law. If the British law 'of the time' anticipated and regarded imperialist excesses as illegal — as with the execution of Chief Unwini — how can these deeds be defended in the 'context of the time'? These problems of the theory and practice of law were central to Plaatje's thinking and the question is as appropriate now as it was then. Similarly, after the war, the British administrators of the Transvaal Colony chose to enforce many Boer laws designed to control the movement and employment of blacks even though these regulations were contrary to British law.

For people like Plaatje this was not an academic argument because these violations of the law led directly to gross human rights abuses on the ground. The implications are wider because it did not require a leap of logic for the engineers of apartheid and the coming European fascists to dispense with the cynicism and translate imperial administrative practice and ideas into policy. It is more difficult to assess whether individuals, such as Baden-Powell, operating in this context, were leaders in heralding these sickening shifts or merely the effects of dishonesty and the abuse of power. In Mafeking, the residents, while regarding the Tshidi as an inferior species, were nonetheless appalled at his treatment of them — while, in Britain, he was regarded as a super-hero even though there was evidence to the contrary. However, the whites in Mafeking would go on to broadly support the Natives' Land Act of 1913 and apartheid. Baden-Powell must, therefore, be considered ahead of his time and a precursor to the coming horrors where the colour of one's skin could be a death sentence. If any doubts linger as to his sentiments, it should be noted that he praised Hitler and Mussolini on numerous occasions and, in 1933, wrote 'the dictators in Germany and Italy [have] done wonders in resuscitating their people to stand as nations.'

Plaatje accused Baden-Powell of 'coolly and deliberately lying' to the Royal Commission. But Baden-Powell was not alone in his deceit and hypocrisy — he merely stretched unwritten policy that it would be bad form, in a white man's war, to admit reliance on blacks. The betrayal of Mahikeng was, further, a microcosm of the plight of blacks throughout South Africa. Like animals, they paid a terrible price in someone else's war, and then, when over, were required to return uncomplaining to their pens, stables and kraals. It now appears foolish, in the light of British behaviour, that men such as

Plaatje and Molema continued to be hopeful that blacks would receive wider recognition in the new political dispensation that must surely come after the war. The supposed folly of this belief was to be portrayed when the British sacrificed their black allies to reconcile with their white enemies. However, the British, to ensure continued black support, fraudulently encouraged this confidence to the extent that it appeared that the racism and duplicity of people such as Baden-Powell were isolated aberrations and not representative of British desire. Lord Salisbury, the British Prime Minister during the war, declared: 'There must be no doubt ... that due precaution will be taken for the kindly and improving treatment of those countless indigenous races of whose destiny I fear we have been too forgetful'. Such enunciations led many blacks to fall into the trap that the South African War was a just crusade to spread equality before the law and to bring 'equal rights for all civilised men'. That nothing could be further from the truth is clear now, it was not then. But there is growing evidence that the black élite were no longer duped and were becoming seriously concerned that hoped for changes would not materialise with the cessation of hostilities. Ghandi himself for many years perceived no means of emancipation other than peacefully through the structures of Empire. This was the crux of the problem – there was no other route, whether people of colour liked it or not, than through constitutional structures because no alternative forum existed. It would require angry black men to lay the foundation for such structures before the physical war for recognition and liberation could begin.

So blatant was the ungraciousness and dishonesty of Baden-Powell, who owed more to black support than any other British commander, that the outraged white residents of Mafeking took up their cause with the British authorities. Bell wrote to his superior stating that the Barolong had 'rendered invaluable services throughout the siege and defended their posts with energy and courage.' So vociferous were these calls for recognition that Lord Roberts sent Wessels, now reinstated, and the Barolong chiefs, a framed address written in gilt letters.

The Chief Wessels, Lekoko, and the Barolong of Mafeking

I, Frederick Sleigh Baron Roberts, K.P., G.C.S.I., G.C.I.E., V.C., of Kandahar and Waterford, hereby testify my approbation of the loyalty to H. M. Queen Victoria, and the good behaviour of the Barolongs under the leadership of Wessels, Lekoko, and the headmen Silas Molema and Paul Montsioa, throughout the long and trying investment of Mafeking by the Boers, from October 13, 1899 to May 17, 1900, and I desire to congratulate these leaders and these people on the successful issue of their courageous defence of their homes and properties against the invasion of the enemy.

However, without compensation or financial support the Tshidi were less able to repair the damage done to their wealth, withstand the pressures to seek employment as farm labourers, or join the hordes of migrant labourers heading for the gold mines. On the other hand, whites, with assistance, were quickly able to get back on their masterly feet.

Me that 'ave been what I've been —
Me that 'ave gone where I've gone —
Me that 'ave seen what I've seen —
'Ow can I ever take on
With awful old England again,
An' 'ouses both sides of the street,
An' edges two sides of the lane,
And the parson an' gentry between,
An' touching my 'at when we meet —
Me that 'ave been what I've been?
KIPLING, CHANT – PAGAN

Baden-Powell, not a hero of the war but *the* hero, was promoted to General and stayed on for a short while as officer commanding the military district of Mafeking, Zeerust and Lichtenburg. In that time he oversaw the repairing of the railway line that linked Kimberley and Bulawayo. His command, however, for the rest of the war, was less auspicious than that of many of his bumbling peers. Farcically, he nearly got himself invested again at Rustenburg. Lord Roberts, who at first ordered him to avoid another investment, was eventually reduced to begging him to avoid the town. He also managed to allow General Christiaan de Wet to slip through his grasp, a very costly mistake.

His promotion to General, at the age of 43, made him the youngest general in the British Army. Wolseley, his benefactor, said in congratulation, 'You now have the ball at your feet, and barring accidents greatness is in front of you.' That accident came soon after with the death of Wolseley. But, already, the writing was on the wall. Baden-Powell, while the hero of the people, was not a luminary among the orthodox military upper echelons. He was still regarded as a dangerous eccentric who had not graduated from Staff College. The powers in the military regarded his promotion to General as a symbolic gesture and he remained excluded from the inner circle. But, more damning, his spectacular ascent to glory made him more famous than even the Commander-in-Chief. It was the type of glory that could wreck a man's career. 'His bright fruition of fortune and success was soon obscured by a chilly fog,' commented Winston Churchill. '[The War Office] resented the disproportionate acclaim which the masses had bestowed on a single man.'

Roberts quickly sidelined him. On 4 July 1900 he wrote to Milner with his recommendation for Inspector General of the South African Constabulary: 'Baden-Powell is far and away the best man I know. He possesses in quite an unusual degree the qualities you specify, viz., energy, organisation, knowledge of the country, and a power of getting on with its people ... you will find Baden-Powell immensely useful.'

Later, in Cape Town to accept this position which effectively removed him from the direct line of command to a support function, Baden-Powell was mobbed by well-wishers who turned out to greet the most famous Englishman alive. Though he would go on to be feted by monarchs and presidents, his military career was effectively capped.

> *Who hath smelt wood-smoke at twilight? Who hath heard*
> *the birch log burning?*
> *Who is quick to read the noises of the night?*
> *Let him follow with the others, for the Young Men's feet are*
> *turning*
> *To the camps of proved desires and known delight!*
> KIPLING, 'FEET OF THE YOUNG MEN'

Fortunately for Baden-Powell, he was not particularly enamoured with generaling. The grass of realised ambition was not green. His world was that of wide, sweet-smelling skies; not the arid boredom of symbolic offices and official duties. He had been a woodcrafter, a big-game hunter and a free man. Cities made him feel pinched, cramped and restless and soon he was considering exploiting his 'damnable notoriety' outside the army.

184

Cooped up in England, after the war, he became more convinced that something had to be done for the 'pale, narrow-chested, hunched-up, miserable specimens' he observed 'smoking, betting and passively spectating at football matches'. Many boys felt the same. He was inundated with fan-mail from those who followed his exploits at Mafeking and were subsequently drawn to his writing.

To prepare the way for his 'second-life' he consciously transformed the Siege of Mafeking, and his role in it, into 'just the sort of yarn we want for the camp-fire or the powwow' in the 'great work towards the prevention of misery and crime and the promotion of some, happy citizenhood.' He romanticised war and militarism as a tool to prepare men who were wholeheartedly patriotic and 'who saw the value of a united Empire as a force for the peace and prosperity of our race.' Order, fitness, courage, brotherhood and a refusal to admit defeat were the underbelly of the Boy Scouts movement he founded in 1907 which, on the surface, promoted the outdoors and playful pandemonium. So, while the Cadet Corps, formed during the siege, probably played only a small role in the establishment of the Boy Scouts, the siege was central because it provided him with the international fame necessary to attract boys to the organisation.

Jimmy Quinlan, the Irish nationalist who had languished in jail throughout the siege, left Mafeking shortly after Baden-Powell. Plaatje is renowned for being meticulous and extremely diligent. Directly after the siege he was kept busy tackling the administrative chaos that had built up during the investment. Also, he was responsible for collecting evidence and formulating cases against rebels of the Cape Colony who had supported the Boers. The most prominent of these was Quinlan, whose case was well known in Mafeking. Not only did he face a charge of High Treason, but many other serious cases which had grown with the inclusion of a charge of sedition in December 1899. Quinlan, above all, was ordered by Cecil to be returned to London for trial for crimes committed as an Irish National Invincible.

The case file containing the charges against Quinlan, however, that reached the authorities, was for High Treason only and contained no supporting evidence. He was released, rejoined the railways and died in 1937 at Seapoint at the age of 76. It remains a mystery as to who 'cleansed' his file as he was a popular man in Mafeking. But, Plaatje, had it been anyone else, would have realised that the charges and file had been tampered with when he collated it and he remains the most likely suspect. It is tantalising to believe that Plaatje realised, as early as the lifting of the siege, that there was a chance that his people may have to face an Ireland scenario before recognition and liberation.

> *Woe unto them that decree unrighteous decrees, and that write grievousness*
>   *which they have prescribed;*
> *To turn aside the needy from judgement, and to take away the*
>   *fruit from the poor of my people, that widows may be their prey,*
>   *and that they may rob the fatherless.*
>   FROM ISAIAH,
>   QUOTED IN SOL PLAATJE'S NATIVE LIFE IN SOUTH AFRICA

Plaatje was 23 years old when the siege ended and he was soon reunited with his wife and son. His siege diary, which he never intended for publication, appears to be an instrument whereby he honed his literary talents, evidenced by his construction of complicated musical metaphors. But, more than that, it is a document which reveals the origins of a new struggle in South African politics which was to culminate in 1994 with the election of the African National Congress as the first non-racial government.

The siege, for him, had been filled with moments of great anger, despondency, loneliness and pessimism. Friends, black and white, and his beloved horse Whiskey were killed or died and he witnessed gross violations of justice and humanity. But it was not all gloom. It was here, in the depths of despair, that his character was shaped and his single-minded crusade to ensure that his people's fate was never again determined by the colour of their skin gained purpose and resolve. He also acquired valuable experience during the investment from working with journalists and compiling reports for the authorities on the 'native situation'. And, within the Barolong community he had matured into a recognised and respected leader because he had access to the representatives of the colonial government, knew his way through the maze of red tape, and could represent and defend them in the political and social situation in which they found themselves.

Plaatje, beyond his official functions immediately after the lifting of the siege, concentrated on improving himself. In December 1900 he made a trip to Cape Town to sit the Civil Service Examination. He was placed first in both the subjects he sat. In a blatantly mean and racist move the practice of publishing the names of the candidates in the order of their results, for these subjects, was dispensed with that year and anyone reading the published results, without being aware they were printed in random order, would have been of the impression that Plaatje was placed third in Typewriting and sixth in Dutch. Plaatje, acutely sensitive to the wrongs perpetrated on blacks, was deeply offended and this could well have contributed to his decision to seek a more rewarding career where a white skin was not the primary qualification for a job.

His discontent, before he resolved to resign, boiled to the surface in March 1901. He was continually frustrated by the resident military authority's arrogance in allowing their cattle to stray into his garden and destroy his crops. On 19 March he snapped, resulting in the only criminal charge ever brought against him:

Solomon T. Plaatje did wrongfully and unlawfully assault one Indalo, a native herd in the employ of the Imperial Government by knocking him to the ground, by tying him with reins, by kicking him while on the ground with the booted foot and by damaging his clothing and other wrongs and injuries to the said Indalo did then and there do.

The case was dismissed for lack of evidence, but it did prove that Plaatje, a man of peace, was no pacifist.

In April 1901 a single sheet Setswana insert, known as *Koranta ea Becoana* (*The Bechuanaland Gazette*), began to appear in the *Mafeking Mail*, which George Whales still edited and now owned. As Whales could neither speak nor write Setswana it was obviously written by someone else. The identity of the writer remains a mystery, but it is suspected that it was Plaatje. His condition of service specifically prohibited him from contributing to newspapers so, if it was him, his involvement had to remain secret. No other Tswana capable of compiling such a sheet would have needed their identity hushed. More compelling is that from this date Plaatje became increasingly involved with the insert.

In September, the same month as Plaatje's second son, Richard, was born, Whales sold his share in *Koranta* for 25 pounds to Silas Molema. In February 1902, the newspaper purchased its own printing press, acquired separate offices and changed its format to an English/Tswana newspaper printed on two pages. Plaatje, in April 1902, handed in his notice to the civil service and took the reins as editor of a newspaper that immediately took an overtly political direction. With this move he joined an élite and influential band as there were only two other black newspapers that appeared regularly. He quickly stated that *Koranta* was committed to the principles of labour, sobriety, thrift and education and that its mission was 'the amelioration of the native.' He now had a mouthpiece from which he could formulate opinion, convey black aspirations and educate his people on the values and beliefs necessary to overcome the increasing wilderness they found themselves in at the end of the war.

Dante, do not weep yet, though Virgil goes.
Do not weep yet for soon another wound
shall make you weep far hotter tears than those!
PURGATORY, CANTO XXX

Part III

Phoenix Rising

Not by lust of praise or show,
Not by peace herself betrayed —
Peace herself must they forego
Till that peace be fitly made.

KIPLING

After partaking of Hot Cross Buns [one Easter Sunday] at the family table of a dear old English family, 'I went to Walthamstow, and there heard a moving discourse ... on the suffering and death of Christ for the redemption of mankind.'

SOL PLAATJE

The British public were also dumb, and with that infinite capacity for being gulled which is so remarkable in a people proud of their common sense, acquiesced in everything.

AH KEENE

Of all the characters of cruelty, I consider that as the most odious which assumes the garb of mercy.

FOX, QUOTED IN SOL PLAATJE'S NATIVE LIFE IN SOUTH AFRICA

11

THE BLACK MAN'S BURDEN

*The Bantu's condition after war has grown worse and worse every year.
Their rights, never many or mighty, have been curtailed systematically
from then to now and the future is dark and dreary.*

DR S M 'MODIRI' MOLEMA, THE BANTU: PAST AND PRESENT

Five days after Plaatje's resignation from the Cape Civil Service, British
and Boer representatives signed the Treaty of Vereeniging, which
finally brought peace to a sub-continent that had been engulfed by three
years of devastating war. For blacks the terms of peace were profoundly
disappointing, particularly Clause 8 of the treaty, which stated that no
decision would be taken on extending the Cape franchise to the black
inhabitants of the former Boer republics until after the introduction of
responsible government. In essence, blacks were to receive no political
reward or recognition for their services to the British imperial
government. And what little they had, in reality, was to be continually
eroded.

The British were concerned with two things – to rebuild the
agricultural capacity of a scorched land and return the gold mining
industry to full production as soon as possible, so that the enormous
debts incurred by the war could be settled and southern Africa be
reconstructed as a Greater Britain in the veld. To achieve this, it was
necessary to reconcile with the Boer and sacrifice the black. Milner
naively believed that the dangers attending this could be nullified by
encouraging massive British emigration to southern Africa to Anglicise
the region and effectively swamp the Boer. This policy was fatally

191

flawed by the simple fact that it would require persuading Englishmen to flock to a region that suffered a history of instability.

In places like Mafeking, however, the immediate reaction to the peace was a sigh of relief as the day-to-day business of life could once more be attended to. Plaatje, on land given him by Silas Molema, built himself a house, 'Seoding' (Riverside), in the Molopo Native Reserve. This house soon overtook 'Moratiwa' as the social hub for 'progressive' blacks of Mahikeng. His great joy, however, was being with his family, particularly his first daughter, Olive – his favourite child, named after Olive Schreiner, whom he had known in Kimberley – who was born in December 1903.

> By the verdant bank of a country spring
> Olive and I sat watching a pen
> of Kalahari partridges on the wing.
> In their Aerial trend they looked peculiarly well off:
> They sipped the precious fluid by Elysian nod.
> Thus Olive softly: LI THABILE.

> O'er the grassy turf 'neath the desert sun
> Olive and I walked picking wild flowers,
> Up sprang a duiker and commenced to run,
> Sprightly and hale he flew and darted across the bowers.
> I speedily fired and shattered his back;
> The nickel bullet also pierced his vivific pluck.
> Said Olive dolefully: E SHULE.

> In the western vale of Mahur'take,
> Olive and I mused of break-(ing our)-fast,
> 'Neath the clear rural sky, our meat to take:
> Comprising wild fruit, 'morama', a handy repast,
> Porridge, winged-game, cocoa beans and cooking,
> Displaying her neat set of youthful ivories,
> Olive quoth SOTTO VOCE: MONATE.

This adoring relationship was to be tragically shattered a few years later by the callousness of the growing oppression that would soon become apparent. Olive contracted the Spanish Flu of 1919 which Plaatje also caught, a virus that would permanently damage his heart. The doctor treating her had recommended the curative and therapeutic waters of the hot springs at Aliwal North but, on arrival, they were turned away because of the colour of their skin. Shortly after, feeling faint, she left school early to go home. At the railway station she was not permitted, even in her condition, to either enter the 'whites only' waiting room or lie on a bench. Outside on the cold concrete she lay down and died.

But Plaatje's growing commitments and workaholic nature meant he spent little time with his family. The new-look *Koranta*, with him as editor, appeared regularly after its launch in August 1902. That he put in a superhuman effort to building the newspaper reflected his concern that his people have a mouthpiece that could articulate their struggle for justice and equal rights. It also revealed his personal realisation that he was only a spokesperson by dint of his control of that medium. Overall it was an exuberant, professional publication that mirrored his universal thinking, assertiveness, humour, optimism and independence. Thus, it consisted of a mix of editorial comment; articles of interest to blacks on the issues of the day; contributed articles from leading black thinkers — particularly African-Americans such as Booker T Washington, principal of the famous Tuskegee educational institution in Alabama; letters from readers and advertising. John Edward Bruce, an American editor, praised the newspaper for its 'virile and well written editorials, its snappy editorial notes and contributed articles which, though brief, were instructive and to the point.'

Though his constituency was the Tswana, and specifically the Barolong, he was convinced that the issues of the day could be better dealt with where there was unity of purpose. It was this thinking that led him to conceive and initiate the Native Press Association in 1903. That other black editors accepted his leadership in this effort is an indication of his growing political stature. And that ascendancy was earned not just through tireless effort in editing, but by actively backing his position. An illustration of this blend of leader-spokesperson is clearly displayed by his actions during Chamberlain's South African tour of 1902/03.

In 1902 a group of white businessmen in Mafeking, dissatisfied with high tariffs between the Cape and Transvaal colonies, decided to present a petition to Chamberlain requesting incorporation of the Mafeking district into the Transvaal. To strengthen their case they persuaded the Tshidi chiefs to support their plea. Plaatje was outraged and castigated them, in the light of Clause 8 of the peace treaty, for taking a leap in the dark which could only result in political suicide. By personal lobbying he got them all to withdraw their support. But his involvement did not end with reacting; he now took a proactive stand.

He briefed Kimberley attorneys to draw up a petition on behalf of the Tshidi-Barolong to present to Chamberlain. In it he reminded the British imperial government of the pivotal role played by the Barolong during the war. He then turned to address Tshidi grievances. Land around Polfontein, just over the border in the Transvaal, had been promised the Barolong during the siege and had, as yet, not been handed over. Also, compensation for war loss had still not been received and should be paid immediately. In conclusion, an assurance was demanded that black rights in the Cape Colony would not be tampered with. As a mark of the distinctive manner in which Plaatje operated, he arranged for a gilded commemorative copy of the petition to be framed and handed to the distinguished guest during the welcoming address.

Chamberlain, greeted by cheering and blaring hooters, was accompanied by a brass band when he entered the *stadt* on the afternoon of 28 January with his wife and other dignitaries. Under the glaring sun Chamberlain's wife was heard to mutter that the blacks before her 'were not a picturesque lot'. But, irrespective of this discourtesy, Plaatje was to regard the visit as a resounding success. Chamberlain, in his address, promised to investigate the issue of compensation, ignored the matter of Polfontein and vowed that the rights of blacks in the Cape Colony would never 'be altered in the slightest respect'. For Plaatje the visit was a personal triumph as he received a signed testimonial from Chamberlain, favourable comment in the *Diamond Fields Advertiser* and praise in the *Cape Argus* that commented 'the young Barolong editor made good use of his opportunities.' The issues of Polfontein and compensation were never resolved, but Plaatje was delighted at the unambiguous public assurance on future rights.

The school chaplain had asked: 'What is the unique importance of the Christian religion?'

My hand went up. My father had supplied me with the answer to that one.

'Well, Sutton?'

'Sir, it makes more promises than any other religion.'

194

'Yes ... What sort of promises?'

'Ridiculous promises, Sir ... like "The meek shall inherit the earth".'

Snorts of laughter burst from my class-mates. The chaplain was studiously neutral: 'Ridiculous. I see.' More laughter – more general.

My face was scorching, but I plunged on: 'The best religions promise the most. It's the promises that matter – not whether they're kept.'

EDWARD RICHARDSON, HALF-BUILT HALL

For Plaatje there were no 'holy cows'. He vociferously condemned the contradiction between the theory and practice of British rule and the habit of repressive functionaries who behaved as if practice was actually government policy. He was critical of illiberal white newspapers, the biased decisions of all-white juries and blacks whenever they appeared to be stagnating or regressing rather than progressing. A teetotaller, he was particularly scathing of businesses that encouraged blacks to consume alcohol and, equally, of those that partook.

His major focus, however, was the British administration in the Transvaal who were out-Boering the Boer in their efforts to enforce discriminatory laws – many inherited from the old Boer republics. 'The benefit of the Pass Law,' he thundered, 'is that thousands of useful unoffending black men, than whom His Majesty has no more law abiding subjects, are daily sent to prison, without having done harm to anybody, and they die as regular gaol-birds even though they had never, during their lifetime, dipped the tips of their fingers in the cup of criminality. ... And we are sure that if there is any Native unrest in existence it is the outcome of the callous and oppressive administration of the Pass Law.' In 1904, after witnessing the Johannesburg Municipality clearing blacks from Nancefield, he commented, 'I saw the misery and hardships which attended the enforcement of the measure, and heard Native viragoes loudly lamenting the fall of Kruger and cursing the new administration, which they termed "remorseless tyrants" (*batana li-sitlhogo*, lit: 'cruel beasts of prey')'. On another occasion he noted that Transvaal blacks 'Unanimously declare that they were far better off under the Field Cornets of the late Government than what they are under the Sub-Native Commissioners. We are sure that never was the name of her late Gracious Majesty, Victoria, dragged in the mire like now, when the cruelty of those officials drives it into the minds of the black people, who lost their life and property to establish British rule in their country, that her reign is worse than Krugerism.'

As Plaatje travelled and campaigned on behalf of blacks, his horizons extended and his reputation grew beyond the Tshidi-Barolong, who were steadily losing control of their affairs. The tribe fought tooth and nail to maintain their autonomy, through a skilful use of the legal system, but the war and the failure of the British to compensate them had fatally weakened them and their efforts to protect themselves became weaker and weaker. Their situation was not helped by the alcohol-seduced Badirile, Wessels' successor, who was 'a hopeless and abandoned drunkard'.

It is wrong to assume that the authorities regarded Plaatje and other black editors as hostile. On the contrary, the black newspapers were generally optimistic about the future because the final shape of South Africa was still to be decided and the British welcomed the medium through which blacks could 'blow off steam'. This cordial relationship was strengthened by the constitutional avenues these editors pursued to solve the 'native problem' rather than exhorting their readers to the much feared 'native uprising'. They were, furthermore, a gauge of 'native opinion' and it was considered judicious to be tolerant of criticism.

If the black press's association with the British was genial, the opposite was true of their amity with the white English press and their readership. What was abundantly clear was that there was no common purpose between the black and local English press. This antagonistic relationship was riven with sinister clues as to the hostile future direction South Africa was taking. *The Natal Witness* reminded its black counterparts that the British were 'the race to which they and theirs owe everything, and which has fostered to an almost continental extent, progress amongst the natives of the sub-continent'. *The Friend*, published in Bloemfontein, who Plaatje dubbed 'The Foe', was less polite in its venom in an editorial on 9 March 1903 regarding a series of articles on discrimination that appeared in *Koranta*.

They decline to accept the fact that they cannot be placed on the same footing with the white man, and it is coming to a nice pass when they refer to white men as 'fellows' and themselves as 'ladies' and 'gentlemen'. Now that the war is over, and the necessity for officers and privates of the British Army chumming with niggers, and – I regret to say – negresses, has passed, it is time for us to bring the native back to the status he was placed in before the war. The first step in that direction would be the suppression of all the nigger papers, for they are spreading a propaganda throughout the country which is the cause of all the trouble in the native question, i.e. the fact that the native is equal to the white man. I am not in favour of slavery, but I think that the time has come to place a firm hand on the native and put him in his place, and keep him there.

The Mafeking Mail, with which relationships were in tatters, went even further because Whales believed Plaatje's attacks on the British verged on sedition: 'Disloyalty, now-a-days, is the refuge of the ignorant. It has sunk down to the level of a kaffir pastime. The editor of the Mafeking kaffir newspaper, "*Koranta ea Becoana*", is a studious person who used to interpret at the Magistrate's Court. He got into the habit of thinking during the course of his duties, and a lot of stored up, compressed thought drove him into journalism as an outlet for it. Thinking, however, is a bad thing to get into late in life, if you haven't been used to it before. One is apt to get a wrong perspective, and when he complains of British rule it is an evidence of it.' Whales's simple solution was that Plaatje should be flogged.

The white English newspapers were perfectly in step with, if not led by, white English opinion. In the colonialist mind the war, and the role blacks played in it, made blacks lose sight of their proper place in a white man's country. There was a confusion within this colonial thinking – not clarified, but exacerbated, by their press – that blacks not only desired political rights but also aspired to white culture and a European way of life. 'Would you want one of them to marry your daughter?' was not a question but a threat that went with the granting of political rights.

Plaatje, recognising this muddled thinking, was very careful to separate the issues in order to pacify white fears. In the third issue of *Koranta* on 13 September 1902 he printed his famous 'Equal Rights' address which he would return to on many occasions:

We do not hanker after social equality with the white man. If anyone tells you that we do so, he is a lunatic, and should be put in chains. We do not care for your parlour, nor is it our wish to lounge on couches in your drawing rooms. The renegade Kaffir who desires to court and marry your daughter is a perfect danger to his race, for if his yearnings were realised we would be hurrying on the path to the inauguration of a generation of half-castes, and the total obliteration of our race and colour, both of which are very dear to us.

For this reason we advise every black man to avoid social contact with whites, and the other races to keep strictly within their boundaries.

All we claim is our just dues; we ask for our political recognition as loyal British subjects. We have not demonstrated our fealty to the throne for pounds.s.d., but we did it to assist in the maintenance of the open door we now ask for, so it cannot be said we demand too much.

Under the Union Jack every person is his neighbour's equal. There are certain regulations for which one should qualify before his legal status is recognised as such: to this qualification race or colour is no bar, and we hope, in the near future, to be able to record that one's sex will no longer debar her from exercising a privilege hitherto enjoyed by the sterner sex only.

Presently under the British Constitution every MAN so qualified is his neighbour's political equal, therefore anyone who argues to the contrary, or imagines himself the political superior of his fellow subject, is a rebel at heart.

Plaatje, further, was not as confident as Milner on the liberating effect British immigration was having. On 4 April 1903 he commented:

We, as the mouthpiece of the Natives of Bechuanaland and the Transvaal colony, are surprised to find the people of the Transvaal inclined to ignore the grand axiom, 'Equal rights for every civilised man south of the Zambezi', by one of Britain's greater statesmen, the late Cecil John Rhodes. The solution of the Native Problem lies in the carrying out of this principle, which we believe is the essence of the British constitution. But the policy of deliberately boycotting and ostracising the Native African and the British Indians, as persisted in by the selfish newcomers of the Rand, leaves a dark future for the generation to take the place of the citizens, both white and black, who inhabit this subcontinent.

Our motto as Native Africans is Africa for all law-abiding citizens, naturalised British subjects and all those foreigners in whose countries we would be treated with respect and political equality. Equal rights for all of them, regardless of race, colour, creed or sex.

Plaatje also fell out with the London Missionary Society. As *Koranta* appeared in both Setswana and English, he was deeply involved in the orthography of the Tswana language. When the London Missionary Society decided to revise the Setswana Bible he commented that they were imposing on the language without referring to Native Tswana, notably himself, who were deeply concerned about the development of the written language. Offended, they referred to him as a 'native editor of a not very respectable paper'. He countered by accusing them of being 'reactionary and blocking the way to progress'. Unable to stomach the views of an outspoken black, they resolved to call a conference to resolve the storm — Plaatje's absence, as he did not receive an invitation, was noticeable.

Regardless of Plaatje's growing influence, *Koranta* and his personal finances were in a mess. Like all its contemporaries, *Koranta*'s potential readership was limited by low black literacy. Silas Molema, the main backer, and Plaatje ran up huge personal debts to keep the newspaper appearing regularly. But by 1906, both had exhausted all potential credit and *Koranta* effectively closed in the middle of that year. Politically, for blacks, this could not have happened at a worse time as every instrument was needed to face the coming years.

By 1905 the political direction South Africa was taking was becoming clear. The British imperial government, to reconcile with the ex-Boer republics, was anxious these colonies be granted responsible self-government as soon as possible. Not only did it appear unlikely that blacks in these colonies would be granted any representation, but, more disturbingly, the British were beginning to warm to the idea of segregation — a policy that local whites, Boer and colonial, were overwhelmingly in favour of — to maintain white economic and political domination. A key element of this thinking was that the occupation of land by black and white be separated. Blacks, whose place it was to provide labour for the mines and farms, would be confined to 'reserves' where they could fulfil their political aspirations.

Plaatje commented that racial territorial segregation was unnecessary: 'Give [the blacks] the franchise, and your confidence, and the problem will solve itself to your mutual advantage.' Moreover, in practice, it was impossible:

> Go to Kingwilliamstown and see the flood of black peasantry pouring through the streets, walking up and down the thoroughfares, meeting and gossiping with friends, staring at the shop windows, purchasing groceries, farming implements and clothes; then imagine these Natives all far away in Katanga and ask yourself the question: 'What will become of the merchants of Kingwilliamstown without the Kaffir? — the Kaffir as a labourer, the Kaffir as a transport rider, the Kaffir as a customer?' and only one possibility suggests itself, namely, that they will be bankrupt. And what is patent in regard to Kingwilliamstown is equally so in regard to Port Elizabeth, to Kimberley, Bloemfontein and Johannesburg, in spite of all that has been urged in the latter two cities in favour of 'a white man's country'.

By 1907, at the time Baden-Powell was launching the Boy Scouts at Brownsea Island, Plaatje had completely changed the political outlook of the Tswana. In the same year his second daughter, Violet, was born. Financially his personal affairs were in crisis. Between 1906 and 1910 he was issued with 16 summonses for unpaid debts. In desperation he even tried his hand at labour recruiting. So severe was the problem that it hampered his ability to fully participate in the most important political discourse of the time and forced him to miss the South African Native Convention held in Bloemfontein from 24-26 March 1909.

Britain believed its long-term interests in southern Africa would be preserved by the four colonies coming together in union. The British, to achieve this, were forced to choose between their racist white kin or their black friends. They chose family and, as a result, there was no place for even a non-racial Cape franchise let alone 'equal rights for all civilised men'. The draft South Africa Bill, negotiated between white South Africans and the British imperial government, made no provision for the extension of the Cape franchise to the other colonies nor provided for effective black representation. Simply, the other three colonies would have rejected union had this issue been forced on them. The convention, at which Silas Molema represented the Barolong, was called so that black South Africans could present a united front to the grave dangers inherent in the proposed union. Never before was such a sense of unity displayed. It was agreed that pressure be brought to bear on the British imperial government to intervene on behalf of black South Africans to ensure proper representation. They also sought assurances that the Cape franchise be protected and demanded the removal of the colour bar from the proposed legislation.

The convention also resolved that it become a permanent structure and it was here that Plaatje became involved as an office bearer. Further, it was suggested that a non-ethnic black newspaper be established as a mouthpiece for all black South Africans. This idea was taken up by wealthy Barolong landowners, from the Seleka clan in Kimberley who provided the funding. This newspaper, *Tsala ea Becoana* — The Friend of the Bechuana — appointed Plaatje its editor.

After Union in 1910 it appeared the first Prime Minister, General Louis Botha, would follow a soft line with regard blacks. False optimism was raised by his appointment of the Cape liberal, Henry Burton, as minister of Native Affairs. But Botha was being squeezed at the hustings. From platform, pulpit and in the press he was derided by Afrikaners for being pro-English and weak on blacks. Further, poor Afrikaners were demanding jobs and upliftment — the cry, caricatured by cartoonists, was 'give, give'. And, those that could be taken from to satisfy these calls, were the unrepresented blacks.

Plaatje, however, was not immediately fearful. Kimberley, where *Tsala* was to be located, was a more central base than Mafeking and a welcome break from the proximity of his creditors. His friends still lived there and it meant he could be closer to his ageing mother at Pniel. This improvement in his social life and his belief that the ideas of the Cape liberals would eventually filter through to the north was reflected in the positive outlook of his early editorials. It would not last.

Tsala first appeared on 18 June 1910 and many saw it as the resurrection of *Koranta*. The first few issues were concerned with the circumstances surrounding Union and Plaatje took particular pleasure in the drubbing some vehemently anti-black candidates took in the election and in the inclusion of well-respected liberals, such as Burton and JW

Sauer, in the cabinet. But, for blacks, matters were becoming bleaker. The Cape liberals were as trapped as Botha. Each action that appeared soft on blacks was pounced on by General Hertzog's supporters, who were calling for tougher 'native policies'. Afrikaner nationalism was growing and the balance of power soon reflected this by shifting increasingly toward the northern provinces. Soon bills such as the Native Labour Relations Act, which tightened control on black labour, and the Mine and Works Act, which reserved certain categories of work for whites, were passed into law. The central issue after Union, however, remained segregation.

Plaatje found himself tirelessly lobbying politicians, travelling and acting as watchdog. He, ever the gentleman, left a deep impression on white politicians because of his meticulous manner in preparation and presentation. In turn, they accepted him as a responsible spokesperson for his people. Isaiah Bud-M'belle commented 'he had a way particularly his own of approaching, interviewing, and placing his case before cabinet ministers of all different shades, and other highly placed authorities of English or Dutch extraction – a rare and valuable quality not possessed by other Bantu leaders.'

By doing freelance work as a columnist for Vere Stent, then editor of the *Pretoria News*, and selling insurance he was slowly able to repair his financial situation. Though his writing was robust, Vere Stent, on introducing Plaatje to his readers, wrote: 'He is no agitator or firebrand, no stirrer-up of bad feelings between black and white.' And soon he was the most widely read black journalist among all South Africans. But *Tsala*'s finances were as precarious as *Korantu*'s and the newspaper closed in June 1912. This time, however, Plaatje was not out of the spotlight long as he was appointed editor of a new newspaper, *Tsala ea Batho*, The Friend of the People, which was funded by Non-Tswana blacks.

More importantly, Plaatje had, since mid 1911, been actively discussing, through the South African Native Convention, the formation of a new national organisation to represent blacks. Unity, particularly as the realisation dawned that worse was still to come, became more urgent. What was perceived was a broader-based organisation than the South African Native Convention which would also have more purpose in overcoming the political impotence conferred on blacks by Union. Envisaged was a movement that would unite politically active black organisations, bring in the chiefs as representative of traditional society and promote the aspirations of emerging black leaders. This was easier said than done because politics can be as much about charismatic leaders as about policy. Personal rivalries, past sleights, competing ideals, ambitions and self interest all required attention before agreement could be reached on the necessity to establish a single, national political organisation. This scenario was perfect for Plaatje's unique brand of perspicacity, persuasion and diplomacy.

By late 1911 it was finally agreed that all parties were ready to hold an inaugural conference and its date was set for 8 January 1912. The atmosphere, on that day, amongst the large number of political and traditional leaders that attended, was pervaded with a sense of optimism that the way was being cleared for the formation of a body capable of attending to black grievances.

'The platform was filled with eminent formally dressed Africans,' wrote Mary Benson in *South Africa: The Struggle for a Birthright*, 'some with frock-coats and top hats, carrying furled umbrellas. A sergeant-at-arms in a tunic with sergeant's stripes, breeches and gaiters, and carrying a hide shield, knobkerrie (a wooden club) and axe, kept order.' After the singing of the hymn *Nkosi Sikelel'i-Afrika*, God Bless Africa, Pixley Seme, an attorney, opened the convention by explaining its purpose:

> Chiefs of royal blood and gentlemen of our race, we have gathered here to consider and discuss a theme which my colleagues and I have decided to place before you. We have discovered that in the land of their birth, Africans are treated as hewers of wood and drawers of water. The white people of this country have formed what is known as the Union of South Africa — a union in which we have no voice in the making of laws and no part in the administration. We have called you, therefore, to this conference so that together we can find ways and means of forming our national union for the purpose of creating national unity and defending our rights and privileges.

Seme concluded by proposing a permanent congress be established. The motion was unanimously accepted with a standing ovation, whistling, singing and cheering that went on and on. The Reverend John Dube was elected president and Sol Plaatje, the first secretary-general — a position that was, in many ways, more important than president because it would be on him that the duty of building up the organisation would devolve. In a decision with which Plaatje was particularly unhappy, it was decided to name the congress the South African Native National Congress (SANNC) – to be changed a few years later to the African National Congress.

The leaders of the SANNC still believed that the tried methods of lobbying, petitions and delegation would be effective in the new dispensation of Union. Thus, there was no question, at this point, of the SANNC working in any way other than within the constitutional framework. Even their modest objectives reflected the desire to foster a greater understanding between black and white in South Africa.

But whites were going in a different direction, made abundantly obvious by the replacement of Henry Burton as Minister of Native Affairs with General Hertzog in June 1912. This move symbolised the triumph of Afrikaner nationalism over Cape liberalism. Plaatje summed up the situation beautifully: 'That the Imperial Government, after conquering the Boers, handed back to them their old republics, and a nice little present in the shape of the Cape Colony and Natal.' The upshot was that the Boers could now take constitutional revenge on Britain's sacrificed, unrepresented allies. But Britain was not passive, she acquiesced fully in the outrages that were to follow over the next 75 years – actions that were nothing short of a declaration of war by the reconciled opponents of a white man's war on the blacks who had ensured Britain's victory.

It was 'like a mastiff long held in the leash' as Hertzog seized the political opportunity to pander to the interests of the mine owners, farmers and poor Afrikaners who funded, fed and fired the new Union. He was not out of step with either the white constituency or Britain, in fact he understood better than any their objectives and was being hailed as the right man for the job and as a future Prime Minister. So, when he set about preparing comprehensive proposals to deal with 'the native problem' and give effect to the desire for segregation, he was doing nothing less than representing the interests of the franchised and of exploitative capitalists.

That black progress was to be arrested with Hertzog's appointment was obvious and any optimism harboured by men such as Plaatje evaporated. But, a measure infinitely worse than anything they contemplated was in store for them. The provisions of the Natives' Land Bill, to become the Natives' Land Act of 1913, were revealed in February 1913. This cynical piece of opportunism encompassed both the white aspirations for segregation while satisfying the labour needs of farmers and mine owners. This single piece of legislation laid the foundation for apartheid and resulted in the mass exploitation of black South Africans.

The Land Act sought to deprive blacks of the right to acquire land, by purchase or leasehold, outside demarcated areas of occupation referred to as 'Scheduled Native Areas.' J Keyter, the MP for Ficksburg, in a speech in support of the legislation said that it was necessary to tell blacks that South Africa 'was a white man's country, that he was not going to be allowed to buy land there or to hire land there, and if he wanted to be there he must be in service.' It also aimed to alter the status of peasants farming on white-owned farms to that of labourer; so severe was this provision that it even prohibited the renting of pasturage. What Keyter did not mention was that the Act, in effect, was a piece of legislation designed by enfranchised whites to steal the country and virtually enslave the unrepresented because the core purpose of this legislation was the provision of cheap labour. This was accomplished by allocating 7,3 per cent of the land surface of South Africa to 80 per cent of the population. It was obvious that this was not sufficient to support the blacks in South Africa and would immediately throw more than a million blacks into the deep end of the labour pool.

The Act was introduced by the tearful JW Sauer, the so-called 'friend of the native' who had replaced General Hertzog as Minister of Native Affairs, who farcically opposed his own legislation. Though he claimed his bill was to preclude something infinitely worse, he was also kowtowing to the new political reality to ensure his career. But parliamentary approved bills still required the signature of the Governor-General, Lord Gladstone, an admirer of General Botha and his government.

Plaatje, realising that Britain's constituency was the mine owners, referred to the black miners in his plea to the British: 'The subterranean heroes who by day and by night, for a mere pittance lay down their limbs and their lives to the familiar "fall of rock" and who ... .in the bowels of the earth, sacrifice their lungs to the rock dust which develops miners' phthisis and pneumonia — poor reward, but a sacrifice that enables the world's richest gold mines ... to maintain the credit of Empire ... Surely the appeal of chattels who render service of such great value deserves the attention of the British people.'

But, as Plaatje suspected, the British, even before this legislation was introduced, had conspired to ensure that this bill's safe passage would not be interfered with. 'With a rush the Natives' Land Bill was dispatched from the Lower House to the Senate,' wrote Plaatje, 'adopted hurriedly by the Senate, returned to the Lower House, and went at the same pace to Government House, and there received the Governor-General's signature, it immediately became law. As regards the Govenor-General's signature, His Excellency, if Ministers are to be believed, was ready to sign the Bill (or rather signified his intention of doing so) long before it was introduced into Parliament. This excited haste sugests grave misgivings as to the character of the Bill. Why all the hurry and scurry, and why the Governor-General's approval in advance? Other bills are passed and approved by the Governor, yet they do not come into operation until some given day – the beginning of the next calendar year, or of the next Freed financial year. But the Natives' Land Act became law and was operating as soon as it could be promulgated.'

'I blush,' said the Reverend Amos Burnett of the Wesleyan Methodist Church, 'to think that His Majesty's representative signed a law like this, and signed it in such circumstances.'

For Plaatje the passing of this Act raised emotions akin to the death of his father. 'Awakening on Friday morning, June 20, 1913,' declared the outraged Plaatje, 'the South African native found himself, not actually a slave, but a pariah in the land of his birth.'

'For to crown all our calamities' he continued, 'South Africa has by law ceased to be the home of any of her native children whose skins are dyed with pigment that does not conform with the regulation hue.'

Addressing the whites, in *Native Life in South Africa*, he wondered:

What have our people done to these colonists, we asked, that is so utterly unforgivable, that this law should be passed as an unavoidable reprisal? Have we not delved in their mines, and are not a quarter of a million of us still labouring for them in the depths of the earth in such circumstances for the most niggardly pittance? Are not thousands of us still offering up our lives and our limbs in order that South Africa should satisfy the white man's greed, delivering 50,000,000 pounds worth of minerals every year? Have we not quarried the stones, mixed, moulded and carried the mortar which build the cities of South Africa? Have we not likewise

206

prepared the material for building the railways? Have we not obsequiously and regularly paid taxation every year, and have we not supplied the Treasury with money to provide free education for Dutch children in the 'Free' State and Transvaal, while we had to find additional money to pay the school fees of our own children? Are not many of us toiling in the grain fields and fruit farms, with their wives and their children, for the white man's benefit? Did not our people take care of the white women — all the white women, including Boer fraus — whose husbands, brothers and fathers were away at the front — in many cases actively engaged in shattering our own liberty? But see their appreciation and gratitude! Oh, for something to —

> Strike flat the thick rotundity o' the world!
> Crack Nature's mould, all germins spill at once!
> That make ungrateful men!

The effects of the Act, passed in the middle of one of the coldest winters on record, were devastating. Desperate peasant families were forced to submit to conditions of labour provision at derisory compensation or abandon homes that had belonged to their ancestors. And the wealthier the peasant, the greater the loss. As peasants were no longer allowed to rent pasturage, those with large herds of cattle or flocks of sheep and goats were forced to give them away or see them die of starvation. Worse, individual farmers made the provisions even more untenable by evicting the wealthier peasants so that they could annex their goods and property by expelling those unwilling to bond themselves to their arbitrary demands. Once prosperous peasant farmers were reduced to impoverished labourers or forced to take the road to nowhere.

Roadsides were filled with animals, children, the old and the sick. They could not stop, for if they did they were charged and arrested for vagrancy. And if their cattle or livestock became sick or starved they were criminally charged for that too. 'It was a sickening procedure of extermination,' said Plaatje who witnessed many harrowing scenes, evocative of the horror of Mafeking, that left him in tears.

It was cold that afternoon as we cycled into the 'Free' State from Transvaal, and towards evening the southern winds rose. A cutting blizzard raged during the night, and native mothers evicted from their homes shivered with their babies by their sides. When we saw on that night the teeth of the little children chattering through the cold, we thought of our own little ones in their Kimberley home on an evening after gambolling in their winter frocks with their schoolmates, and we wondered what these little mites had done that a home should suddenly become to them a thing of the past.

Kgobadi's goats had been to kid when trekked from his farm; but the kids, which in halcyon times represented the interest on his capital, were now one by one dying as fast as they were born and left by the roadside for the jackals and vultures to feast upon.

This visitation was not confined to Kgobadi's stock, Mrs. Kgobadi carried a sick baby when the eviction took place, and she had to transfer her darling from the cottage to the jolting ox-wagon in which they left the farm. Two days out the little one began to sink as the result of privation and exposure on the road, and the night before we met them its little soul was released from its earthly bonds. The death of the child added a fresh perplexity to the stricken parents. They had no right or title to the farm lands through which they trekked: they must keep to the public roads — the only places in the country open to the outcasts if they are possessed of a travelling permit. The deceased child had to be buried, but where, when and how?

This young wandering family decided to dig a grave under cover of the darkness of that night, when no one was looking, and in that crude manner the dead child was interred — and interred amid fear and trembling, as well as the throbs of a torturing anguish, in a stolen grave, lest the proprietor of the spot, or any of his servants, should surprise them in the act. Even criminals dropping straight from the gallows have an undisputed claim to six feet of ground on which to rest their criminal remains, but under the cruel operation of the Natives' Land Act little children, whose only crime is that God did not make them white, are sometimes denied that right in their ancestral home.

Numerous details narrated by these victims of an Act of Parliament kept us awake all that night, and by next morning we were glad enough to hear no more of the sickening procedure of extermination voluntarily instituted by the South African parliament. We had spent a hideous night under a bitterly cold sky, conditions to which hundreds of our unfortunate countrymen and countrywomen in various parts of the country are condemned by the provisions of this Parliamentary land plague. At five o'clock in the morning the cold seemed to redouble its energy and never before did we so fully appreciate the Master's saying: 'But pray ye that your flight be not in the winter.'

Plaatje, in *Native Life in South Africa,* had no doubt who was to blame for the predicament his people found themselves in.

It is doubtful if we ever thought so much on a single bicycle ride as we did on this journey; however, the sight of a policeman ahead of us disturbed these meditations.

In a few moments the policeman was before us and we alighted in presence of the representative of the law, with our feet on the accursed soil of the district in which we were born. The policeman stopped. By his looks and his familiar 'Dag jong' we noticed that the policeman was Dutch, and the embodiment of affability. He spoke and we were glad to notice that he had no intention of dragging an innocent man to prison. We were many miles from the nearest police station, and in such a case one is generally able to gather the real views of the man on patrol, as distinct from the written code of his office, but our friend was becoming very companionable. Naturally we asked him about the operation of the plague law. He was a Transvaaler, he said, and he knew that Kaffirs were inferior beings, but they had rights, and were always left in undisturbed possession of their property when Paul Kruger was alive. 'The poor devils must be sorry now,' he said, 'that they every sang "God Save the Queen" when the British troops came into the Transvaal, for I have seen, in the course of my duties, that a Kaffir's life nowadays was not worth a . . . ., and I believe that no man regretted the change of flags now more than the Kaffirs of Transvaal.' This information was superfluous, for personal contact with the Natives of Transvaal had convinced us of the fact. They say it is only the criminal who has any reason to rejoice over the presence of the Union Jack, because in his case the cat-o'-nine-tails, except for very serious crimes, has been abolished.

'Some of the poor creatures,' continued the policeman, 'I knew to be fairly comfortable, if not rich, and they enjoyed the possession of their stock, living in many instances just like Dutchmen. Many of these are now being forced to leave their homes. Cycling along this road you will meet several of them in search of new homes, and if ever there was a fools errant, it is that of a Kaffir trying to find a new home for his stock and family just now.'

'And what do you think, Baas Officer, must eventually be the lot of a people under such unfortunate circumstances?' we asked.

'I think,' said the policeman, 'that it must serve them right. They had no business to hanker after British rule, to cheat and plot with the enemies of their Republic for the overthrow of their Government. Why did they not assist the forces of their Republic during the war instead of supplying the English with scouts and intelligence? Oom Paul would not have died of a broken heart and he would still be there to protect them. Serve them right I say.'

While the Siege of Mafeking represented a turning point for Plaatje, this Act was his life's central event. Not only did the suffering deeply anger him, but for him the Act was a sacrilege that outraged the concepts of both law and humanity. It did, however, provide an opportunity – though one he would happily have foregone – to mobilise the SANNC because the provisions of the Act were so far reaching that they touched the lives of each black person. From now on he was at the forefront of organising opposition to an Act of parliament that had placed South African blacks on the long road to national exclusion and apartheid. It was this act, by sophisticated manipulation, that would later form the basis of the apartheid 'homeland' system which sought to denationalise black South Africans by making them citizens of the homelands created from the once 'Scheduled Native Reserves.' It was not long before the concept 'foreign-native' entered the lexicon.

An academic debate exists as to whether Plaatje can be called a 'freedom fighter' or whether he was merely a patriot. It is always pointed out that he was a man of peace, worked within the system and never contemplated taking up arms. On the other hand, his tireless lobbying in England, Europe and the United States of America were a precursor of the successful diplomatic route the future ANC would take. This effort alone should be enough to confer on him the honour of being the ANC's first 'freedom fighter' because war is fought on many levels — diplomatic, physical and psychological — that one cannot discount the efforts of the person, above all others, who paved the way for the future successful liberation of South Africa.

But Plaatje went further, because he clearly regarded the actions of a reconciled Boer and Britain as a declaration of war and the Land Act as an act of war. 'If, after a proper declaration of war,' he wrote, 'you found your kinsman delivered from pillar to post in the manner that the South African natives have been harried and scurried by Act no. 27 of 1913, you would, though aware that it is part of the fortunes of war, find it difficult to suppress your hatred of the enemy.' In 1913 there was no structure, other than diplomatic channels, to conduct that war. But he foresaw what was coming and he warned whites of the consequences of their actions and the nemesis to follow. And the looming conflagration he perceived was not far removed from that consuming Ireland, and he was not opposed to that route if whites did not change direction. Quoting from Shakespeare, he cautioned with a crystal clear message, 'If you prick us, do we not bleed? If you tickle us, do we not laugh? If you poison us, do we not die? And if you wrong us, shall we not revenge? If we are like you in the rest, we will resemble you in that.'

Finally, turning to Mafeking, he enquired, 'What must be the feelings of these people ... now that it is decreed that their sons and daughters can no longer have any claim to the country for which they bled?'

And the migrants streamed in on the highways and their hunger was in their eyes, and their need was in their eyes. They had no argument, no system, nothing but their numbers and their needs. When there was work for a man, ten men fought for it — fought with a low wage. If that fella'll work for thirty cents, I'll work for twenty-five.

If he'll take twenty-five. I'll do it for twenty.

No, me, I'm hungry. I'll work for fifteen. I'll work for food. The kids. You ought to see them. Little boils, like, comin' out, an' they can't run aroun'. Give 'em some windfall fruit, an' they bloated up. Me, I'll work for a little piece of meat.

And this was good, for wages went down and prices stayed up. The great owners were glad ... And pretty soon now we'll have serfs again ...

And the companies, the banks worked at their own doom and they did not know it. The fields were fruitful, and starving men moved on the roads. The granaries were full and the children of the poor grew up rachitic, and the pustules of pellagra swelled on their sides. The great companies did not know that the line between hunger and anger is a thin line. And money that might of went to wages went for gas, for guns, for agents and spies, for blacklists, for drilling. On the highways the people moved like ants and searched for work, for food. And the anger began to ferment.

JOHN STEINBECK, THE GRAPES OF WRATH

THE GRAPES OF WRATH

In the souls of the people the grapes of wrath are filling and growing heavy, growing heavy for the vintage.
JOHN STEINBECK, THE GRAPES OF WRATH

Ripe persecution, like the plant
Whose nascent Mocha boasted,
Some bitter fruit produced, whose wrath
Was never known till roasted.
SOL PLAATJE, NATIVE LIFE IN SOUTH AFRICA

In 1977 Mafeking became Mafikeng. Mafikeng, in 1994, was capital of the nominally independent Bantustan of Bophuthatswana – the place where the Tswana gather. The architects of Grand Apartheid had refined the Natives Land Act of 1913 to create ethnic 'independent homeland' states. By making each black person a citizen of a homeland, so the National Party government believed, it could solve the 'native question' by wishing away the vast bulk of South Africa's citizens.

Chief Lucas Mangope, a National Party puppet and staunch believer in separate development, was elected Bophuthatswana's first president when it was granted statehood in 1977. He would have done well to have read Anton Lembede, a legal partner of Pixley Seme, in *Inkundla ya Bantu*, a black newspaper in Natal:

The history of modern times is the history of nationalism. Nationalism has been tested in the people's struggles and the fires

213

of battle and found to be the only antidote against foreign rule and modern imperialism. It is for that reason that the great imperialistic powers feverishly endeavour with all their might to discourage and eradicate all nationalistic tendencies among their alien subjects; for that purpose huge and enormous sums of money are lavishly expended on propaganda against nationalism which is dismissed as 'narrow', 'barbarous', 'uncultured', 'devilish', etc. Some alien subjects become dupes of this sinister propaganda and consequently become tools or instruments of imperialism, for which great service they are highly praised by the imperialistic power and showered with such epithets as 'culture', 'liberal', 'progressive', 'broadminded', etc.

Of the four homelands to be granted independence, Mangope's was the most successful and it became the showpiece of apartheid engineering. In reality Bophuthatswana was a one-party fiefdom, rife with corruption and nepotism, ruled with an iron fist by the slight, doleful ex-school teacher and his Christian Democratic Party.

Bophuthatswana, in the build-up to South Africa's first democratic election, was the only one of these Bantustans committed to preserving its artificial independence. But, this was doomed to end in tears because the ANC campaigned for a unitary, non-racial democratic South Africa in which all the structures of apartheid were swept away. For added leverage Mangope joined the right-wing Freedom Alliance, which was involved in the pre-election negotiations process but was composed of groups, black and white, who refused to participate in the polls and favoured partition.

The white groups within the Freedom Alliance had formed a loose front called the Afrikaner Volksfront (AVF). This sub-alliance was composed of some 80 disparate Afrikaner groups still mired in the myth of racial supremacy and who still hankered after the apartheid dream. Though their total support base was less than 5 per cent of the population, it was the most heavily armed sector. In 1993 the AVF drew up secret plans to secede should their demands not be met. Their war-plan included the neutralising of all hostile generals in the South African Defence Force in 48 hours and the mobilisation of their supporters for a conventional civil war. While most of the defence force did not support this group, many of the rural commando structures did. Some of these had even replaced the South African flag fluttering above their barracks with the old South African Republic's Vierkleur. General Constand Viljoen was in command of this right-wing alliance's military capability. His overriding problem was that nearly all the groups that made up the AVF possessed their own private armies and individual leaders were extremely reluctant to lose direct control of their forces.

Mangope, while taking part in the negotiations, vociferously refused to take part in the elections or to allow political parties to campaign in his territory. The South African ambassador warned him of the implications, but he remained resolute. While his actions contributed to fermenting a national crisis, matters in Bophuthatswana were beginning to unravel. The focus of a series of strikes, go-slows and demonstrations by civil servants and industrial workers, concerned about the security of their pensions in a new dispensation, was subtly shifted by the ANC to a demand for reincorporation. This internal crisis resulted in a complete breakdown in services by the beginning of March and Mangope clung to his fantasy power only through the wavering support of his security forces.

Students of the University of Bophuthatswana, spoiling for action, barricaded themselves behind boulders and trash cans. Simmering anarchy exploded as liberation fever swept the town. Soon black palls of smoke, from burning barricades, hung over Mafikeng. The air was thick with the acrid smell of teargas, burning tyres and the wail of sirens. Demonstrators armed themselves with petrol bombs, rocks, bottles and road signs ripped from the ground. On 10 March, as looters tore through shopping centres, the scared police mutinied and joined the demonstrators. As cars with blaring horns roared round the town – the occupants shouting 'Viva!', 'Freedom!' and raising clenched fists as they passed the statue of Rhodes pointing to the north – Mangope phoned Viljoen and pleaded for assistance in suppressing the uprising and undertook to provide automatic weapons, armoured vehicles and rations. Viljoen promised to immediately bring 3 000 men to stabilise the situation.

A convoy of AVF supporters arrived on the night of 10 March and established their command post at the airport to the north of Mafikeng. Journalists and television crews, sensing an explosive story, also invaded the town. The problems for the AVF started immediately with the uninvited arrival of 500 members of the undisciplined ragtag far-right Afrikaner Weerstandsbeweging (AWB), calling themselves Boers and proclaiming loudly that they had come on a 'kaffir shooting expedition'. The white chief of the Bophuthatswana Defence Force requested the AWB to leave. They refused. Mangope then issued an order that they could stay on condition they removed their rank insignia and submitted to the command of the AVF. They refused. The leaders of the AWB and AVF then began a showdown in full view of their bearded supporters, who were dressed in khaki shorts, short-sleeve shirts, long socks and veldskoene.

On learning that the AWB was part of the force and hearing their intention, black members of the Bophuthatswana Defence Force began to mutiny and flatly refused to issue the automatic weapons. As the stand-off developed, FW de Klerk, the then President of South Africa, could dither no longer and ordered South African Defence Force troops into Mafikeng. But when the South African force did arrive they found the mutinied Bophuthatswana soldiers successfully driving the AVF out of the town. The ease with which the AVF was expelled ended the threat of a right-wing civil war when it became abundantly clear that armed farmers were no match for trained soldiers. By the end of the day the right-wing alliance was in tatters and the major obstacle to the election process was cleared.

The AWB, however, had decided, before the South African Defence Force arrived, to take matters into their own hands with their personal weapons. They had driven away from the airport and sped through Mafikeng randomly firing from their cars and warning residents to get off the streets or be shot. The Bophuthatswana Defence Force managed to round up most of these lawless men and herd them over the Molopo River. One convoy, however, broke away and headed over the railway line and cut a swathe into the old *stadt*, firing indiscriminately. They passed 'Moratiwa' as they entered and again when they left. Between Plaatje's old residence and the fort where Eloff had been trapped, they rejoined the Vryburg road. Here they fired on a Bophuthatswana police patrol, which returned their fire, disabling the last car in the convoy. The blue Mercedes Benz, with three occupants, pulled up on to the dusty verge under a billboard for soap that proclaimed 'Sunlight Mildness.'

Alwyn Wolfaardt, the driver and a 'colonel' in the AWB, got out and moved round the back with his hands in the air. 'Don't shoot,' he shouted. When he got to the passenger door he opened it and the wounded Nic Fourie slipped from the seat and lay bleeding to death in the dirt. Fanie Uys, who had been lying on the back seat opened the door and slipped out. He was pale and shaking uncontrollably as he propped himself against the rear wheel.

216

'Please God help us, get us some medical help,' pleaded the brawny, bushy bearded Wolfaardt as he crouched at the passenger door with his hands still in the air. Television crews arrived and began filming the men as two nervous Bophuthatswana policemen guarded them. Wolfaardt again pleaded for assistance. 'Fuck it — someone just get a fucking ambulance.'

'Black bastards,' muttered Uys as one of the policemen pulled Wolfaardt onto his stomach and frisked him for weapons. The policeman, his mouth as thin as the blade of a knife and his eyes sweeping like a raptor, glared at Uys who quickly shouted, 'Sorry! Sorry!'

The policeman, Ontlametse Menyatsoe, already enraged by the indiscriminate shooting of his people, stood, his R4 rifle at his hip. 'Who do you think you are? What are you doing in my country?' A journalist tried to calm him, but he continued. 'We want to shoot these fucking dogs! They have killed women! They are animals, not people!' With that, he released hundreds of years of pent-up anger as he raked the three jerking, twitching men with a hail of bullets that orchestrated the death rattle of apartheid.

I KHUTSU MOROLONG: MODIREDI wa AFRIKA
THE INSCRIPTION ON SOL PLAATJE'S GRAVE, MEANING
'REST IN PEACE MOROLONG: YOU SERVANT OF AFRICA'

SELECTED READING

Sol Plaatje's *Mafeking Diary*, for those wishing to experience a day-to-day account of the Siege of Mafeking, is highly recommended, as is his *Native Life in South Africa* for the horrors of the Natives' Land Act. Brian Willan's *Sol Plaatje: A Biography* is a brilliant biography of this amazing South African.

Tim Jeal's *Baden-Powell* is comprehensive, albeit sycophantic – in particular there is no better treatment of Baden-Powell's sexuality or his relationship with McLaren. Brian Roberts' two books, *Churchills in Africa* and *Those Bloody Women: Three Heroines of the Boer War*, are recommended for those wanting to read more on Lady Sarah Wilson, as is Thomas Packenham's *The Boer War* for those wanting more on the South African War.

BIBLIOGRAPHY

Baden-Powell, Robert: *Sketches in Mafeking and East Africa.* London, 1907.

Baillie, Major FD: *Mafeking: A Diary of the Siege.* Westminster, Constable, 1900.

Bateman, Philip: *Generals of the Anglo-Boer War.* Cape Town, Purnell.

Bottomley, John: '"Garrisoning the moon against an attack from Mars"; The Siege of Mafeking and the Imperial mindset', in *New Contree.* Dept of History, University of the Northwest, Lichtenburg, September 1997.

Bottomley, John: 'The Siege of Mafeking and the Imperial mindset as revealed in the diaries of TWP (Tom) Hayes and WP (William) Hayes, District Surgeons', in *New Contree.* Dept of History, University of the Northwest, Lichtenburg, September 1997.

Bradford, Mary & Richard (Editors): *An American Family on the Africa Frontier: The Burnham Family Letters, 1893–1896.* Durban, Bok Books, 1993.

Brendon, Piers: *Eminent Edwardians.* London, Secker and Warburg, 1980.

Brogan, Hugh: *Mowgli's Son's: Kipling & Baden-Powell's Scouts.* London, Jonathan Cape, 1987.

Cock, Mrs Ada (Franklin): *Petticoat in Mafeking: The Letters of Ada Cock, With Annotations and Vindication of Baden-Powell, by John F Midgley, etc.* Kommetjie, JF Midgley, 1974.

Connell, Charles: *The World's Greatest Sieges.* London, Oldhams Books, 1967.

Doyle, Arthur Conan: *The Great Boer War.* London, Nelson, 1903.

Gardner, Brian: *Mafeking: A Victorian Legend.* London, Cassell, 1966.

Gardner, Brian: *The African Dream.* London, Cassell, 1970.

Grinnell-Milne, Duncan: *Baden-Powell at Mafeking.* London, Bodley Head, 1957.

Hamilton, John Angus: *The Siege of Mafeking.* London, Methuen, 1900.

Holmberg, Ake: *African Tribes and European Agencies.* Stockholm, Scandinavian University Books, 1966.

Jeal, Tim: *Baden-Powell.* London, Pimlico, 1989.

Kiernan, RH: *Baden-Powell*. London, Harrap, 1939.

Kipling, Rudyard: *The Five Nations*. London, Methuen, 1903.

Kipling, Rudyard: *Collected Verse*. New York, Doubleday, 1910.

Mandela, Nelson: *Long Walk to Freedom*. Randburg, Macdonald Purnell, 1994.

Maylam, Paul: *A History of the African People of South Africa: From the Early Iron Age to the 1970s*. David Philip, Cape Town, 1986.

Le May, GHL: *British Supremacy in South Africa*. Oxford, Oxford University Press, 1965.

Molema, SM: *The Bantu — Past and Present*. Cape Town, Struik, 1963.

Molema, SM: *Montshiwa — Barolong Chief and Patriot (1814-1896)*. Cape Town, Struik, 1966.

Neilly, J: *Besieged with Baden-Powell*. London, C Arthur Pearson, 1900.

Pakenham, Elizabeth: *Jameson's Raid*. London, Weidenfeld and Nicolson, 1960.

Pakenham, Thomas: *The Boer War*. London. Macdonald & Co, 1979.

Plaatje, Sol T: *Native Life in South Africa*. 4th Edition, Kimberley, Tsala ea Batho, 1916.

Plaatje, Sol T: *Mafeking Diary: A Black Man's View of a White Man's War*. Edited by John Comaroff. Cambridge, Meridor Books, 1973.

Plaatje, Sol T: *Mhudi*. Cape Town, Francolin Publishers, 1996.

Roberts, Brian: *Churchills in Africa*. London, Hamish Hamilton, 1970.

Roberts, Brian: *Those Bloody Women: Three Heroines of the Boer War*. London, John Murray, 1991.

Rosenthal, Michael: *The Character Factory: Baden-Powell and the Origins of the Boy Scout Movement*. London, Collins, 1986.

Ross, Edward: *Diary of the Siege of Mafeking, October 1899 to May 1900*. Ed Brian P Willan. Cape Town, Van Riebeeck Society, 1980.

Setiloane, Gabriel M: *The Image of God Among the Sotho-Tswana*. Rotterdam, A.A. Balkema, 1976.

Sparks, Allister: *The Mind of South Africa*. London, Arrow, 1997.

Stafleu, Abraham: *Die Beleg van Mafeking: Dagboek van Abraham Stafleu*. Raad vir Geesteswetenskaplike Navorsing, Pretoria, 1985.

Steinbeck, John: *The Grapes of Wrath*. Pan Books, London. 1975.

Taylor, AJP: *The Struggle for Mastery in Europe 1848-1918*. Oxford, Oxford University Press, 1971.

Wilkinson-Latham, Christopher: *The Boer War*. London, Osprey Publishing, 1977.

Willan, Brian (Editor): *Sol Plaatje Selected Writings*. Johannesburg, Witwatersrand University Press, 1996.

Willan, Brian: *Sol Plaatje: A Biography*. Johannesburg, Ravan, 1984.

Wilson, Lady Sarah: *South African Memories, Social, Warlike and Sporting, From Diaries Written at the Time*. London, Edward Arnold, 1909.

Young, Filson: *The Relief of Mafeking*. London, Methuen, 1900.

INDEX

222